Gervase Phinn taught in a range of schools for fourteen years until, in 1984, he became General Adviser for Language Development in Rotherham. Four years later he was appointed Senior General Inspector for English and Drama with North Yorkshire County Council and was subsequently made Principal Adviser for the county. He is now a free-lance lecturer and adviser, and Visiting Professor of Education at the University of Teesside.

He has published collections of his own plays and stories and has contributed to several anthologies. His own anthology of poems, *Classroom Creatures*, has been published by Puffin in an expanded edition called *It Takes One to Know One*. His first book of reminiscences, *The Other Side of the Dale*, and *Head over Heels in the Dales*, which continues the story of his career as a School Inspector, are also published by Penguin.

Gervase Phinn is widely sought after as a speaker and was an immediate star on Esther Rantzen's television show, *Esther*, appearing a second time due to public demand. He is married with four children and lives in a village just outside Doncaster.

OVER HILL AND DALE

Gervase Phinn

PENGUIN BOOKS

PENGUIN BOOKS

Published by the Penguin Group
Penguin Books Ltd, 80 Strand, London WC2R 0RL, England
Penguin Putnam Inc., 375 Hudson Street, New York, New York 10014, USA
Penguin Books Australia Ltd, 250 Camberwell Road, Camberwell, Victoria 3124, Australia
Penguin Books Canada Ltd, 10 Alcorn Avenue, Toronto, Ontario, Canada M4V 3B2
Penguin Books India (P) Ltd, 11 Community Centre, Panchsheel Park, New Delhi – 110 017, India
Penguin Books (NZ) Ltd, Cnr Rosedale and Airborne Roads, Albany, Auckland, New Zealand
Penguin Books (South Africa) (Pty) Ltd, 24 Sturdee Avenue, Rosebank 2196, South Africa

Penguin Books Ltd, Registered Offices: 80 Strand, London WC2R 0RL, England

www.penguin.com

First published By Michael Joseph 2000
Published in Penguin Books 2001

20

Copyright © Gervase Phinn 2000
All rights reserved.

The moral right of the author has been asserted

Printed in England by Clays Ltd, St Ives plc

I should like to record the immense debt of gratitude that I owe to Jenny Dereham, my editor, for her invaluable advice and support and for her wisdom and patience.

The Inspector Calls (facing page) and *Remember Me?* (page343) both appear in *It Takes One to Know One* published by Puffin Books, 2001.

The Inspector Calls

Miss, miss, there's a man at the back of the classroom
With a big black book and a smile like a crocodile.
Miss, he asked me if I got a lot of homework,
And when I said, 'Too much!' – he wrote it down.

Miss, miss, there's a man at the back of the classroom
With a long sharp pencil and eyes like a shark.
Miss, he asked me what I liked best about our school,
And when I said, 'The dinners!' – he wrote it down.

Miss, miss, there's a man at the back of the classroom
With a big square badge and hair like a hedgehog.
Miss, I asked him what he liked best about our school,
And he said he was not there to answer my questions,
He said he was just 'a fly on the wall'.

Miss, miss, why don't you tell him to 'BUZZ OFF!'

Dr Gore, Chief Education Officer for the County of Yorkshire, smiled like a hungry vampire, the sort of thin-lipped,
self-satisfied smile of Count Dracula before he sinks his
fangs into a helpless victim.

'And how are you, Gervase?' he mouthed softly, showing
a glimpse of teeth.

'Oh . . . er . . . very well, thank you, Dr Gore,' I replied,
attempting to sound cheerful and relaxed.

'Good, good,' the CEO murmured. He stared for a
moment over the top of his small, gold-framed spectacles
and then, resting his elbows on the large mahogany desk in
front of him, steepled his long fingers and nodded thoughtfully. 'And how have you found your first year with us in
Yorkshire?' he asked. His voice was as soft as the summer
breeze.

'Oh . . . er . . . very well, thank you, Dr Gore,' I replied
for the second time and shifted nervously in the chair. He
continued to smile and steeple his long fingers without
saying a word. In the embarrassed silence which followed
I heard the slow ticking of the clock on the wall, squeaking footsteps in the corridor outside, the distant hum of
traffic on the High Street and a slight buzzing of a faulty
fluorescent light in the outer office. 'I think, well, quite
good actually, quite successful . . .' My voice trailed off.
I sounded incredibly inarticulate for the County Inspector
of Schools for English and Drama. 'Not too bad,' I said
finally.

'Good, good,' the CEO said almost in a whisper. 'I

expect you are wondering why I sent for you so early in the new academic year?' he continued, smiling and steepling.

'Yes, I *was* wondering,' I replied nervously.

The morning had started off so well. I had arrived at the Education Office in Fettlesham that first day of the new term, bright and early and keen to be back at work. A warm September sun had shone in a cloudless sky, the air had been fresh and still, the birds singing and everything had seemed right with the world. Over the summer break, while the schools had been on holiday, I had managed to clear my desk of the mountain of paperwork. Reports had been completed, guidelines written, courses planned, correspondence dealt with and documents had been filed away neatly. I had surveyed the empty desk with a sense of real satisfaction and achievement.

It had been a fascinating first year, occasionally exhausting and frustrating, but for most of the time full of variety and challenge. The colleagues with whom I worked and shared an office had been immensely supportive during my induction into the profession of school inspector. There was Dr Harold Yeats, the Senior Inspector, Sidney Clamp, the unpredictable and larger-than-life creative and visual arts inspector and David Pritchard, the small, good-humoured Welshman responsible for mathematics, PE and games. We got on well together and were supported and kept in order by Julie, the inspectors' secretary.

That first year, I had worked alongside teachers in the classroom, organised courses and conferences, directed workshops, run seminars and attended governors' meetings and appointment panels. The most interesting part of the job, however, had involved visiting the small rural primary schools in the heart of the beautiful Yorkshire Dales, to spend a morning or an afternoon observing lessons, looking at the children's work and reporting on the quality of the teaching and learning.

As I sat at my empty desk, thinking about the quiet, uneventful, stress-free day ahead of me, I heard a clattering on the stairs, telling me that a moment later Julie would totter in on those absurdly high-heeled shoes she was so fond of wearing. In my first year Julie had been invaluable. Not only was she very efficient, good-humoured and extremely comical, she had those qualities often possessed by Yorkshire people – generous to a fault, hard-working but with a blunt nature and a fierce honesty, characteristics which often got her into trouble. With her bright bubbly blonde hair and bright bubbly nature, Julie was a breath of fresh air in the drab and cramped office. That morning she struggled into the room, breathing heavily and loaded down with assorted bags, papers and files. I jumped up to help her.

'I feel like some sort of peripatetic car boot sale!' she cried, dropping her load noisily on the nearest desk. Before I could open my mouth she continued, 'I started off with a handbag and a bit of shopping but collected all this little lot on my way from the bus stop. As I was passing Committee Room 1, Debbie – you know, the big woman with the peroxide hair who always wears those awful pink knitted outfits – asked me to take Mr Pritchard's briefcase which he left there last term. Forget his head if it wasn't screwed on. I mean that briefcase has been there for six weeks. It wouldn't have done Debbie any harm to bring the briefcase up herself. The climb up the stairs would have given her a bit of exercise. She could do with losing a few pounds. Anyway, when I got to the Post Room that Derek – you know, the gangly lad with the spectacles and big ears – asked me to pick up the inspectors' mail since I was going that way anyway. Then I had these confidential staffing files pushed into my hands when I reached Personnel. They weigh a ton. I don't know why Dr Yeats didn't pick them up himself. I must have looked like an old pack horse, stumbling along the corridors of County Hall.' She shook her head and breathed out heavily. 'I'm too good-natured by half, that's my trouble. And I've snagged a nail.' She began to root about in her handbag and continued chattering on without pausing. 'Anyway, how are you?' I attempted a response but without success. 'I had a nail file in here somewhere, I'm sure I did,' she continued. 'I don't know about you, but I could murder a strong cup of coffee.' Without waiting for an answer she disappeared out of the room.

'Good morning, Julie!' I shouted after her, at last getting a word in. I thought of the wonderfully descriptive and rather unkind Yorkshire expression to describe a person, just like Julie, who so enjoys talking about anything and everything that it becomes almost a running commentary: 'She's got a runaway gob – talks and says nowt and she's said nowt when she's done.'

A few minutes later, when I was sorting through my mail, Julie returned with two steaming mugs. I watched as she set one mug down on my desk and cupped her hands around the other.

'You're very quiet today,' she said. 'Is something wrong?'

'Nothing at all, Julie,' I replied amiably, putting my letters into the in-tray on my desk. Then I asked a question which I immediately regretted, for it started her off on another monologue. 'How was your holiday?'

'Don't ask!'

'Not too good then?' I hazarded, looking up and reaching for the coffee.

'Awful! I went to Majorca with my boyfriend. It took months to persuade him, because Paul's about as adventurous as a dead sheep when it comes to holidays and, of course, his mother has to put her two pennyworth in about foreign food, plane crashes and hijackers. Anyway, the flight was delayed so we had a four-hour wait at Manchester Airport with him moaning and groaning. Then I was stopped at customs by a horrible little man in black. I got Spanish tummy the day after I arrived and Paul fell asleep in the sun and woke up like a lobster with an attitude problem. Then he came out in blisters the size of balloons and wouldn't leave the room. He said he looked like something out of a horror film and when I agreed he didn't speak to me for two days. The hotel was only half built and the pool was full of spoilt, screaming children. We had karaoke every night until two in the morning with a tone-deaf Dutchman singing "I Did It My Way" at the top of his voice and a woman from Dudley who sounded like a sheep about to give birth. And if you got down after eight o'clock in the morning you could say goodbye to the sunbeds. We'll go to Skegness next year in his auntie's caravan. Anyway, what was your holiday like?'

'Oh, very restful,' I told her. 'I managed to get away for a few days and –'

Before I could elaborate Julie dived in with her characteristic bluntness. 'And did you see much of that sexy teacher you were taking out?'

'Unfortunately, not a great deal,' I replied smiling and thinking of what Christine's reaction would be to Julie's comment about her.

I had met Christine almost exactly a year earlier when I had visited the infant school where she was the Headteacher. She had appeared like some vision and I had been bowled over by those large blue eyes, warm smile, fair complexion and soft mass of golden hair. After a long period spent summoning up the courage, and with constant nagging from my colleagues in the office, I had asked her out. We had been to the theatre and the cinema, to a concert and various school events and as each day passed I felt sure I was falling in love with her.

When I had first met Christine she had had a boyfriend – Miles. He was everything I was not: strikingly handsome, with the sort of sculptured features of a male model. He was lean, athletic, sophisticated and suave and he was also very wealthy. But Miles had those flaws of character often possessed by men who are rich and handsome: he was arrogant and self-centred. To my delight, Christine had, in Sidney's words, 'given him the old heave-ho', which was when I had chanced my arm and asked her out. Over the recent summer holidays I had not seen very much of her. She had spent three weeks in Chicago, staying with a cousin and a further week writing up a dissertation for a masters degree. We had enjoyed a day walking on the North York Moors and been to the theatre and out to dinner a couple of times. This term I was determined, I was going to see a whole lot more of her.

'So what's happening with you two then?' asked Julie. She was not one to beat about the bush.

'What do you mean, what's happening?'

'Well, are you getting it together? Is it serious?'

'I'm not sure . . .' I started.

Julie folded her arms and pulled a face. 'Typical of men that – "I'm not sure." Just like Paul.' She put on a sort of whining voice. ' "I'm not sure about going to Majorca, I'm not sure this is the right flight, I'm not sure I'll like this Spanish food, I'm not sure – " '

I decided to change the subject. 'Am I the only one in the office this morning?'

'It's always the woman who has to make the decisions. What did you say?'

'I asked if I was the only one in the office this morning?'

'Just you. Mr Clamp's planning his art course, Mr Pritchard's meeting with the newly qualified teachers and Dr Yeats is at a conference. There's not much mail either, by the look of it.'

'So,' I said happily, 'it looks like a quiet start to the term.'

'Not necessarily,' said Julie. 'Mrs Savage phoned last Friday.' At this point her lip curled like a rabid dog and her voice became hard-edged. 'She wondered where you were. I said, "People do take holidays, you know." If she'd have bothered to look at those wretched inspectors' engagement sheets I have to send over to Admin. every week, she'd have seen that you were on leave. She just likes the sound of her own voice and it's not her real voice anyway. She puts it on. I don't know who she thinks she's trying to impress.'

I began to chuckle and shake my head. 'You've really got it in for Mrs Savage this morning, Julie, and no mistake. She's not that bad.'

'She's *unbearable*. "Ho," says she, "well tell Mr Phinn, when he returns, thet Dr Gore wishes to see him in his room has a metter of hurgency at nine hey hem prompt." Made you sound like a naughty schoolboy. Then she slams the phone down with no trace of a "please" or a "thank you".' Julie's face screwed up as if she had chronic indigestion. 'That awful voice of hers really gets under my skin.'

Mrs Savage, the CEO's personal assistant, was not the most popular of people in our office nor was she the easiest woman to get on with. She had a formidable reputation with a sharp tongue and a stare that could curdle milk; she definitely was not a person with whom to cross swords. I had kept a wary distance after battling with her the previous year.

'And speaking of getting under people's skin,' said Julie, 'I reckon she's had her face done.'

'Who?' I asked.

'Mrs Savage. When I saw her last week in the staff canteen I didn't recognise her. Her skin's been stretched right back off her face. She looks as if she's walking through a wind tunnel. All those wrinkles have disappeared. And she did have some lines on her face, didn't she? Looked like some-thing out of that shop in the High Street where they sell all those wrinkled leather coats. Those two pouches under her chin have gone as well.'

'I don't remember her having pouches.'

'Of course you do! She looked like a gerbil with mumps. And I think she's had that rhinosuction because she looks a lot thinner as well.'

'Liposuction,' I corrected.

'She's that thick-skinned, I think I was right first time. She gave me such a glare. I tell you, if looks could maim, I'd be on crutches.'

'And she said Dr Gore wanted to see me?'

'She's unbearable that woman,' said Julie with venom, 'you would think —'

'Julie!' I snapped. 'Did Mrs Savage say that Dr Gore wanted to see me?'

'At nine o'clock prompt. That's what Lady High and Mighty said.'

'I wonder what it's about?'

'She puts on that posh accent and that hoity-toity manner but it doesn't fool me. Marlene on the switchboard remem-bers her when she started as an office junior. That's when her hair colour was natural. She had a voice as broad as a barn door and as croaky as a frog with laryngitis. Then she went through all those husbands like a dose of salts and was promoted far beyond her capabilities and she now speaks as if she's got a potato in her mouth.'

'I think the expression is "a plum in her mouth".'

'With a mouth like hers, it's definitely a potato. When I think of the times —'

'Did she say what Dr Gore wanted?' I interrupted. I was feeling rather uneasy about this interview with the CEO so early on in the term. A small cold dread was settling into the pit of my stomach.

'No, I never gave her the chance. I keep all conversations with that woman as short as possible. Anyone would think she was royalty the way she carries on. It might be promotion.'

'Pardon?'

'Why Dr Gore wants to see you. You know, a step up. Doubtful though – you've only been here a year and a bit. Could be a complaint from a governor or an angry headteacher.'

'That's all I need the first week back,' I sighed.

'Then again,' said Julie, with a mischievous glint in her eye, 'it could be one of his little jobs.'

'Oh no!' I exclaimed. 'Not one of his little jobs! Please don't let it be one of his little jobs!' I was well acquainted with Dr Gore's little jobs, having been given several in my first year – and they were never 'little' jobs. There had been the county-wide reading survey and the full audit of secondary school libraries followed by a detailed report to the Education Committee. There had been the investigation into the teaching of spelling, the production of a series of guideline documents for teachers, and the organising of the visit of the Minister of Education. All this was extra work on the top of the courses, inspections and report writing. I prayed it was not one of Dr Gore's little jobs.

Dr Gore, Chief Education Officer for the County of Yorkshire, continued to smile like a hungry vampire as he leaned forward in his chair. He peered over his glasses, his eyes glinting like chips of glass. 'Well, Gervase,' he murmured, stroking his brow with a long finger. I just knew what he was going to say. He was going to say, 'I have a little job for you.'

'I have a little job for you,' he said.

Ten minutes later Julie was waiting for me at the top of the stairs. 'Well?'

'One guess.'

'A little job?'

'Right first time.'

'I'll put the coffee on.'

I followed her into the office. 'Actually it's not too bad,' I said cheerfully, rattling the change in my trouser pocket. 'Dr Gore's asked me to organise a visit of one of Her Majesty's Inspectors for later this term. He wants to look at some schools as part of a national information gathering exercise on literacy standards. I just have to nominate a number of schools and arrange things, nothing massively demanding in that. I can ring round the schools this morning and get a letter off to the Ministry. There's not much else for me to do today. The only fly in the ointment is having to liaise with Mrs Savage.'

Julie pulled the screwed-up face again and clattered out of the office. 'Forget the coffee,' she said, 'I'll get the brandy.'

One bright morning a week later I was looking casually through my post when I came upon a frighteningly official-looking document. On the envelope there was a large royal crest with a lion rampant and rearing unicorn and topped with a crown. The letter inside had a black embossed heading – *The Ministry of Education* – and ended with a large flourish of a signature. I recognised the name: Miss W. de la Mare.

Miss de la Mare, Her Majesty's Principal Divisional Inspector of Schools, had contacted me the previous year when I had been given the 'little job' of arranging the visit of the Minister of Education. She had barked down the telephone at Julie that she had wanted to speak to me to discuss the visit and then had promptly hung up. Julie had told me that the speaker 'was like a grizzly bear with toothache' and had given a name which sounded like

'Deadly Stare'. In the event Miss de la Mare's bark was far worse than her bite. In the letter I had now, she requested that I arrange a series of visits to schools 'which demonstrate good practice in the teaching of reading and writing' and which 'show good breadth, balance and continuity in the curriculum'. She was particularly interested in poetry.

I knew just the school for her to visit: Backwatersthwaite Primary, the very first school I had called at when I had started in my new career as an inspector a year earlier.

It had been the first week of the job. After a frustrating two-hour search up and down the dale, along muddy, twisting roads, across ancient stone bridges, up dirt tracks and through countless picturesque villages, I had eventually discovered Backwatersthwaite School. The Headteacher, Mr Lapping, a tall, lean man with grey, frizzy hair like a pile of wire wool, had not been expecting me but was entirely unperturbed when I informed him that I was a County School Inspector visiting to examine the children's work and scrutinise the school documentation. I had called at the school again a couple of times during the year and had been immensely impressed by the quality of the education. The children were polite and well-behaved, they answered questions with enthusiasm and perception, read with confidence and expression and wrote the most poignant and vivid poetry.

I replied promptly to the letter from the Ministry of Education suggesting five schools for Miss de la Mare to visit and offering to accompany her to Backwatersthwaite. I certainly did not want her to spend half the day, as I had done, travelling backwards and forwards through the dale in search of the elusive school.

A couple of days later a second rather sharp-sounding letter arrived from the Ministry of Education informing me that Miss de la Mare was grateful for the list of suitable schools and for my offer to accompany her on one of the visits, but she would prefer to go alone. I immediately telephoned the headteachers at the chosen schools fore-warning them of the HMI's visitation.

'Well, thank you very much,' sighed George Lapping down the line. 'Thank you very much indeed. I know now who my friends really are.' I could guess from the tone of his voice that he was secretly pleased but he made the pretence of displeasure. 'I have attempted, Gervase, over the many years I have been a teacher and headteacher in this vast and beautiful county, to avoid the attentions of school inspectors. My school is isolated, difficult to find and subtly disguised to resemble the façade of a private dwelling. I have kept my head down, got on with my teaching and not done too bad a job, even if I say so myself. Now, with your recent arrival in the county, Backwatersthwaite has been put firmly on the map. I guess there will be coaches creeping up the dale full of educationalists and researchers, maybe day trippers and school parties. Now I have an HMI putting me under the microscope.'

'You should be very flattered that I recommended your school, George,' I replied. 'It's a mark of the excellent work which your pupils achieve. As Shakespeare would have it, "Some are born great, some achieve greatness and some have greatness thrust upon them."'

'But I have an *HMI* thrust upon me. Well, I just hope he has the same difficulty finding the school as you did when you first came here, Gervase. I can't be doing with visitors. They interrupt my teaching routine with all their questions. Anyway, when is this visit likely to take place?'

'Oh, some time this term,' I replied. 'I'm not exactly sure, but I should imagine that you'll be given very good warning. By the way, George –' I was about to tell him that the HMI in question would be a woman but he cut me off.

'And I do not intend putting on anything special for him.

He'll just have to take us as he finds us. Anyway, if he intends coming out in November or December, he had better reconsider. It's like Tibet up here in the winter.' I tried again to explain that the HMI intending to visit him was not a man but Miss de la Mare, and quite a forceful character at that, but he never gave me the chance. 'I shall have to go. Break is over and there's children to teach. I'll let you know how I get on.' With that the line went dead.

As soon as I had replaced the receiver, however, the telephone rang. I snatched it up.

'George,' I said, assuming it would be the previous speaker, 'I meant to say that the HMI –'

The voice which replied was coldly formal. 'This is Mrs Savage.' I jumped as if someone had poured a bucket of cold water down my back. 'Is that Mr Phinn?'

'Yes, yes, Mrs Savage,' I said. 'I thought you were someone else.'

'Mr Phinn,' she said primly, 'it was my understanding that you and I were going to liaise?'

'Going to what?' I asked.

'Liaise,' she repeated. 'I understood from Dr Gore that we were going to liaise over the visit of the HMI.'

'Oh yes, he did sort of mention something about that.'

'Mr Phinn, Dr Gore does not sort of mention something. Dr Gore is always very specific and precise and he clearly informed me that you were going to get in touch to liaise about this intended visit of the HMI. I was to deal with all the administrative arrangements.'

'I see,' I said lamely.

'Clearly you do not see, Mr Phinn.'

'I'm sorry?'

'I have not heard a thing,' she said tartly. When I did not respond she continued. 'I did telephone earlier in the week but your secretary – who is not the easiest person to deal with I have to say – was in rather a tetchy mood. Something had obviously got under her skin that morning.' At the mention of 'skin' and Julie I recalled the earlier conversation about Mrs Savage's plastic surgery. I winced and held my breath to keep from laughing.

'Are you still there?' came a strident voice down the line.

'Yes, yes, I am.'

'And then this morning, as I was dealing with Dr Gore's correspondence, I came across a letter from the Ministry of Education informing him that the visits have already been arranged.'

'The thing is, it was a pretty simple task, Mrs Savage,' I said. 'I saw no reason to bother you about it.'

I heard a sort of clucking noise down the telephone. 'So I take it that you have contacted the schools, arranged the visits and organised everything else as well?' I could imagine the stiffening of the shoulders, the hawk-like countenance and the flashing eyes.

'Yes, I have.'

'I see. Well perhaps you will do me the courtesy, next time we are asked to liaise, of letting me know that you intend to do it all yourself.'

'As I said, Mrs Savage, it was not an onerous task and –'

'I shall, of course, be informing Dr Gore of the situation. I expect you have sent him all the details?'

'It is in draft now,' I said, pulling a clean pad of paper towards me, 'and he will have it in the morning.'

There was an embarrassed silence followed by the clucking noise again. 'Well, there seems little more to say.' With that she replaced the receiver.

I took a deep, deep breath, turned to the window and exhaled noisily. The morning had started off so well. How things can change in a matter of hours, I thought to myself. I prayed that I would see little of Mrs Savage in the term ahead. As things turned out, my prayers were not answered.

'Miss, who's that funny man at the back of the classroom?'
The speaker was a small, stocky boy of about nine or ten
with a shock of thick, red hair.

'That's not a funny man, Oliver,' replied the teacher
smiling and colouring a little, 'that's Mr Phinn.'

'Well, who is he, miss?' asked the child.

'He's a visitor, come to see how well we are getting on.'

'But what does he do, miss?' persisted the little boy staring
intently at me with clear quizzical eyes. 'He's just sitting
there not doing anything.'

'That's because he's an inspector –'

'A policeman!' whispered the child excitedly.

'No, Oliver. Mr Phinn's not a *police* inspector. He's a
school inspector and –'

'And he just sits and watches people then does he, miss?'

'Well, yes, he does, but he has lots of other things to do.'
Mrs Peterson took a slow, deep breath. 'Mr Phinn listens
to children read, for example.'

'Listens to children read?' Oliver repeated shrilly. 'And
does he get paid for it, miss?'

'Yes,' replied the teacher wearily, 'he does get paid for
it, Oliver, but come along now, settle down, there's a good
boy.'

Oliver returned to his desk, all the while staring intently
in my direction. He then shook his head like an old man
despairing at the excesses of youth, before commenting,
'Nice little number that.'

I was sitting in the junior classroom of Highcopse County

Primary School, the second week into the new school term, watching the children settle at their tables, wriggling to get comfortable on the hard chairs.

It was a gloriously sunny September morning and through the open classroom window I could see a great rolling sweep of green, dotted with lazy sheep, rise to the austere, grey-purple fells beyond. An old stone farmhouse crouched against the lower slopes, tiny wisps of smoke curling from the squat chimney into the clear blue sky. A kestrel hovered in the warm air. I could hear the trickling of the small stream outside as it dribbled amongst the white limestone rocks and smell the fresh peaty tang of the countryside. It was idyllic. The boy was right – it was a 'nice little number'.

I was brought back from my reverie by the teacher's voice. 'Now, is everyone ready?' she asked. 'Will you all face the front, and pay attention? Do stop shuffling your feet, Penny, and Oliver, don't do that with your pencil, please. You know what happened last time. Thank you. It will not have escaped your notice, children, that we have a very special visitor in school today.' Those children who were not busy clearing away looked warily in my direction. My smile was greeted by a sea of solemn faces. 'Our special visitor is called Mr Phinn, and he will be with us all morning. I hope you will have a good view of proceedings from the back, Mr Phinn?'

'I'm sure I will, thank you,' I replied smiling.

'I wouldn't want you to miss anything.' I detected a hint of sarcasm in the teacher's voice.

'I can see everything very well, thank you, Mrs Peterson.'

'And you are not too uncomfortable on the small chair?'

'No, I'm fine, thank you,' I repeated, still smiling.

'Let's give Mr Phinn a really nice warm welcome, shall we, children, with a cheerful "Good Morning"?'

The children chanted half-heartedly: 'Good morning, Mr Phinn.'

'Good morning, children,' I replied cheerily, still smiling widely.

'Mr Phinn,' continued the teacher, 'will be hearing some of you read, looking at your writing and having a little chat about the work which you have been doing. That's right, Mr Phinn, isn't it?'

'It is indeed,' I replied, with the fixed smile beginning to make my cheeks ache.

'Oliver!' snapped Mrs Peterson, her eyes becoming suddenly cat-like, 'will you stop doing that with your pencil, please? I have told you once and I don't want to have to tell you again. We do not want a repetition of last term and the incident with the wax crayon, do we?'

'No, miss,' answered the child brightly.

'Oliver managed to get a piece of wax crayon lodged in his ear, Mr Phinn, and we had the devil's own job to get it out, didn't we, Oliver?'

'Yes, miss.' There was no trace of contrition in the cheerful voice.

'Peter, turn round please, dear, and pay attention. And do you know, Mr Phinn, Oliver always has an opinion or an answer. I do encourage the children to ask questions and express their views but sometimes they do need to listen, don't they?'

'They do indeed,' I agreed, wishing that she would not include me at every turn.

'And if Oliver listened a little more and talked a little less he wouldn't have all these mishaps, would you, Oliver?' The subject of the teacher's comments understood that this was an occasion for listening and he stared back silently with wide eyes. 'When I asked him what he was doing pushing a wax crayon in his ear, do you know what he replied, Mr Phinn?' I shook my head. 'He replied, "To see if it fitted."' The teacher pursed her lips and a pair of hard, glittery eyes rested on the child. 'Now then, Oliver, you can perhaps remember what I said Mr Phinn does for a living?'

'Not a lot by the sound of it, miss,' replied the child seriously.

The teacher sighed. 'Can you remember what I said his job was called?' she asked sharply.

'Yes, miss. He's a suspecter.'

Mrs Peterson shook her head, shrugged and mouthed in my direction, 'There's always one!'

I knew exactly what she meant. In the twelve months that I had been a County Inspector of Schools, I had come across countless little Olivers: lively, inquisitive children who were full of questions (and answers) and, like Julie, bluntly honest and outspoken.

'Mr Phinn is a school inspector,' the teacher corrected, mouthing the words slowly, 'and it's lovely to have you with us, Mr Phinn.' Judging by her expression and body language, I was not convinced of the sincerity of this statement. Mrs Peterson held out her hand suddenly in a dramatic gesture. 'Oliver, bring that pencil to me, please.' The little boy trudged to the front of the room and placed the pencil on the teacher's palm. 'Thank you.' She glowered at him as he returned to his seat before turning her attention back to the class. 'Now this morning, because it is a Monday, we start the day as we normally do with "Newstime". And we love "Newstime", don't we?' The class remained impassive. Mrs Peterson turned in my direction. 'It's an opportunity, Mr Phinn, for the children to tell us what they have been doing over the weekend. I don't know whether it's considered good practice or not these days. Things in education seem to shift like the sands of time.'

'It *is* good practice,' I reassured her, smiling still. 'It encourages the children to speak clearly, confidently and with enthusiasm.'

'Just what I think.' She nodded and proceeded. 'Though

with some children' – she glanced in the direction of Oliver – 'a little more listening and a little less speaking would be preferable.' The subject of her observation had his elbows on the desk and was propping his chin in his hands. He had a faraway look on his face. Clearly he was not listening. 'Well, this week, let me see whom I shall ask.' She scanned the classroom. 'Portia, would you like to come out to the front and tell us what interesting things you and your family have been doing over the weekend?'

A large, moon-faced, rather morose-looking girl with hair in enormous bunches and tied by large crimson ribbons, rose slowly from her seat and headed sluggishly for the front. She stared motionless at the class as if caught in amber, a grim expression on her round pale face.

'Come along, then, Portia,' urged Mrs Peterson.

'Nowt 'appened, miss,' the girl answered sullenly.

'Something must have happened, Portia. Did you go anywhere?'

'No, miss.'

'Well, what did you do all weekend?'

'Watch telly, miss.'

Mrs Peterson sighed and turned in my direction. 'It's like extracting teeth, getting some of the children to speak, Mr Phinn,' she confided in a *sotto voce* voice. 'Some of them are very economical in their use of words.' She turned her attention back to the large girl at the front of the classroom, who was staring vacantly out of the window. 'Now, come along, Portia, there must be something you can tell us all?'

'Miss, we found an 'edge'og on our lawn on Saturday and it were dead,' the child announced bluntly.

'Oh dear,' said Mrs Peterson, pulling a dramatically sympathetic face. 'I wonder why that was? Do you think something could have killed it?' She then looked in my direction, an expectant expression playing about her eyes. 'Possibly a cat, Mr Phinn, do you think?'

'Very possibly,' I replied.

'My dad said it were probably next door's dog,' said Portia. 'It's allus killing things that dog. My dad says it wants purrin' down. It's a reight vicious thing. It bit 'im when he was fixing t'fence and last week it chased this old woman who were collecting for the RSPCA right down t'path. We could hear t'screaming from our back room.'

'Dear me, it does sound a rather fierce creature, Portia,' said Mrs Peterson.

'It bit 'er on t'bottom by t'gate. All her little flags were ovver our garden. My dad said she wouldn't be coming back in an 'urry!'

Mrs Peterson sighed wearily, gave me a faint smile and picked on another newsgiver: a small, pale boy with large glasses. 'Come on down to the front, Simon, and tell us all what interesting things you have been up to this weekend.'

'Miss, we're going to Disneyland again next year,' said the boy scurrying down to the front. 'We went into town to book it.'

'Well, that does sound exciting. Simon is a very lucky little boy, Mr Phinn,' remarked Mrs Peterson, swivelling again in my direction and giving me a look as if to say: 'His parents have more money than sense.' 'He's just got back from America and he's off there again next year. My goodness.'

'It's really good fun, miss. There's lots to do at Disneyland,' said Simon enthusiastically.

'Have you been to Disneyland, Mr Phinn?' asked Mrs Peterson.

'No,' I replied, 'I haven't.'

'Neither have I. Whitby was as far as I got this summer and it rained for the whole week. Perhaps when teachers get that well-deserved pay rise, Mr Phinn, I'll be able to go to Disneyland.' I smiled faintly and nodded.

'Thank you, Simon. Now let me see. Oh, come on then, Oliver. I can see your hand waving in the air like a palm tree in a tornado. Come on down to the front and tell us what interesting things have happened to you during this weekend.'

Oliver scampered to the front excitedly, drew himself up to his full height and proclaimed in a loud and confident voice: 'Miss, some white worms came out of my bottom yesterday.'

Mrs Peterson screwed up her face as if she were sucking a lemon. 'Oh dear me, Oliver. I don't think we want to hear about that.'

'My mum's going to the chemist's today to get some pink stuff to get rid of the white worms that came –'

'I think we've heard quite enough about the white worms, thank you, Oliver. Is there something nice you can tell us about?'

'But, miss, my mum said lots of people get them. When she was a girl she said that all her class –'

'Yes, well, Mr Phinn's not travelled all the way from Fettlesham to hear about white worms, have you, Mr Phinn?' I smiled faintly and shook my head. 'I'm sure the medicine will work wonders tonight.'

'But, miss, when I first saw these white worms they sort of wriggled and –'

'*Oliver!*' snapped Mrs Peterson with such a wild gleam in her eye that she looked like a cat ready to pounce. '*Enough!* Back to your place, please.' Then, turning to Portia she said, 'Perhaps the hedgehog ate something which didn't agree with him. What do you think might have happened, Mr Phinn?'

This was like some double act, with me as the stooge. I was becoming a regular feature in 'Newstime', and now I was the resident expert on hedgehogs.

'Well, it could have been that,' I said. 'They do scavenge.

Quite a lot of people put out bread and milk for hedgehogs which is bad for them. It makes their stomachs swell, so it's best to let them find their natural food.'

'And does anyone know what the hedgehog's natural food is?' asked Mrs Peterson, addressing the children.

'Worms!' exclaimed Oliver, grinning widely.

Mrs Peterson smiled thinly with noble resignation.

Towards the end of the morning I took the opportunity, whilst the children were writing up their news, to look at the exercise books. Portia was writing carefully in large, clear rounded letters as I approached, but on catching sight of me she froze, dropped her pencil and stared up like a terrified rabbit in a trap.

'May I look at your work?' I asked gently. She slid the book across the desk, all the while staring and blinking nervously. She had written the date at the top of the page in bold writing and then underneath in four large capital letters the word 'E G O G'.

'What does this mean?' I asked.

''Edge'og!' she replied, looking at me as if I was incredibly stupid.

` Try as I might, I just could not get her to speak to me above the single word so I tried another tack, to re-assure her that I was really quite friendly.

'It's a lovely name, Portia,' I said. She eyed me suspiciously. 'You are named after one of the most famous characters in a wonderful play by William Shakespeare. Portia was a very clever and beautiful woman.' I was just about to launch into a rendering of 'The quality of mercy is not strained' when Mrs Peterson approached, bent low so her lips were nearly in my ear and informed me in slow and deliberate tones that 'The name is spelled "P-O-R-S-C-H-E" not "P-O-R-T-I-A!", Mr Phinn. Her father told me, when I asked him about the unusual spelling on Parents' Evening that he always wanted a Porsche car but couldn't afford one. She's the next best thing.' Mrs Peterson shook her head, shrugged and mouthed: 'There's always one!'

Little Simon, with the large spectacles and the pale, translucent face, had produced a lively little account about his recent trip to Disneyland, which concluded:

> On Saturday we booked again for Disneyland but next year we are not taking my nanna with us. My dad said she wouldn't stop talking all week and she got on his nerves and was a pain in the neck. He said it was like taking a parrot with us.

Finally I arrived at Oliver's desk. The little boy had his head down and was scratching away furiously with a large, fat fountain pen. It appeared to be leaking because there was ink everywhere. As I peered over the shock of red hair I read, with some difficulty, a simple little account of the white worms and their dramatic appearance on the day before.

'It's an interesting piece of work, Oliver,' I commented, 'but your writing is hard to read.'

'That's because miss took my pencil away, so I'm having to make do with this.' He scrutinised the writing implement before observing, 'And this pen's got a life of its own.'

After morning playtime I joined the infant class in a spacious room which was neat and orderly with colourful displays depicting various fairy story characters covering the walls. There were six large, low tables with small, orange melamine chairs at each, a selection of bright picture books on a trolley, a carpeted area, a big plastic tray for sand and another for water, and at the front a square, old-fashioned teacher's desk and hard wooden chair. The windows looked out on a magnificent view up the dale: a vast expanse of pale golden-green rolling to the grey-purple fells and clear sky beyond.

The five- and six-year-olds were in the charge of a serious-looking teacher in a grey jumper and dark brown skirt, called appropriately Mrs Dunn. She had iron-grey hair pulled back severely across her scalp and wore a pained expression throughout the hour-long lesson. She had the rather unsettling habit of twitching nervously before glancing in my direction. The children read competently and their writing, though slightly below the standard I would have expected from children of this age, was sound enough. There was a great deal of copied writing, a few simple stories and no poetry.

At the end of the morning I returned to Mrs Peterson's class to make my farewells. The teacher beamed effusively as I entered her room.

'Now, children, look who's back – it's Mr Phinn.' The children looked up indifferently.

'I've just popped in to say goodbye, Mrs Peterson.'

'It's been a pleasure, Mr Phinn. We do like to have special visitors, don't we, children?' One or two children nodded unenthusiastically. 'It's been a real treat for us and I hope it is not too long before you come back and see us again. That would be nice, children, wouldn't it? My goodness, Mr Phinn, we do have such a lot of fun in this classroom, don't we, children?' The class stared impassively. 'We really do have so much fun, don't we?' There were a few nods. I caught sight of Oliver in the Reading Corner. He looked up from his book, *Creepy-Crawlies and Minibeasts* and shook his head. Mrs Peterson had spotted him too.

'Yes, we do, Oliver! We're always having fun.' She fixed him with a rattlesnake look and gave a little laugh. It was not a pleasant little laugh. 'Too much to say for himself, that young man, Mr Phinn,' Mrs Peterson confided in me in an undertone. 'We do have a lot of fun.'

As I passed Oliver on my way out, I heard him mutter, 'I must have been away that day.' I suppressed a smile.

'Oliver,' continued Mrs Peterson, her face now rather more leering than smiling and her voice with quite a sharpness of tone to it, 'would you go and ask the school secretary to ring the bell for dinnertime, please, there's a good boy.' The last phrase was said with some emphasis. 'And shall we all now say a nice, warm "Goodbye" to Mr Phinn?'

'Goodbye, Mr Phinn,' the class intoned.

'Goodbye,' I said.

Oliver and I walked down the corridor together. 'Can I ask you something, Mr Phinn?' he said.

'Of course.'

'How do you become one of these suspecters, then?'

'Inspectors, Oliver.'

'How do you become one?'

'Well, you have to work hard at school, read a lot of books and when you go up to the big school you have to pass your exams and go on to college. You then take more exams and that takes a long, long time.'

'How old do you have to be?' he asked.

'You have to be twenty-one to be a teacher and even older to be a school inspector, so you have a long way to go.'

'And then you can sit at the back of classrooms and watch people?'

'That's right.'

'And hear children read?'

'That's right.'

'And look at their writing?'

'And look at their writing,' I repeated.

The little boy looked up and then scratched at the shock of red hair. 'And you get paid for it?'

'And get paid for it,' I intoned. He still looked very thoughtful, so I said, 'Would you like to ask me anything else?'

3

'You've had a telephone call,' announced David, when I arrived at the office one damp, depressing, early October afternoon. He gave a wry smile before adding, 'You have been summoned to an audience with the Ice Queen herself.'

'Who?'

'Mrs Savage.'

'Oh, no,' I moaned. 'Whatever does she want now?'

Sidney looked up from his papers, shook his head, adopted a pitiful expression and sighed dramatically.

'She left a message that you are to go up and see her,' continued David. 'She was quite insistent.'

'Sounds like Mae West,' said Sidney suddenly. He mimicked the slow American drawl of the star of the silver screen. 'Come up and see me sometime, honey.'

'Anyone less like Mae West, I could not imagine,' I told him caustically.

'My goodness,' said David, taking off his reading glasses and folding them on the desk in front of him, 'someone is in a rather fraught condition this afternoon.'

'I can't seem to escape from the woman,' I said, banging my briefcase down on a chair. 'She was on the phone to me the very first day of term and since then I keep on getting messages and memos every other day.'

'She's perhaps taken a shine to you,' said David, finding the whole situation highly amusing. 'You want to watch out.'

'Huh!' I grunted.

'Or a certain young, attractive headteacher might start getting a trifle jealous.'

'David, I've already had the third degree from Julie about my love life. Could we leave Christine out of it, do you think? I wonder what Mrs Savage is after now?'

'Did you know,' said Sidney, pushing aside his papers and leaning back expansively in his chair, 'that she once tried to lure a bishop up to her room?'

'Who? *Mrs Savage?*' exclaimed David.

'No, no! Mae West. She met this bishop at some fancy function or other and said to him, "Come up and see me sometime," and this bishop replied, with a very serious face, "I'm sorry, Miss West, but that is quite impossible. It's Lent." Mae West was reputed to have quipped back, "Well, bishop, when you get it back from the person you lent it to, come up and see me."'

'I'm sure you make all these stories up, Sidney,' said David sniggering, and returning to his work.

'Did she say what she wanted?' I asked.

'Who? Mae West?' asked Sidney.

'Sidney, *will* you be serious! Mrs Savage. Did she say what she wanted to see me about?'

'No, no,' said David. 'Just for you to go up and see her in the Annexe and that it was a matter of some urgency.'

'When is it not?' I asked in an exasperated voice.

'Now don't start getting comfortable, Gervase,' continued David, as I began taking a bundle of papers from my briefcase, 'putting off until tomorrow what you can do today. She won't just disappear, much as we would like her to, you know. My old Welsh grandmother used to say that it is always best to meet adversity head on. "Grasp the nettle, David," she used to say. "Take the bull by the horns and face the music. Doing nothing, solves nothing." She's working late tonight and wants you to go up and see her at about six o'clock. She will be waiting.'

'Your old Welsh grandmother?' asked Sidney, facetiously.

'You are becoming very tiresome, Sidney,' replied David,

putting his glasses back on and looking at him over the top of them. 'I am endeavouring to convey an important message and then complete this report. It is nearly six o'clock and I do have a home to go to.'

'Go and see her now, Gervase,' advised Sidney. 'David's quite right, it's best to get such a deeply unpleasant and potentially hazardous experience over and done with – like having an ulcerated tooth pulled or a giant boil lanced.'

'Yes, I think you're right,' I said wearily, stuffing the papers back into my briefcase. 'I'd better see what she wants.'

'And if I were you, Gervase,' said David, looking up from his papers, 'I should enter her labyrinth with a great degree of caution. She becomes even more of a Gorgon after six o'clock.'

'No, no!' exclaimed Sidney. 'It was Theseus who entered the labyrinth to face the Minotaur. You're thinking of Medusa, one of the Gorgons, who had great sharp shoulders, barbed claws, enormous teeth and who could turn you to stone with an icy stare. Come to think of it, sounds rather like Mrs Savage.'

'Thank you for the potted history of Greek mythology,' said David, removing his glasses again. 'I am well aware of the difference between the Minotaur and a Gorgon. We were taught the classics at my Welsh grammar school. One can't say anything around here without receiving a lecture from you, Sidney, or some clever comment or other. All I was attempting to say was that Gervase ought to be on his guard, to proceed with extreme caution. She's obviously taken a liking to him –'

'No, she has not!' I exclaimed.

'And may have an ulterior motive for these late meetings. You are a very vulnerable young man. The woman has been through husbands like a killer shark through a shoal of sprats, and before you start to tell me, Sidney, that killer sharks don't eat sprats –'

I left them both in hearty discussion and departed, thinking to myself, if only David knew.

I had never divulged to my colleagues the entirely unexpected and dreadfully embarrassing confrontation which had taken place in Mrs Savage's office a few months into my new job. We had worked closely together on a number of projects and Mrs Savage had been uncharacteristically good-humoured and co-operative. When I had been given one of Dr Gore's 'little jobs' to organise – the visit of the Minister of Education – Mrs Savage had been enormously helpful and highly efficient. The visit had gone really well and she and I were on first-name terms by the end. Then I had visited Mrs Savage's office late one March afternoon. She had looked like the star of an American soap opera, dressed in a scarlet and black suit with huge shoulder pads and great silver buttons and with what, I imagined, she considered an alluring look on her face. She had tilted her head, moved near and confided in me that she had been so lonely following the death of her last husband. When she had moved closer, breathing heavily and fluttering her eyelashes, I had made hurried apologies and departed at high speed. Since then I had kept my distance and, on the few occasions our paths had crossed, Mrs Savage had remained coldly formal. I had sensed, however, that beneath the icy exterior there was something still simmering.

It was with some trepidation, therefore, that I headed for the dreaded meeting. The school inspectors occupied the top floor of what could only be described as an Edwardian villa, some distance away from the main County Hall. We saw little of the occupants of the ground floor – the educational psychologists – who, like us, spent most of their time in schools. One of the villa's former bedrooms had been converted into our office, another was used as a store and the third, which was not much bigger than a box-room, was where Julie worked. The trip from our office to County Hall was a pleasant stroll on a bright summer's day and a bracing walk on a fresh winter's morning, but when the weather took a turn for the worse, I would arrive for a meeting wet and windblown and wishing I worked in an office near to the main Education Department.

But then I would be closer to Mrs Savage which would be worse, I now mused as I quickly skirted the formal gardens, well-tended lawns and neat footpaths which surrounded the grey stone edifice of County Hall. It was a dark, rain-soaked evening and a ragged grey curtain of cloud hung from the sky and the wind drove the rain at a sharp slant, thoroughly soaking me. Once inside the main building, wet and cold, I headed for the cloakrooms where I dried my face and combed my hair in preparation for the ordeal ahead of me. I then set off for the Annexe and Mrs Savage's room.

The interior of County Hall was like an empty museum, hushed and cool, with a succession of wandering marbled corridors, long leather-covered benches and ornate highly polished doors. The walls were full of portraits of former councillors, mayors, aldermen, leaders of the council, high sheriffs, lord lieutenants, members of parliament and other dignitaries, many of them bearded and all of them looking gloomy. They stared from their gilt frames in solemn disapproval, adding to my dismal mood. A jagged streak of lightning lit up the dark corridors, followed seconds later by a grumbling of thunder and a downpour of rain which lashed fiercely at the windows. As I turned the corner leading to Mrs Savage's room, the clock on the County Hall tower struck six deep, melancholy, echoing notes. It sounded like a funeral bell.

The office of Dr Gore's Personal Assistant was at the very top of a modern three-storey structure attached to the rear of County Hall. The Annexe clung to the sturdy imposing Victorian building like some great glass limpet and looked entirely out of place. The architect, no doubt constrained by the Finance Department, had designed something large, utilitarian and cheap and had made no attempt to match the style or construction of the original building. The Annexe housed the administrative and clerical support offices and the Print Room.

Mrs Savage's office was palatial compared to mine. The desk, which dominated the room, was a vast asymmetrical affair in rich mahogany. There were filing cupboards and cabinets of various sorts, an expensive-looking bookcase, an occasional table and two easy chairs. The walls, which were plain and the colour of sour cream, had four large paintings in metal frames, positioned at exact distances from one another. They were the sort of art Sidney described as meaningless, abstract splatters. There was a thick shag-pile carpet and long pale drapes at the window. Mrs Savage was sitting stiffly at her desk with icy imperturbability, a computer humming away on a console beside her.

'Do come in, Mr Phinn, and take a seat,' she said, catching sight of me hovering in the doorway like a naughty schoolboy waiting to see the Headteacher. 'I won't be a moment.' There was a note of sharp command in her voice. I sat in one of the easy chairs, crossed my legs casually and flicked through my diary, attempting to give the appearance of being entirely at ease. Inwardly I felt as nervous and anxious as a patient waiting to hear the results of some medical test. Mrs Savage scratched away with a sharp pencil, for what seemed an interminable amount of time, glancing up occasionally as if to make sure I was still there. I watched her out of the corner of my eye. She looked haughtier than ever. I had not seen her since the previous term and, as Julie had remarked recently, she seemed to have lost weight and a number of wrinkles and creases into the bargain. She was dressed in a close-fitting, pale green silk suit splashed with great crimson poppies which matched exactly the colour of her lipstick and nail varnish. She certainly was a striking-looking woman.

'Now then, Mr Phinn,' she said suddenly, looking up from her papers, 'thank you for coming up to see me.' She was making it perfectly clear that we were no longer on first-name terms. So be it, I thought.

'That's all right, Mrs Savage,' I replied, attempting to sound relaxed. 'I believe you mentioned that it was urgent?'

'It is,' she said sharply. 'It's about the Feoffees.'

'I beg your pardon?'

'The Feoffees,' she repeated, picking at the word like a pigeon with a piece of bread. She stared and waited and it was clear that she had no intention of enlightening me as to what a Feoffee actually was. Well, two can play at this cat and mouse game, I thought to myself.

'What have the Feoffees got to do with me, Mrs Savage?' I asked.

'As you may be aware, Mr Phinn, Lord Marrick, the Vice-Chairman of the Education Committee, is to take up the office of Greave and Chief Lord of the Feoffees in the New Year.' She paused for effect.

'Really?'

'Next year is the five hundredth anniversary of the foundation of the Feoffees. I don't know whether you knew?'

'No, I didn't.'

'Lord Marrick, who is a great one for tradition, as you know, is keen to mark this very significant juncture in the Feoffees' history by hosting an open day at Manston Hall at the end of May, and he wants various events, involving a wide range of local institutions and organisations, to celebrate such an auspicious occasion.'

'I see,' I said, nodding and trying to appear knowledgeable. I had not the first idea what a 'Fee-Fo', or whatever it was called, was but I was not going to let on to Mrs Savage. 'And how do I come in?'

'Dr Gore wishes you to attend a planning meeting at Manston Hall in November in his place. I have checked your engagement sheet and note that you have no important commitments at that time. Of course, Dr Gore would have represented the Education Department himself but it is quite impossible for him to attend the meeting. As you are no doubt aware, he has been asked by the Minister of Education to sit on a major Government committee and will be exceptionally busy for the foreseeable future. It is, of course, a great honour for the CEO to be invited by the Minister to be part of such a prestigious group.' She gave a slight smile as if she were privy to some secret. 'Dr Gore would not, under normal circumstances, have delegated such an important task to someone else, particularly to a relative newcomer to the county, but Dr Yeats is leading a major school inspection in November and is not available. Dr Gore understands that you had a number of dealings with Lord Marrick last year so he is not unfamiliar to you.'

'I see,' I said again, still totally in the dark.

'He would have seen you personally to explain what is involved but he is the guest speaker at the Fettlesham High School Presentation this evening so has asked me to deal with it. He would like this matter expedited immediately.' She leaned over her desk and clasped her hands before her. There was a huge solitaire diamond ring on one red-nailed finger and a cluster of gold hoops on another. 'He has also, Mr Phinn, asked me to liaise with you over this.' Her voice had taken on an even sharper edge. 'I sincerely hope that we will, in fact, liaise and that you will not take it upon yourself, as you did with the HMI visits, to do everything on your own.'

I had guessed that she would raise that little matter but decided not to get into a further discussion about it.

'Yes, of course, Mrs Savage,' I said pleasantly. 'And what does this particular initiative involve?'

'It involves joining the planning group and contributing where appropriate. Of course, the Education Department will have a significant part to play in the celebration of five hundred years of the Feoffees. I guess it will mean displays of various sorts, children's presentations, that sort of thing, reflecting the life and work of the Feoffees.' It was as if she were speaking in a foreign language.

'Of course,' I nodded.

There was a portentous pursing of the lips. Mrs Savage eyed me for a brief moment before continuing. 'Dr Gore has asked me to deal with all the administration. I have already informed Lord Marrick that you will be representing the Education Department and I shall send you the agenda and the accompanying papers for the meeting just as soon as I receive them.' She paused and gave me a frosty look. 'And I would be very appreciative, Mr Phinn, if you would see to it that I am kept fully informed. It makes my life so much easier if I know what is happening, when it is happening and how it is happening. I hope I make myself clear.'

'Perfectly clear, Mrs Savage.'

She ran her eyes over me critically as a doctor might observe an interesting patient. 'Good,' she said. I stood up to go. 'One moment, Mr Phinn, I haven't finished with you yet.' She gave a small, quick smile before rising from her chair and straightening the creases in her skirt. I felt a tingle of apprehension. Was she going to leap across the desk, launch herself on top of me in wild abandon, drag me on to the thick shag-pile carpet, throw me over the occasional table? I stepped back as she moved stealthily around the desk like a predatory cat. I could smell her heavy perfume. The eyelashes began to flutter. My apprehension turned to cold fear. This was going to be a re-enactment of the earlier deeply embarrassing incident. I was going to have to fight the woman off!

'What about a date?' she asked.

'Date?' I whispered. 'What date?'

'You need a date for the meeting at Manston Hall.'

'Ah,' I sighed, 'that date.' In my anxiety to get the meeting over quickly, I had completely overlooked that the date had not yet been mentioned. I had thought, for one appalling moment, that Mrs Savage was propositioning me for a date.

'The twenty-fifth of November at ten o'clock.' I stared, wide-eyed, open-mouthed, rooted to the spot as if looking into the face of Medusa herself. 'Is there something else, Mr Phinn?' asked Mrs Savage.

'No, nothing,' I replied and headed at a brisk pace for the door.

Sidney and David were putting on their coats when I arrived back at the office.

'You managed to escape unscathed then,' commented David, straightening the papers on his desk.

'He does look a little flushed and out of breath, don't you think?' said Sidney. 'I hope your dealings with Mrs Savage were entirely professional, Gervase. What did she want?'

'Have either of you heard of the Feoffees?'

'Are they a pop group?' asked David.

'I once went out with an amazing American girl at Oxford called Fifi,' sighed Sidney. 'Very good sculptor. Had wonderful muscles and flaming red hair. Ate nothing but lentils. Remarkable woman.'

'I have a drawer in my filing cabinet marked "Fifi",' said David. 'It's stuffed full of papers, dead documents, reports and memoranda. Stands for "File it and forget it". Most of Mrs Savage's missives are consigned to that drawer.'

'Will you two be serious for a moment,' I said. 'It's not "Fifi", it's "Feoffee". I have to attend a meeting at Manston Hall. Evidently Lord Marrick is becoming the top Feoffee, whatever that involves, and wants to arrange some events to celebrate it. Could it be some sort of Masonic order?'

'Druids,' suggested Sidney, putting on his raincoat. 'Probably the Yorkshire version of the druids. Old men in white sheets dancing around the monoliths at Brimham Rocks. Like the daft sort of thing the Welsh go in for. Dressing up in those funny costumes and waiting for the eclipse.'

'Daft!' exclaimed David. 'I'll have you know that the druids are part of a long cultural tradition which stretches back centuries. They do not dress up in funny costumes. The Celts –'

'Oh, please spare us the Celts,' begged Sidney, 'or we will be here all night.'

A heavy laboured tread could be heard on the stairs leading up to the office.

'Well, I can't offer any more help,' announced David, glowering in Sidney's direction before reaching for his umbrella.

'But those light steps on the stairs,' said Sidney, cupping his hand around his ear, 'tell me that our esteemed leader is about to enter and I feel certain he will be able to furnish you with detailed information about these Feelies.'

'Yes, you'd best ask Harold, Gervase,' agreed David. 'There is nothing on which Harold Yeats is not an expert.'

'Isn't that a double negative?' asked Sidney. '"Nothing on which he is not". I think it would be rather better expressed as "Harold is an expert on everything".'

'I am going to do something extremely unpleasant with this umbrella in a minute, Sidney, if you don't shut up! Firstly I am picked up on my knowledge of Greek mythology, then you have a go at the druids and now you see fit to correct my grammar.'

'Well, we have the English expert here, he can arbitrate. Am I right or am I right, Gervase? Was that not a double negative?'

'Don't bring me into it,' I said, 'I've got other things on my mind at the moment.'

At this point Harold breezed in, wet and windblown, but smiling a great toothy smile. The Senior County Inspector was a giant of a man. Six foot, three inches in height, he looked a daunting figure with his great broad shoulders, heavy bulldog jaw, large watery eyes and prominent teeth but he was the gentlest and most unassuming person I had ever met. He was a man of sincerity, generosity and unfailing courtesy, someone who always looked for the best in everybody and had a deep interest in the needs of children. He was also a walking encyclopaedia and turned out to know everything there was to know about the Feoffees. He became quite animated when asked to explain what they were and what they did.

'A very interesting group of men, the Feoffees,' he enthused. 'They were originally a collection of civic worthies and dignitaries, usually prominent landowners and gentry, founded in the reign of Henry VII to keep law and order. All justice in a parish or town was administered by them and they ensured the sick and needy were cared for. They were responsible for no end of things – repair of bridges and roads, keeping the water supply fresh, isolating plague victims, making sure the pillories and ducking stools were kept in good working order.'

'Are you sure we're talking about the same thing, Harold?' I asked.

'Oh, yes, indeed. The Feoffees served a very important function in Tudor and Stuart times. They appointed the swineherd, clerk of the market, overseer of the roads and provided all the liveries for the beadles, pipers, town criers and organ blowers – the whole company of minor officials. Of course, the Feoffees varied from area to area but –'

'That's fine, Harold,' I interrupted, 'but what is their function today?'

'Well, it is largely a charitable institution. Why are you so interested in the Feoffees anyway, Gervase?'

I explained about the meeting with Mrs Savage, the proposed visit to Manston Hall and my involvement in the forthcoming celebrations.

'I see,' said Harold. 'It sounds a very interesting undertaking. I would have very much liked to have attended that meeting myself. I mean I am the inspector who covers history. It's strange that I wasn't approached.'

'Mrs Savage said that you are leading an inspection on the twenty-fifth of November when the meeting takes place but if you can re-arrange things, Harold, I should be delighted for you to go instead.'

'No, no,' said Harold. 'I can't cancel an inspection. Mrs Savage is quite right.'

'It would have been nice to have been asked or at least consulted though, wouldn't it, Harold?' said David. 'That woman takes far too much on to herself. She's only an office clerk, for goodness sake. Anyone would think she was the CEO, the way she carries on.'

'Well, I'm glad she didn't approach me!' said Sidney. 'It sounds a complete and utter waste of time! What has all this got to do with education? I thought our job was to inspect schools not join a group of anachronistic, undoubtedly well-heeled geriatrics who have nothing better to do than spend their time repairing pillories and ducking stools, and isolating victims of the plague.'

'Sidney,' snapped Harold, 'it has everything to do with education! First, the Feoffees are part of our rich, cultural heritage, which is something we should be proud of and cherish.'

'Like the druids,' interposed David.

'It is important,' continued Harold, 'that young people should know about the history of their country. Furthermore, the Feoffees still help the poor and afflicted, particularly orphans and deprived children. They continue to promote good conduct in the rising generation, provide financial support and give scholarships and bursaries to deserving causes.' The clock on the County Hall tower began to strike seven but Harold, who had now got the bit firmly between his teeth, continued undeterred. 'The Feoffees, who number amongst their ranks of anachronistic, well-heeled geriatrics our own Dr Gore, do a great deal of good, so when you ask –'

'For whom the bell tolls,' interrupted Sidney, 'it tolls for me to get on home. Seven o'clock and I might, with any luck, have missed the traffic. Oh, and Harold, I do hope the Feoffees have ensured that the roads are in good repair, that Hawksrill Bridge is still standing and there are not too many crowding around the pillories or in the stocks. I need to get back in good time for the football tonight.'

I headed for the office one splendidly bright autumnal Friday afternoon, tired and road-weary. The mild weather had brought the caravaners out in force and I, at the back of a queue of five or six other frustrated car drivers, followed a dangerously swaying box on wheels for three miles as it meandered at 20 mph along the twisting narrow country roads. When at last I became the car directly behind the caravan, I noticed stuck on the back window a little cut-out hand which waved as the caravan teetered. Its message read 'Have a nice day' and next to it was a large yellow circle with the injunction in bold black capital letters: **STAY BACK! BABY ON BOARD!** I would have a much nicer day, I thought to myself irritably, if the driver of this creeping death-trap would pull over and let me pass.

When I finally managed to overtake, I noticed that various other messages and signs had been plastered on the side window, including a bright red rectangle with the information: 'I've been down The Black Hole at Alton Towers.' Who actually would be interested in this piece of totally fatuous information, I asked myself. I caught sight of the driver: he was an exceptionally old man, and incongruously sported a bright orange baseball cap. He beamed through the window and gave me a shaky wave. There was certainly no possibility of this geriatric having a baby on board, and as for a journey down The Black Hole at Alton Towers . . .

I was not in the best of moods as I raced towards the main road. On the grassy verge stood an extremely dirty-looking individual with a tangle of hair and dressed in a filthy raincoat. He was holding aloft a large piece of cardboard on which was written: 'I am going to York'. Not in this car, mate, you're not, I thought to myself, speeding up.

Sidney and David were busy at their desks as I pushed through the door a short while later and collapsed into a chair.

'I met the ever-ebullient Mrs Peterson on my art course yesterday,' observed Sidney, looking up from his work, 'and she was not best pleased with your report on her school.'

Before I could answer, David, placing his pen down carefully and smiling beatifically, added, 'Makes a change from all those adoring women who are constantly telephoning him and writing little *billets-doux* and singing his praises.'

'What did she say?' I asked Sidney, deciding to ignore David's comment.

'That your report was full of criticisms,' Sidney told me blithely.

'It wasn't that bad,' I said glumly, looking through the mail on my desk.

'She said that you said the reading wasn't up to much at Highcopse County Primary School,' continued Sidney casually.

'I never said anything of the sort!'

'That the writing was pretty ordinary, the children didn't speak much and the teachers didn't bother at all with any poetry.'

'Sounds pretty damning to me,' commented David, still smiling like a cat with the cream.

'It would be if I had, in fact, said it,' I replied bristling. 'My report judged the school to be sound enough but there needs to be more challenge and variety in the work. It was pretty positive overall but I suggested that –'

'She also said you were not very impressed with Mrs Dunn.'

'Not very impressed with Mrs Dunn!' I exclaimed. 'Not very impressed with Mrs Dunn?'

'That is what she said.'

'An unusual woman, Mrs Dunn!' exclaimed David suddenly. 'I remember first meeting her on one of my mathematics courses, with that dour expression of hers, wild-looking hair and hooded eyes. She was, I have to admit, a deeply unimpressive woman. She sat in the front row with a face like a death mask until I asked the teachers to break into groups for the activities. Then she looked as if I had asked her to take all her clothes off and do a tap dance on the table. I recall saying to Mrs Peterson, when she said what a good teacher she was, that Mrs Dunn was such a sombre and serious person and that she didn't sparkle for me. "I don't employ Christmas tree fairies, Mr Pritchard," she replied tartly. "I employ teachers."'

'She never smiled the whole lesson,' I said, still stinging at the criticism of my report. I tore open a letter so savagely that I nearly ripped it in half.

'Doesn't make her a poor teacher,' said David. 'We had a classics master at grammar school called "Smiler" Jones. He always had a smile on his face. Terrified of him, we were. He was always leering and grinning from the front. He had these tiny, shining eyes and a big hooked nose and always wore a tattered black academic gown. He was like some great dusty crow. Fearful teacher was "Smiler" Jones. Now, I wouldn't consider him a good teacher.'

'That might explain why you are rather dodgy on the Greek myths,' remarked Sidney.

I shook my head and sighed heavily. 'I merely wrote that the teacher of the infants could be a little more lively and enthusiastic.'

'You know, Gervase,' said David, 'you of all people, being in charge of English, should know that one should never judge a book by its cover or, as they say in this part of the world, "Never judge a blade by its heft". I've seen Mrs Dunn teach, and whilst I have to admit she is not the most dynamic and inspirational of teachers in the world and unlikely to win the "Teacher of the Year Award", she is a good, solid, reliable classroom practitioner, well-intentioned, dedicated and willing to learn. She improves with knowing, does Mrs Dunn.'

'And Mrs Peterson said that you said the children were unusually quiet,' continued Sidney, leaning back on his chair and obviously enjoying imparting this next piece of information.

'Well, they were. There was only one child who got a word in.'

'That was because, as Mrs Peterson said, you frightened them.'

'What?'

'She said you sat at the back with your big black clipboard like someone about to take the measurements for a coffin.'

'I was of the opinion, Sidney, that that is what school inspectors do – sit at the back of classrooms and observe lessons.'

'She said your constant smiling put the children off.'

'I don't believe it,' I sighed.

'Of course that's what "Smiler" Jones used to do,' remarked David. 'His smile was quite unnerving. He put the fear of God into us with his funereal expression.'

'She said that when you had gone,' continued Sidney, 'one of the juniors asked if that funny man with the smile like the shark was coming back?'

'You seem to have taken an unusually thorough interest in my visit to Highcopse School, Sidney. It appears you have gone through the report with Mrs Peterson in some detail.'

'Just forewarning you, old boy, that's all.'

'Oh heck, I'll give her a ring later and sort it out.'

'Might be a wise move,' added David, nodding sagely, 'bearing in mind who her husband is.'

'And who *is* her husband?' I asked.

'County Councillor George Peterson. He's on the Education Committee. One of the most vociferous, self-opinionated and tiresome members. Rambles on for hours, does old George.'

'What an end to the week,' I sighed.

'I have had a most enjoyable week, actually,' said Sidney mischievously, clearly enjoying my discomfiture. 'The art course was a great success, all schools visited, reports completed, letters written, documents filed.'

'And pigs fed and ready to fly,' added David.

'I shall choose to disregard that remark, David,' retorted Sidney. 'I feel on top of everything at the moment and, being Friday, I am in the very best of moods. Nothing and nobody will interfere with my good humour and well being today. It has been such glorious weather for this time of year, I might just take the caravan out this weekend. You can join us if you like, Gervase. It might cheer you up.'

I did not respond.

The following Monday I telephoned the school.

'Hello,' came a loud, confident voice down the line, 'Highcopse County Primary School. Mrs Peterson, Head-teacher, speaking.'

'Hello, Mrs Peterson, it's Gervase Phinn here.'

'Oh, hello Mr Phinn. How are you?' She certainly did not sound upset or angry, quite the reverse in fact.

'I'm very well, thank you. Now, er, Mrs Peterson, my colleague Sidney Clamp has had a word with me. He tells me that you are rather upset about the report I wrote after my visit.'

'I wasn't upset, Mr Phinn,' she said sweetly, 'just a little disappointed, that's all.'

'Would you like me to call in and discuss it with you?' I asked.

'Oh no, there's no need for that. I do know how busy you inspectors are. Of course, we in schools are busy people too. Mrs Dunn and I do try very hard, Mr Phinn, but there's only so many hours in the day and there's so much to cover on the curriculum these days. I do appreciate your comments about poetry, although I have to say we were somewhat surprised with the extent of the criticisms in the report, but you see it's not one of Mrs Dunn's strong points. Not mine either, if I'm truthful. She is very good at the things she feels confident with but when it comes to poetry and –'

I interrupted the monologue. 'Mrs Peterson, I really would be happy to call in to talk about the report and suggest various approaches and offer some ideas.'

'Oh, I'm sure you have lots of suggested approaches and ideas, Mr Phinn.' That same hint of sarcasm was in her voice which I had detected when I had observed her lesson. 'What would be useful, rather than just talking about the report and suggesting what we should be doing, would be for you to come and show us just what you mean.'

'In what way?'

'Well, could you take the children for a poetry lesson? Do a demonstration?'

I have walked straight into that little trap, I thought. 'Well, yes, I suppose I could,' I replied.

'Next week?' came the smug voice down the telephone.

I flicked through my diary. 'Thursday morning?'

'Splendid. I look forward to seeing you then. Mrs Dunn will be so excited.' The Headteacher rang off. I could imagine Mrs Dunn's reaction at the thought of my taking her class for poetry and the word 'excitement' did not spring readily to mind. It would probably be a shrug of the shoulders, a shake of the head and a weary look of resignation.

★

46

I arrived at Highcopse School the following week on another bright, clear morning to take the children for poetry writing. I paused for a moment before entering the building, breathed in the fresh air and surveyed the swath of green rising to the misty fellside, dotted with browsing sheep. I could see rabbits cropping the grass at the edge of a nearby field, and a fat pheasant strutted along the craggy limestone wall bordering the school. A squirrel ran up the trunk of an ancient tree by the road and then peered at me between the yellowing leaves. High above in a vast and dove-grey sky, the rooks screeched and circled. Here was poetry indeed.

The junior class was ready and waiting, paper in front of them, pencils poised. I spent the first part of the morning encouraging the children to write poetry based on several large prints of paintings by famous artists which depicted figures and faces. I asked them to concentrate on the shapes, colours, distinctive features, dress, facial expressions and surroundings, prompting them through questions: 'Who is this person? Where does she live? Is she feeling happy or sad, angry or thoughtful? How would you describe the expression?' In a relatively short time the range of responses and ideas covered the blackboard and helped the children compose some impressive pieces of writing. Mrs Peterson was quite taken aback when she read Porsche's poem which was based on the large colour print of Mary Cassatt's 'Child with a Red Hat'.

> It looks as if her head's on fire.
> Great flaming hat as red as a furnace.
> Tongues of yellow in the golden hair,
> Like burning corn.

Simon's effort was also very descriptive. His poem was based on 'The Ironers' by Degas.

She yawns with a mouth like a gaping cave,
In a face as fat as a football.
She has the fists of a boxer
And arms as thick as tree trunks.
It must be all that ironing.

Mrs Peterson took me aside. 'They are most striking pieces of writing, Mr Phinn. The children have written such lovely poems. I must say you have certainly brought out their creativity.'

I was feeling confident and pleased with myself when I appeared after morning playtime in the classroom of Mrs Dunn. I gathered the small children around me on the carpet in the Reading Corner and we talked about several large colour photographs of various animals which I had brought with me. I explained that we were going to write some little descriptive poems about the different creatures which included a mole, rabbit, squirrel and dormouse. We were to look at each picture in turn and it was my intention to encourage the children to talk about the colours and shapes. I did not, however, get very far. When I held up the large photograph of the mole, one of the older children, a large round child called Thomas, remarked casually that his granddad killed moles.

'Does he really?' I replied equally casually and attempted to move on. 'Now look at his little fat black body. He's an unusual little creature, the mole. Can you see his big flat paws like pink spades and the sharp claws? Can anyone tell me what –'

'They dig and dig wi' them claws, deep underground they go and chuck up reight big mounds of soil,' explained Thomas to no one in particular. 'Do a lot o' damage to a field, do moles. They're a real pest my granddad says. Some farmers put down poison but me granddad traps 'em and hangs up their bodies on t'fence.'

I decided to look at another picture. 'Here we have a grey squirrel. I saw a squirrel this morning peeping from between the branches of the tree outside. Look at his large black eyes and long bushy tail. Can anyone tell me what –'

'Tree vermin,' commented the same boy. 'My granddad shoots them an' all. Ruin trees, they do. My granddad says squirrels are a damn nuisance. They eat all t'corn put out for t'hens. Rats wi' bushy tails, that's what squirrels are. My granddad goes out in t'morning with his shotgun, shoots 'em and hangs up their bodies on t'fence.'

'Just listen a moment, will you, Thomas,' I said, catching sight of Mrs Dunn sitting at the back of the room with a self-satisfied smile on her face. She seemed to be quite enjoying my discomfort. 'We can perhaps talk about that later on. Now I want us all to look very carefully at this picture of the rabbit. I saw quite a few rabbits this morning as I –'

'My granddad kills them an' all,' said Thomas. 'He pegs a little string net ovver t'rabbit warren holes and lets one of his jills down.'

'Jills?' I asked.

'His ferret. He keeps her half fed to make her keen. If he underfeeds her, she eats t'rabbit and won't come up out of t'ole. If he overfeeds her she won't go down at all. He lets her down t'hole and she chases t'rabbits out into t'net. Then my granddad breaks their necks. He's reight good at that.'

'Really,' I said feebly. 'Well perhaps later on we could hear all about that, Thomas, but for the moment let's look at the picture and think of the shapes and colours in it.' I selected the final large photograph of a dormouse and decided on a pre-emptive strike. 'And what about dormice, Thomas? Does your granddad kill those as well and hang them up on the fence?'

'No, he quite likes dormice. They don't really do any harm.'

Thank goodness for that, I thought. 'Right then,' I said cheerfully, 'let's all look at this shy little dormouse, clinging to a stalk of wheat. Look carefully at the colour of his fur and his large round eyes which –'

'Sheba kills dormice, though,' said Thomas in his flat, matter-of-fact voice.

'Sheba?' I sighed.

'Our farm cat. She catches 'em in t'fields, carries 'em into t'kitchen and plays with 'em before killing 'em. We try to get 'em off of 'er but she runs off.'

'I see,' I said wearily.

'And sometimes she brings shrews into t'kitchen an' all, and bites their 'eads off and –'

'Is there anyone else who would like to say anything about animals?' I interrupted, in the hope of changing the subject. A small, pixie-faced little boy sitting right under my nose raised his hand eagerly.

'Yes?' I said pleasantly, looking into the keen little face. 'What have you to tell me?'

'I've got frogs on my underpants,' he announced proudly.

By the end of the morning the children had produced some short, interesting poems about the animals. Most were not about little, soft-furred moles, adorable little dormice, gambolling rabbits or playful squirrels but were blunt, realistic descriptions of the animals that they knew so much about – far more than I ever would. They clearly did not need a set of large photographs to prompt them. There were images of 'fierce, sharp-toothed badgers', 'crows which picked at the dead animals on the road', 'fat, black rats that hid in the hay' and 'red foxes creeping behind the hen coop'. Thomas's effort was quite clearly the best:

On a frosty morning, my granddad
Takes his jill to catch rabbits.
She has a little blue collar and a silver bell,
Tiny red eyes and creamy fur,
And she trembles in his hands.

'Thomas lives on the farm at the top of the dale,' explained Mrs Dunn as we headed in the direction of the school hall for lunch. She was quite animated and talkative. 'Like most farming children, he's been brought up to be unsentimental about animals. They are on the farm for a purpose, not as pets, and any creature which affects their livelihood is regarded as a pest. You should hear what he's got to say about foxes.' She paused for a moment before adding, 'Thomas has a great deal to say for himself, hasn't he? You might have guessed, Mr Phinn, he's Oliver's younger brother.'

At lunch I sat between Thomas and an angelic-looking little girl. The boy surveyed me for a moment. 'Meat and tatey pie for lunch,' he said rubbing his hands. 'My favourite.' He stared at me for a moment. 'I reckon you won't be 'aving any.'

'Why is that?' I asked, intrigued.

'You're probably one of those vegetarians. Me granddad doesn't like vegetarians. He says they take the meat out of his mouth. "There's nothing better than a good bit o' beef on your plate or a nice bit o' pork on your fork." That's what my granddad says. He doesn't like vegetarians, my granddad.'

Woe betide any vegetarian foolish enough to cross his granddad's land, I thought to myself. They'd end up, along with the moles and the squirrels, hanging up on t'fence.

Before I could inform Thomas that I was not, in fact, a vegetarian, the little angel sitting next to me whispered shyly, 'I like rabbits.'

'So do I,' I replied.

'My daddy likes rabbits too.'

'Does he?'

'And my mummy likes rabbits.'

'That's nice.'

She took a mouthful of meat and potato pie before adding quietly, 'They taste really good with onions.'

I am certain that I learnt more from the children that morning at Highcopse Primary School than they did from me. Heading back to the office after lunch, on that bright autumnal afternoon, along the twisting ribbon of road, I came once more upon the swaying box on wheels with the cut-out hand waving 'Have a nice day' in the back window. I glanced again at the driver as I overtook. He gave me his shaky wave. I smiled and waved back. I was in such a good mood that had the extremely dirty-looking individual still been at the side of the road intent on getting to York, I might very well have stopped to give him a lift.

Later that afternoon, on my way back from collecting some guideline documents from the Print Room, I bumped into George Lapping in a corridor in County Hall.

'Hello,' he said laconically.

'What are you doing at County Hall, George?' I asked. 'I thought you rarely ventured out of Backwatersthwaite.'

'I've been dragooned,' he said.

'Pardon?'

'Enlisted, press-ganged, selected to sit on one of these advisory committees. I got the sort of invitation you couldn't refuse from the CEO. It's on "Key Skills". Now what do I know about key skills? You're responsible, putting me in the spotlight and encouraging that HMI to visit me. I knew it would happen.'

'I meant to give you a ring about the HMI. She's been then, has she?'

'Oh, she's been all right,' he replied with a wry chuckle.

'Have you got a minute, George?' I asked him. 'Just let's pop into one of the empty committee rooms and you can fill me in.'

A moment later George was giving me a blow-by-blow account of the visitation of Miss Winifred de la Mare, HMI.

'For a start,' began George, 'I didn't remember receiving this letter which she said she sent, saying when she would be coming, so it was a real shock when she arrived on my doorstep. I was walking up the path to the school one morning just before half past eight and, as I always do, I paused to admire the view. Anyway, as I approached the entrance a huge brown creature jumped out at me. It gave me the shock of my life. I thought at first it was a grizzly bear. When I had calmed down a bit, I realised it was, in fact, a large woman in thick brown tweeds, heavy brogues and this hat in the shape of a flowerpot.

'"You were expecting me!" she snaps.

'"Was I?" I replied.

'"Yes!" says she.

'"Oh!" says I.

'"I wrote you a letter," says she.

'"Did you?" says I.

'"Did you not get it?" she asks.

'"I might have," I replied.

'"It was very important," says she.

'"Was it?" says I.

'"Official!" says she. "In a large brown envelope."

'"Really?" says I.

'"The name is de la Mare," says she. "Do you not remember?"

'"Can't say as I do," says I.'

As George recounted his meeting with the HMI, it brought back memories of his and my first meeting and the verbal badminton we had played for a good few minutes before he had discovered that I was not the man to fix the guttering but a school inspector. I thought to myself that he might have learnt something from that experience. He clearly had not.

'So what happened?' I asked.

'I told her that I received lots of letters but, because I was a teaching head, I had to deal with correspondence and such when I could find the time. She followed me into the school, peering around her as if it were a museum, declined a cup of tea, plonked herself down on my chair, took the flowerpot off her head and got out this thick wedge of paper from her big black bag.

'"I'm ready to commence," says she.

'"Are you?" says I.

'"I am," says she.

'I pointed out to her that the children had not yet arrived so there was not much point in "commencing" anything, but at nine o'clock after the register she could get started. I asked her if she wanted to begin with the infants and work up or with the juniors and work down.

'"I wish to start with you, Mr Lapping," she says, fixing me with those gimlet eyes of hers. "I want to discuss the teaching of spelling, grammar and punctuation, approaches to poetry, drama and story writing, standards of literacy, the handwriting policy, reading in the early years and the level of comprehension." It was like an educational shopping list.

'"Hang on, Miss Mare," I says.

'"De la," says she, "it's de la Mare."'

I shut my eyes and groaned inwardly – I could guess what was coming.

'"OK, Della," I says, "I don't have all that information at my fingertips, you know."'

Bingo!

'"Well, don't you think you ought to, Mr Lapping?" says she.

' "What?" says I.

' "Have that information at your fingertips. After all you are the Headteacher!"

'I tried to explain to her that document after document arrived at the school like the plagues of Egypt, that I'd got a broken boiler, faulty pipes, toilets which wouldn't flush, a leaking roof, three children with chicken pox and a member of staff suffering from stress who, having just returned from one of Mr Clamp's art courses, was ready to chuck herself down a pothole at Hopton Crags.

' "Nevertheless, Mr Lapping," says she, "it would be helpful to have some information on all these matters."

' "Well, it's a new one to me," says I. "It's the first time in nearly forty years of teaching that the nit nurse has wanted that sort of information from me." '

I winced. 'You thought she was the school nurse?'

'Well, of course I did. How was I to know she was one of these HMIs? I've only ever met one in the whole of my career and he was an old man in a suit, with a hangdog expression and about as happy as a jockey with haemorrhoids. I was certainly not expecting a strapping great woman in tweeds. I mean, she looked like the nit nurse.'

'How did she react?' I hardly dared ask.

'She stared at me for a moment with a sort of glazed expression and then she smiled.

' "Let's start again, Mr Lapping," she said. "My name is Winifred de la Mare, HMI."

'We got on like a house on fire after that, particularly when she had met the children and read their poetry and stories. She liked what she saw so much she's coming back in the spring.'

'I really am delighted,' I said. 'Maybe I could come out to meet her when she returns?'

'Oh, you'll be meeting her all right, Gervase,' George Lapping replied. 'She was very interested in the creative writing we were doing, said it was very innovative, so I told her I got the ideas from one of your literacy courses and I suggested that she might care to join you on the next one you direct. Those little gimlet eyes of hers lit up at the thought. She said it was an excellent suggestion and that she will, no doubt, be getting in touch with you.'

'Well, thank you very much,' I replied.

'You should be very flattered,' he told me, with a mischievous ring in his voice. 'It's a mark of the excellent in-service you provide that I have recommended you.' With that, he made for the door, waved his hand dramatically and departed with the words: ' "Some are born great, some achieve greatness and some have greatness thrust upon them." '

There was a witch waiting for me outside the school. The hideous creature had long, knotted black hair which cascaded from beneath a pointed hat, a pale green-tinged face and crimson slit of a mouth, and she was shrouded in a flowing black cape. As I approached, the red-rimmed eyes fixed me with a glare and a long white-fingered hand with sharp red nails reached out like the talon of some great bird of prey and beckoned. The ghastly crone smiled widely to reveal a mouthful of blackened teeth.

'Hello, Gervase,' she crooned, 'how nice to see you.'

Before me stood the woman I was pretty sure I loved. Beneath the green and red make-up, the tangle of hair and the cloak of black was Miss Christine Bentley, Headteacher of Winnery Nook Nursery and Infant School. That particular morning I had agreed to visit the school as part of the Children's Reading Day celebrations to take the school assembly, talk to the children about stories and reading, and judge the competition for the best fancy-dressed characters out of literature. I had looked forward immensely to seeing Christine again and, even dressed as a witch, thought she looked wonderful.

I had arrived at the Education Office earlier in the day feeling on top of the world.

'You're looking pretty chipper, Gervase,' remarked Sidney as I entered the room, humming.

'I am feeling pretty chipper actually, Sidney,' I replied cheerfully.

'Certainly a lot more buoyant than a couple of weeks ago,' remarked David, looking up from his papers and removing his spectacles. 'I take it you have placated Mrs Peterson and have dear little Mrs Dunn eating out of your hand following your latest visit to Highcopse School?'

'Yes, things went well, thank you, David. You were quite right, she is a dedicated teacher and perhaps I was a little hard on her.'

'And is the Bride of Frankenstein leaving you in peace?'

'Things have gone blissfully quiet in that direction,' I said brightly. 'Not a memo or a message or a telephone call all week from Mrs Savage.'

'There's a definite spring in your step,' continued Sidney, 'an eagerness in your eye and rather a smug little smile playing about your lips. I could hear you whistling up the stairs like a blackbird with the early morning worm.'

'It would hardly be whistling, this blackbird of yours,' observed David, putting down his pen, 'if it had a beak full of worms.'

'Oh, don't be so pedantic,' retorted Sidney. 'I didn't say the blackbird had the worm in its beak, did I?'

'Well, where would it have the worm then, if it's not in its beak – tucked under its wing? In a shopping basket?'

'Look, the worm is immaterial –' began Sidney.

'Is this conversation leading anywhere?' I interrupted. I had heard quite enough about worms recently – enough to last me a lifetime. Sidney ignored me.

'What I meant, David, is that Gervase looks like the cat that has caught the mouse. Now is that comparison acceptable to you?'

I had heard enough about mice as well. 'When you two have quite finished –' I attempted to get a word in but had no success.

'Not really,' continued David. 'That's a cliché, that is. What about: like a proud, powerful lion surveying his jungle

58

kingdom. Much more original, precise and descriptive, don't you think?'

'Now I wonder why our young colleague here is looking so very pleased with himself this bright morning?' remarked Sidney, swivelling around on his chair to face me. 'It has rather more to it than having a successful visit to Highcopse School, I'll wager.'

'Possibly because today is Children's Reading Day,' I suggested, 'and for most of the time I shall be doing what I really enjoy – touring schools encouraging children to read.'

'Or could it, by any chance, be because you are about to see the woman of your dreams, the Venus of Fettlesham, the Aphrodite of the education world, the delectable Miss Christine Bentley of Winnery Nook Nursery and Infant School?'

'How do you know I am visiting Winnery Nook this morning?'

'You can't keep anything from me, dear boy. Julie mentioned that you had the visit on your engagement sheet for this week. Now do tell us, how are things going with that Nordic beauty of yours?'

Before I could reply, David looked up again from his papers. 'She's a real cracker is that Miss Bentley,' he said. 'As my grandfather – he was the one who had the sheep farm near Builth Wells – used to say, "*Fyddai hi yn berffaith petai hi yn Gymraes.*"'

'I could not have expressed it better myself,' remarked Sidney. 'And what in heaven's name does that mouthful of gutteral gibberish mean? Whenever you start spouting Welsh I always think you're choking on a bone.'

'It means, "If she were Welsh, she'd be perfect"!' replied David. 'And I'll tell you this, if I was fancy-free, with a bit more hair on my head and less of a spare tyre around the tummy, I'd be after her like a rat up a drainpipe.'

'"Like a rat up a drainpipe"!' Sidney repeated, snorting.

'What a wonderful way with words you Welsh have! "Like a rat up a drainpipe." Most original and descriptive. I don't know how you have the brass neck to criticise my choice of words when you use that sort of hackneyed expression.'

I had begun to sort through the papers on my desk to check that there was nothing urgent to deal with, trying not to get involved in the endless badinage between Sidney and David. It was impossible, however, not to listen. They were like a comedy duo. One would set off on a line of thought and then the other would respond with a witticism or a clever riposte, each trying to outdo the other. It was like playing verbal ping-pong.

After a moment's silence, when I thought my two colleagues had returned to their work, Sidney jumped up from his desk, hurried over to where I was standing, put his arm around my shoulder and looked at me with an intense expression upon his face and a gleam in his eye.

'What is it?' I asked.

'Now come along, Gervase, you have been particularly elusive when a certain young enchantress is mentioned. How are things going with you and the delightful Head-teacher of Winnery Nook?'

'Oh, all right,' I replied, shuffling my papers.

'Another master wordsmith. "Oh, all right",' Sidney snorted again. 'Ever the master of understatement. You are supposed to be an inspector for English, for goodness sake. Can't you do better than "Oh, all right"? What about splendid, fantastic, magnificent, marvellous, amazing, incredible, miraculous, phenomenal, spectacular –'

'All right! All right! Things are going pretty well. I just don't want to tempt fate.'

'So we can assume that you are, in Harold's quaintly old-fashioned words, "walking out" with Miss Bentley, or in Julie's more down-to-earth description "cooartin" and that wedding bells will soon be in the air?'

'No, you certainly cannot assume any such thing. I have taken her out a few times. There's nothing serious at the moment.' I was feeling rather embarrassed and irritated by the way the conversation was going. 'Have you completed this form on school resources yet?' I asked holding up a yellow sheet of paper, endeavouring to change the subject.

'Oh, you won't get out of answering quite so easily as that,' Sidney told me, plucking the paper from my hand and returning it to the pile on my desk. 'Now do tell. Are things developing satisfactorily in that direction?'

'Look, Sidney,' I groaned, 'I would rather not talk about it. It's gone eight thirty and I have to be in a school in fifteen minutes.'

'Well, you want to go for it, Gervase,' remarked David, leaving his desk to join us. 'You are only young once. And as my grandfather used to say –'

'Oh dear, here we go,' sighed Sidney. 'Another dose of Welsh wisdom.'

'"Live for the moment, for time runs away like the wild horses in the wind." Very imaginative was my old grandfather. One of the Welsh bards he was. He had a very poetical turn of phrase. You know, I think about that little saying of his more and more these days. I feel as if time is running away with me like the horses in the wind.' He turned to the window and stared out in the direction of County Hall. 'I've felt decidedly past it recently, I can tell you. Last week a child asked me if I wore knickerbockers when I was a boy, and then the games teacher at St Walburga's wondered if I might care for a chair while I watched the rugby match. Then I got this memorandum from Mrs Savage outlining the advantages of early retire-ment. People will be standing up for me on buses next and helping me cross the road.' He sighed, turned to face me and rested a hand on my shoulder, 'But about Miss Bentley . . .'

As the conversation was now developing into an in-depth analysis of my love life, I decided to leave. Snatching up my mail, I crammed it into my briefcase and headed for the door, nearly knocking Julie over in the process as she entered with three mugs of coffee.

'Somebody's in a hurry!' she exclaimed. 'Rushing around like a rabbit with the runs.'

'Look,' I said quietly but deliberately and addressing all three of my companions, 'this morning I have been compared to a blackbird with a beak full of worms, a cat that has got the mouse, a lion in the jungle, a rat up a drainpipe, a horse in the wind and now a rabbit with the runs. To continue the animal similes, may I add one of my own? I feel like a fox pursued by hounds. I would be very pleased if you left me and my love life alone! And so that no one is in any doubt where I am going, I am off to Winnery Book School for Nook Day, I mean Winnery Nook for Book Day, to see Christine, I mean Miss Bentley, purely, I may add, in my professional capacity.'

'Of course you are!' they all chorused loudly.

'I thought you were dressing up for Children's Reading Day,' I teased, returning Christine's smile.

'Cheeky thing!' she exclaimed. 'You had better come in. And any more clever comments of that kind and I'll put a spell on you.'

But Christine had already put a spell on me. She had captivated and charmed me, if only she knew it. I walked with her down the school corridor past excited, chattering children dressed as all sorts of characters, fussing parents who were putting the final touches to their children's outfits, and teachers in costume attempting to organise things.

'How was Chicago?'

'Marvellous,' Christine replied.

'And the dissertation?'

'All finished and sent off.'

We had arrived at the main hall by this time and were surrounded by a knot of colourful little characters all excited to show themselves off to the Headteacher.

'Look,' Christine whispered, laying a red talon on my arm, 'things are a bit frenetic at the moment, but I'm free this weekend. Let's go out and I can tell you all about it and you can tell me what sort of summer you've had.'

'That would be great,' I said, chuckling. 'I'll give you a ring.'

'What are you laughing at?' she asked.

'You just look so ridiculous in that witch outfit.'

'I've told you once,' she said, showing a mouthful of black teeth, 'I'll put a spell on you. I promise we'll catch up on everything this weekend, but now I must welcome the parents and children, Gervase, so if you would like to wait in the staff room, I'll see you in a moment. Make yourself a cup of coffee if you like. Oh, by the way, you'll find the Chairman of Governors in there. She'll be judging the competition with you.'

In the small staff room I found a large, elderly woman with hands on hips and legs planted well apart, staring intently out of the window at the view. She had really gone to town on her costume and was dressed in a wonderfully bizarre outfit. The heavy, old-fashioned suit was a mustard yellow with red and green checks and was as shapeless as a sack of potatoes. The thick stockings were of the darkest brown and the shoes of the heavy, sensible brogue variety with little leather acorns attached to the front. To complete the effect, she wore a wide-brimmed red hat sporting two long pheasant feathers, held in place by a silver brooch in the shape of a stag's head. She held a battered old handbag and an ancient umbrella with a swan's head handle. She looked magnificently outlandish.

The multicoloured figure, like some overfed, exotic bird,

turned full circle when she heard me enter. 'Mornin'!' she snapped.

'Good morning,' I replied. 'You really do look the part.'

She stared at me perplexed. 'Do I?'

'Yes, indeed. Are you Miss Marple?'

'I beg your pardon, young man?'

'Miss Marple?'

'No, I'm not. I'm Sybil Wainwright, Chairman of Governors.'

'But who are you dressed as? Are you not Agatha Christie's sleuth, Miss Marple?'

'Why do you keep going on about a Miss Marple? I've already told you, my name is Mrs Wainwright.'

'Yes, but what character are you supposed to be? Are you Mary Poppins?'

'Character? What are you blathering on about? I've not come as any character.' It then dawned upon me that she was wearing her usual apparel. 'I always dress like this.' I urgently wanted the ground to open and swallow me up.

'Of course.' I held out my hand which she shook charily. 'It's my feeble attempt at humour. I'm Gervase Phinn, school inspector, here to judge the competition with you.'

'Pleased to meet you, I'm sure,' said Mrs Wainwright, grimacing and eyeing me suspiciously. 'I had not the first idea what you were going on about.'

After a short and rather strained conversation, I extricated myself from the company of the colourful Chairman of Governors and went in search of Christine. I found her in the small reading area of the school. The Wicked Witch of the West was sitting in the corner with her arm around a small boy who was crying piteously. His little body was shaking uncontrollably and great tears streamed down his round red face. Christine held him close with a claw-like hand and tried to comfort him. The child was dressed in twisted yellow tights over which he wore a pair of close-fitting, electric-blue underpants. He had on a baggy white T-shirt with SUPAMAN written incorrectly across the front in large, shaky letters.

'Well, *I* don't think you look a prat, Gavin,' said the witch.

'I do, miss, I do,' whimpered Superman. 'Everyone says I look a prat.'

Christine caught sight of me peering through the bookcases. 'Well, look who is here!' she cried, beckoning me over. 'It's Mr Phinn.' Superman looked up and stifled his sobbing for a moment. He wiped away his tears with a grubby little fist, leaving long streaks across his cheeks, and stared sorrowfully in my direction. 'Now, Mr Phinn is a very important visitor, Gavin, and knows everything about everything because he's an inspector.' The child sniffed loudly and wiped his nose on his hand. 'Do you know what an inspector does?'

The child nodded pathetically before answering. 'He collects bus tickets.'

Christine stifled a laugh before telling the child that I was a school inspector and something of an expert on costumes. 'Shall we ask Mr Phinn what he thinks about your outfit, Gavin?' The child sniffed, wiped his nose again and nodded. 'Well, Mr Phinn,' said Christine, 'do you think Gavin looks a prat?'

'I certainly do not think he looks a prat!' I exclaimed dramatically.

The little boy started to weep and wail again. 'I do! I do! I know I do. Everybody says I do!'

'And I have in my pocket a special piece of paper which says you do not look a prat.' I reached in my jacket, produced a visiting card and wrote on it: 'Superman does not look a prat.'

The little boy took it from me, scrutinized it for a moment and asked: 'Is that what it says?'

'It does,' I replied.

He tucked the card down the back of his electric-blue underpants, sniffed, smiled and scurried off.

Christine came over and put her hand on my arm. 'That was sweet,' she said. 'Now let's see how you fare taking the school assembly.'

The infants by this time had gathered in the hall and were sitting cross-legged in their resplendent costumes, facing the front.

'Good morning, children,' said Christine brightly.

'Good morning Miss Bentley, good morning everyone,' they chanted.

'Don't you all look wonderful this morning,' she said, scanning the rows of children who gazed back with expectant, happy faces. 'Everyone looks really, really super. My goodness, what a lot of different characters we have in the hall today. It's going to be really hard to judge which of you are the best, so I have asked two of my friends to help me. I think you all know Mrs Wainwright' – she indicated the Chairman of Governors sitting at the side – 'and some of you may remember Mr Phinn who visited our school last year. Well, Mr Phinn is going to take our assembly this morning and then help us decide which of you are the most imaginatively dressed characters. Over to you, Mr Phinn.'

I had decided that I would read the children the parable of the lost sheep. It's a short account and I thought it would be very appropriate for an assembly and would relate to the children, many of whom came from farming backgrounds.

'Good morning, children,' I said, striding to the front of the hall. 'Today, as you know, is Children's Reading Day and Miss Bentley has asked me to talk to you about some of my favourite books.' I held up a large crimson-coloured volume, on the front of which the title, *Stories from the Bible*, was picked out in large golden lettering. 'This book was given to me by my mother many years ago when I was a little boy. It is a very special book, full of wonderful stories which were told by a very special man. Does anyone know who I mean?'

'Jesus,' chorused the children.

'Yes, it's Jesus, and although Jesus never wrote down any of his stories, his friends did, and millions of people have read what he said nearly two thousand years ago. Jesus wanted everyone to be kind and love each other and was often surrounded by people who did not have much money, people who had done wrong, people who had got into trouble, people who were sick and lonely, people who were looked down upon by the rich and powerful. In this story, which is called "The Story of the Lost Sheep", Jesus tries to help us understand how we should feel about the poor and weak.'

Every eye was on me as I read the story. 'Imagine that a shepherd had a hundred sheep. One day, when he counted them, he found that there was one missing. He could have said, "Well, it's only one, I've got ninety-nine more. I won't bother looking for it." But he didn't say that. He left all the other sheep untended and went in search of the one lost sheep until he found it. Now why do you think he did that?' I hoped that the children would appreciate the meaning of the parable, that every single one of us is valuable in the eyes of God and that 'there is more joy in heaven when one sinner turns back to God than ninety-nine who see no need to repent'. But the point was missed.

'Why do you think the shepherd risked losing all the other sheep just for the one which was lost?' I asked again.

A thoughtful-looking little boy on the front row raised a hand. ''appen it were t'tup!' he said.

I pressed on, explaining what parables were and how they taught us all how to lead better lives. I could see by the fidgeting and turning of heads that I was not having a massive impact on the children who were obviously keen to get on with the judging of the costumes, so I decided to finish. But not before posing one final question.

'And what would you say to Jesus,' I asked, holding high the red book like some preacher of old, 'if he were to walk into the hall this morning?'

The boy on the front row thought for a moment, then raised his hand a second time and said loudly, 'I'd give 'im that book, Mester Phinn, and I'd say, "Jesus Christ – this is your life!"'

The judging of the competition went a great deal better. Before us paraded a whole host of book characters: Long John Silver and Peter Rabbit, Paddington Bear and Peter Pan, Robin Hood and Cinderella, Toad of Toad Hall and Little Red Riding Hood. Last of all came a pathetic-looking little boy in wrinkled yellow tights, electric-blue underpants and a T-shirt with SUPAMAN written incorrectly across the front. I heard a few suppressed giggles and whispers from the other children and saw their smirks and smiles.

Mrs Wainwright and I awarded the first prize to the Little Mermaid, the second prize to Aladdin and the third prize to a very pleased little boy in yellow tights, electric-blue underpants and a T-shirt with SUPAMAN written incorrectly across the front. As he scampered out to the front of the hall, his weeping and whimpering ceased and the frowns were replaced by a great beaming smile.

I said my farewells to the children and Mrs Wainwright and headed for the door. Christine followed me and when she had made sure we were out of sight of everyone slipped her hand through my arm.

'That was really nice of you,' she said, giving me a quick peck on the cheek and then rubbing out the greenish smear which had been left behind. 'Gavin won't stop talking about that for weeks. You're an old softie really, aren't you?'

'I think the assembly was a bit over their heads,' I said.

'Just a bit. I've got to go. Don't forget to ring me.'

A large, round-faced boy appeared from the hall. He wore a bright red blouse, baggy blue pants, large red floppy hat with a small silver bell on the end and huge black shoes. His lips were crimson, his eyes lined in thick black mascara and two scarlet circles adorned each cheek. It was a grotesque parody of Noddy.

'Mr Phinn!' he gasped. 'Mr Phinn! I need one of those pieces of paper which you gave to Gavin which says I don't look a prat.'

Driving on to my next appointment, I recalled when I had been in exactly the same situation as little Gavin. I was seven at the time and my sister, at home from teacher training college, had made me the most magnificent red and yellow outfit from crêpe paper for a fancy dress event. I was to go as the Pied Piper of Hamelin and had set off for school with her in my colourful doublet and little red and yellow hat. People on the top deck of the bus had craned their necks to get a view of the little figure who had strutted along, passers-by had stared and then smiled, and old ladies had peered through the curtains. I had felt the centre of attention and so proud. Half way there, the sky had opened and the rain had fallen as thick as umbrella spokes. In seconds the crisp crêpe paper had turned into one soggy, orange mess and I had arrived at school soaked to the skin and sobbing uncontrollably. Miss Franklin, the Headteacher, had taken charge immediately and I had been dried and given a clean pair of shorts and yellow T-shirt to wear. By this time, my great heaving sobs had become a pathetic sniffle and snuffle but when I had seen myself in the mirror I had returned to the howling. The dye from the red and yellow crêpe paper had run and looking back at me in the mirror had been a small boy with brilliant orange streaks down his face, arms, hands and legs. Miss Franklin had calmed me down, given me a cuddle and had ushered me into the hall where all the other children were waiting in their colourful costumes. I remembered their smirks and grins and the whispering and giggling and, like the child in the electric-blue underpants and yellow tights, I had felt a complete prat.

'Who's he come as, miss?' one of the older children had sniggered.

'Well, can't you tell, Jimmy Everett?' Miss Franklin had said with exaggerated surprise in her voice while putting her arm protectively around my shoulder. 'He's come as the Gingerbread Man. Fancy you not knowing that.'

Like little Gavin, I had won third prize, had talked about it for weeks and had fallen in love with my very first infant Headteacher, the beautiful Miss Franklin.

6

My next appointment on Children's Reading Day was at Hawksrill Primary, a school deep in the heart of the Dales, where I had agreed to take another school assembly on the theme of reading. As I drove up the twisting snake of a road, I determined that this assembly would be without incident and decided that I would abandon my plans to read again the parable of 'The Lost Sheep' and I would talk about something completely different.

One day during the summer holidays, Christine and I had walked from deep within the North York Moors to the coast at Ravenscar. The journey followed the old Viking route known as The Lyke Wake. Legend has it that the Vikings carried the 'lyke' or corpse across the bleak moors to the sea, where the body was given up to the waves. With the coming of Christianity, the practice was continued but it took on a deeper meaning and the walk came to symbolise the journey of the soul towards Heaven.

When we had arrived at Ravenscar Christine had bought me a very readable little book about The Lyke Wake. The central character was a brave and noble Viking called Thor who helped carry his dead father across the lonely, desolate land to his final resting place. The story starts in modern times, when a school party stumbles across a silver bracelet or torque glistening in the bracken. This short, lively tale, I thought, would be ideal for reading in the assembly.

Hawksrill was a small stone building enclosed by a low, craggy limestone wall. It was surrounded by a vast expanse of pale and dark green fields which rose to the thick, now dead bracken slopes, long belts of woodland and the faraway, cold grey fells. The Headteacher, Mrs Beighton, was a stout, squarely built, ruddy-complexioned woman with a wide, friendly face and short cropped white hair. Her assistant, Mrs Brown, was uncannily like her. They both wore rather old-fashioned, floral-patterned dresses and cardigans and carried capacious handbags. Both were widows and shared a small cottage within walking distance of the school.

Mrs Beighton and Mrs Brown were inseparable. They came on courses together, could be seen each Saturday, shopping in Fettlesham, and on Sundays they attended the primitive Methodist chapel and sat side by side in the front pew in their Sunday hats. Mrs Beighton and Mrs Brown were typical of many Yorkshire folk: industrious, good-humoured and plain speaking, with strong views and an ironic sense of humour. On my last visit to the school towards the end of the previous term, I had remarked that they were so typical of the forthright and friendly people I had met on my travels about the county.

'Well, you know, Mr Phinn,' Mrs Beighton had explained, 'I think you can always tell someone from Yorkshire.'

'But you can't tell them much,' Mrs Brown had added, chuckling.

Both teachers now greeted me with warm smiles when I entered the one large, bright classroom during morning playtime.

'Hello, Mr Phinn,' said the Headteacher cheerily. 'How kind of you to come to see us.'

'Most kind,' echoed Mrs Brown. 'Do come in.'

'It seems an age since you visited us, out here at Hawksrill,' said Mrs Beighton.

'A good few months, I should say, Mrs Beighton,' remarked her companion.

'And the children are so looking forward to meeting you again.'

'They are indeed,' added Mrs Brown.

After morning break, the sixteen junior and twenty infant children gathered around me in the large classroom for the assembly. They listened attentively to the story of The Lyke Wake with no interruptions and everyone was completely still and hushed when I arrived at the dramatic conclusion. Mrs Beighton and Mrs Brown, mouths open, hands resting on their laps, sat transfixed at either end of the classroom like bookends and made no effort to move.

'Well, I hope you all enjoyed that,' I said cheerfully when I finished. The children and their teachers nodded. 'Are there any questions?' I looked across a sea of silent children. 'There might be something someone wishes to ask?' There was still no response. 'Anything at all?'

'Come along now, children,' came Mrs Beighton's voice from the back. 'I'm sure there are lots of things you would like to ask Mr Phinn.'

A young frizzy-haired boy with a pale, earnest face raised a hand.

'Ah, there's someone,' I cried, relieved that at least one child had found the story sufficiently interesting to ask a question. 'Yes, and what would you like to ask?'

'What's a condom?'

'Pardon?' I jumped up in my chair as if I had been poked with a cattle prod.

'A condom? What's a condom?' repeated the child. I was completely lost for words.

Mrs Beighton and Mrs Brown leapt to their feet like synchronised puppets with their strings being yanked.

'Well, it's . . .' I began, looking appealingly towards the teachers.

'It's a snake,' snapped Mrs Beighton quickly.

'No, that's an anaconda, miss,' volunteered a young, helpful, red-headed boy.

'It's a bird,' announced Mrs Brown with great assurance.

73

'Condor,' exclaimed the child at the back. 'You're thinking of a condor, miss.'

'Well, what *is* a condom?' persisted the frizzy-haired child, looking straight into my eyes.

'Well, it's . . .' I began a second time.

'Vikings didn't have big horns on their helmets, John,' said Mrs Beighton, moving to the front of the class and taking centre stage, 'and they definitely did not have condoms either.'

The little boy, entirely undeterred, continued with the grilling. 'But what *is* a condom?'

'It's something you will learn about when you are older,' replied Mrs Brown firmly, as she joined her companion. She had the pious face of a Mother Superior.

'Is it a rude word, miss?' asked the innocent.

'No, it's not a rude word, John.'

'Can I call somebody a condom then, miss?'

'No! You certainly cannot!' snapped Mrs Beighton.

'Certainly not!' echoed her companion.

'Somebody called me a condom, miss,' the infant told the teacher.

'Well, they shouldn't have,' said Mrs Beighton.

'Ignore them,' added Mrs Brown sharply.

'Does it begin with a curly "C" or a kicking "K"?' asked a fresh-faced little girl at the front.

'A curly "C", Sarah, but –' replied Mrs Brown.

'And is it spelt C–O–N–D–O–M?' she asked, articulating every letter slowly and deliberately.

'It is but –'

'Oh, just look at the time!' cried the Headteacher, coming to her colleague's aid. 'We haven't started writing yet.' The frizzy-haired child continued to persevere and still had his hand in the air.

'Right, children. Put down your hand now, John. Everyone sit up straight, look this way, arms folded and when we are ready we can go to our desks and start our writing.'

Mrs Beighton explained that the older children were going to recount the story I had told in assembly in their own words and the younger ones were to draw a picture and add some captions which she would write on the blackboard. Soon books were out and the children were scribbling away industriously and peace descended on the classroom. I spent the remainder of the morning working with groups of children and looking through the reading scores.

'Thank you, Mrs Beighton,' I said over a cup of coffee at lunch-time, 'you really saved my bacon.'

'I'm sorry, Mr Phinn?' she said with a quizzical expression on her face.

'The condom,' I reminded her.

'Oh that. Well, children do tend to get straight to the point in this part of the world. Do you remember what you were saying on your last visit about bluff Yorkshire folk, Mr Phinn?' she asked.

'Yes, I do,' I replied.

'I believe in being honest and open with children, don't get me wrong, but sometimes it is necessary to evade the difficult question. As my sainted mother used to say, there is a time and a place for everything.'

'And everything in its proper place,' added Mrs Brown.

'Children grow up too early these days, in my opinion, Mr Phinn,' continued the Headteacher. 'The time when they were innocent until they reached the big school has sadly passed.'

'Like wild horses in the wind,' I murmured, remembering David's words.

'I blame the television,' added her companion and then, almost as an afterthought, sighed noisily, 'I was thirty-three before I knew what a condom was.'

When the time came for me to leave, I paused at the gate of the small school to marvel at the panoramic view which stretched out before me: soft green pastures dotted with grazing sheep and heavy, square-bodied cattle; a vast, hazy-blue sky streaked with creamy clouds; nestling, sunlit farmsteads; the country lane which twisted and turned over the hill. It had, no doubt, remained the same for centuries. There was a great sense of tranquillity and timelessness around me, as if the noises and concerns of the modern world had been swallowed up by those rolling fields, thick bracken slopes, dark, mysterious forests and misty fells.

I was brought out of my reverie by the sound of voices. Out of sight, behind the craggy stone wall which enclosed the school, I observed three or four young boys gathered around the red-haired pupil who had tried to put his teachers right about what a condom was. He was explaining to his fascinated companions that 'You can get them in different sizes, different colours, different flavours . . .'

My next appointment was at the Staff Development Centre to plan the in-service course for secondary school librarians with Mike Spiller, Principal Librarian for the county, and the children's writer, Irene Madley, who lived locally. I arrived at the unattractive, red-brick building, which had once been a secondary modern school, with only a few minutes to spare. At the entrance was a large notice with the words WELCOME TO THE STAFF DEVELOPMENT CENTRE, underneath which was written, THESE PREMISES ARE PROTECTED BY GUARD DOGS. The car park, formerly the school playground, was littered with great red and yellow cones and resembled the test course for advanced motorists.

Connie, the caretaker, was awaiting my arrival. She was standing, as was her wont, in the entrance hall, with arms folded tightly over her chest and with the pained expression of one who is wearing uncomfortably tight shoes. She was an ample woman with a bright copper-coloured perm, round florid face and the small sharp eyes of a hungry bird. She was dressed in her usual brilliant pink nylon overall and clutched a feather duster magisterially like a field-marshal's baton.

'You can always tell when the Caretaker from Hell is approaching,' Sidney had once said after a particularly acrimonious exchange with Connie. 'She fair crackles in that nylon overall. Touch her and you'd electrocute yourself.'

Connie was not Sidney's favourite person and he was certainly not hers. She complained about him frequently and he about her. Sidney – extrovert, unpredictable, creative – was just the sort of man to ruffle Connie's feathers and he had experienced the sharp edge of her tongue on many an occasion.

Connie, in fact, complained about most things and most people. If one were to ask her how she was, she would invariably reply with the phrase, 'Mustn't grumble' which was followed immediately by a long diatribe. She was a woman of a certain reputation and famous for her bluntness, thick skin, memorable malapropisms and amazingly inventive *non sequiturs*. Connie was also very good-hearted, down-to-earth and had a dry wit to rival Sidney's. On my first visit to the Centre, I had walked cheerfully into the main hall, with an armful of books and folders, to be stopped in my tracks by a stentorian voice echoing down the corridor behind me.

'I say!' she had boomed. 'I've just mopped that floor!'

I had promptly dropped everything I had been carrying. Later in the day she had informed me gravely that she liked things neat and tidy and that she had so much work cleaning up after the inspectors that she 'could barely keep her feet above water'.

Connie greeted me that afternoon with her usual grimace, which I ignored.

'Good afternoon, Connie,' I said in the most agreeable of voices. 'What a lovely day it is.'

'I wouldn't know, I've been inside cleaning,' she answered glumly.

'The weather has been perfect today,' I continued cheerfully. 'Beautifully mild and sunny.'

'Aye, that's as may be,' she mouthed, 'but I reckon we'll be paying for it next week.' Before I could respond, she launched into the attack. 'You came into the car park like a squirrel with its tail on fire. You want to slow down.' What is it, with all these animal similes, I thought to myself. Now Connie had jumped on the band wagon. 'You don't need to go so fast,' she continued, gesturing with the feather duster. 'It's a good job it isn't icy, or you'd have been into the wall and then the sparks would have really hit the fan.'

'I thought I was running a bit late for the meeting,' I explained.

'Well, there's only you here.'

Connie set off up the corridor in the direction of the kitchen, still determined to prolong the conversation about my speedy arrival at the Centre. 'You nearly had my bollards over. I put them bollards there for a reason, not for decoration, you know. They're to stop people from driving recklessly and from blocking my entrance. It's a health and safety hazard it is, parking in front of my entrance. That Mr Clamp's always doing it, when he runs his artery courses. I'm tired of telling him not to obstruct the fire exit, but does he listen? Then there's Mr Pritchard. He left his equipment propped up there on the Monday when he had his PE course and –'

'I've parked well away from the entrance, Connie,' I assured her, 'and your bollards are intact and all in place.'

'Just as well,' she snorted, flicking at the window sills as she walked ahead of me. We soon arrived at the small kitchen.

'Did Mr Spiller or Mrs Madley ring through to say they'd be late?' I asked her.

'No,' she replied curtly.

'Well, they should be here any time now. I'll go and put the papers out in a minute, if you'll tell me what room we're in.'

'I've put you in Room 9, well away from the psychologists. They've got a meeting here today which, knowing the way they talk, will go on into the early hours.'

'Connie, I was wondering –' I began.

She read my mind. 'And I suppose you'll be wanting a cup of tea?'

'That would be most welcome.'

'Well, you're out of luck with the biscuits. Mr Clamp polished off the last custard creams on Tuesday and I'm all out of Garibaldis.'

Connie disappeared into the small kitchen and I heard her rattling and clattering as she made the tea.

'And did you have a nice holiday this summer?' I shouted after her.

'No,' came the quick reply.

'I thought you and your husband were going to Ireland?'

'We did.'

'And you didn't enjoy it?'

'No, I didn't!' She emerged a moment later with a mug of tea which she thrust into my hand. 'Be careful, it's hot.'

'Well, I had an absolutely marvellous time in Ireland,' I told her. 'It was one of the best holidays I have had. The scenery was stunning, the food magnificent, the people really friendly. What was the problem?'

'The crossing. I had a dreadful time. I thought I was going to die, I really did. As soon as I set foot on that ferry I just knew I was going to be sick. We'd barely got out of the harbour when it started to move and it got worse and worse. I was up and down those steps like a shuttlecock.' I assumed she meant 'like a yo-yo' but I felt it politic not to interrupt. 'If I vomited once, I vomited ten times.' I took a sip of tea and attempted to look concerned. 'All the way over, the sea was heaving and splashing outside and I was heaving and splashing inside in the ladies' lavatory. And where was Ted?' Ted was Connie's long-suffering husband. 'I'll tell you where Ted was,' she continued, not waiting for or expecting a response. 'He was in the restaurant with a full English breakfast, two rounds of toast and a pot of tea for two, that's where Ted was. I said to him later, when I decided to talk to him again, that if I'd have fallen overboard he'd have never known. If he'd have been on the *Titanic* he wouldn't have got up from his egg and bacon and sausage. No little thing like an iceberg would have shifted Ted from the table. Up and down, up and down, went that boat. I'll tell you this, I've never been so glad to get my feet on terra cotta.' I spluttered, nearly choked and covered my tie in tea. 'I told you that tea was hot,' she said.

'No, no, it's fine,' I replied, wiping my tie with a handker-chief, 'I was just thinking it was about time for me to see if my colleagues have arrived.'

'And leave the room tidy,' Connie told me, disappearing into the kitchen where she resumed the clattering and clanking. A moment later, as I was half way down the corridor, I heard her echoing voice, 'And I hope they've parked away from the entrance.'

Following the planning meeting, I headed for my final engagement of the day. Connie watched eagle-eyed from the window as I crawled out of the car park, negotiating the line of large red and yellow, strategically placed cones. I was still in good spirits when I arrived at the market town of Masonby to give an evening talk on Reading

Development to parents and governors, but things were about to change.

Westgarth Primary School was a large, sprawling building surrounded by high iron railings. I had visited the school the previous year with Harold Yeats and we had received a rapturous welcome. The beaming caretaker had announced our arrival in grand style, the secretary had very nearly swooned with pleasure and the Headteacher, Mrs Thornton, a horse-faced woman with a vigorous handshake, had exclaimed: 'At last! I cannot tell you how pleased we are to see you!' She had then discovered that we were not from the Premises and Maintenance Section of the Education Department, as she had thought, there to deal with the smell in the boys' lavatories, and her attitude had instantly changed for the worse. She had regained her good humour, however, when Harold had delivered a very good report on the school curriculum and promised to take up her cause of the boys' lavatories at County Hall.

My talk now at Westgarth Primary School started later than planned. In the Headteacher's room, I was collared by the particularly garrulous and self-opinionated Chairman of Governors who owned the large hardware shop near the school. I had passed the premises on my way down the High Street and smiled after reading the notice prominently displayed in the window: 'Bargain Basement Upstairs'. The owner was a loud, flop-eared, extremely portly individual with a nose as heavy as a turnip and great hooded eyes. He berated me about the drop in standards, the decline of homework, the lack of manners in the young and the increase in juvenile crime. The Headteacher tried in vain to intervene and move the conversation on to more pleasant and inconsequential topics but she failed singularly. The Chairman of Governors, stabbing the air with a fat finger and with eyes shining with the intensity of a zealot, carried on regardless. Mrs Thornton's face took on the long, gloomy expression I had observed on my visit to the school the previous year, when Harold had informed her that we had not come to fix the plumbing. It was the look of weary resignation, that of a saint approaching certain martyrdom. Clearly that was her way of dealing with this pretentious and irritating man.

'Mr Parsons,' she began, glancing at her wristwatch, 'do you think we might make a start? It is –'

The Chairman, who clearly thought that school inspectors were part and parcel of some conspiracy to depress standards and were largely responsible for all the ills of society, continued to harangue me without even acknowledging her. In his opinion it was all the fault of the 'educational establishment'. It was the 'long-haired professors' and 'trendy, bearded progressives' who were to blame with 'their wishy-washy, airy-fairy ideas'. I was just too nonplussed to reply, and listened to the tirade with a bemused expression on my face, thinking how he would have reacted to Sidney and Sidney to him.

The ranting speaker was clearly rather disconcerted when I failed to respond. My mother, a nurse and health visitor for many years, had had to deal with many an awkward and sometimes aggressive patient. She had always advised me that, when faced with antagonistic and belligerent people, bristling for a quarrel, the best plan of attack was to disarm them with affability. It never failed to work. So, I looked at the large blustering face before me and merely smiled and nodded.

It was the janitor, knocking noisily on the door before bursting in, who rescued the situation. 'Are we startin' or what, Mrs Thornton?' he demanded loudly. 'We've got upwards of fotty people out theer and they're getting restless.'

'We are just coming, Mr Smails,' the Headteacher replied, clearly relieved by the interruption and grasping this ideal opportunity to get the proceedings started. 'If you'll follow me, Mr Phinn,' she said, ignoring the Chairman of Governors, who was mid-sentence at the time, 'we'll make a start, shall we?'

Three rows of parents and governors faced a bare table and chair at the front of the school hall, most of them with weary expressions and folded arms. As I arranged my books and sorted out my papers, Mr Parsons launched into his introduction as if addressing a Nuremberg rally. He told parents that we were 'all labouring under a misconception' if we thought reading was in a healthy state. He had read in the paper about the three million illiterates in the country and thought that it was a 'national scandal'. This evening, he told them, the expert would tell them just what the Education Department would be doing to raise standards. The expert, I thought to myself, would be doing no such thing. He would be speaking about the excitement of books and how parents might help in encouraging their children to read and enjoy them.

As Mr Parsons droned on, I glanced at the solemn faces in front of me, and recalled Sidney's reassuring comments after one of his talks had not gone as well as he had expected. He had addressed a group of reactionary elderly ladies at a luncheon club event on the theme of modern art. He had said he had felt like a garlic salesman at a vampire convention. The Madame Chairman had told the audience at the end of his talk that she was grateful to Mr Clamp for sharing his interesting views and that he had very kindly waived his fee. As a result, she had said, beaming widely, they could save up to get a really good speaker for the following year.

Finally Mr Parsons finished and introduced me. Once I started reading extracts from books and peppering the talk with anecdotes about children, the atmosphere in the hall improved. I heard a number of chuckles and saw people smiling and nodding in approval. During the talk I glanced occasionally in the direction of the Headteacher and the Chairman of Governors. Each time I looked their way, I saw Mrs Thornton, perched motionless on the edge of her chair, staring into space like someone who had been told some devastating news. I guess the anxiety over the boys' lavatories paled into insignificance compared with the problem sitting on her right.

The vote of thanks was not the most effusive I have received. 'Thank you,' said the Chairman of Governors, when I sat down to a ripple of applause. 'I'm not taking any questions,' he said, pushing out his chin, 'because time is getting on and I'm sure Mrs Thornton and the janitor are anxious to get to bed.'

A pained expression crossed the Headteacher's face.

'And I shan't be far behind them,' added Mr Parsons, oblivious to the titters from the audience.

The Headteacher walked with me to the school gate. 'Thank you very much for coming, Mr Phinn,' she said. She sounded exhausted. 'It was good of you to give up your evening. I know the parents very much enjoyed your talk. As for Mr Parsons . . .' She did not finish the sentence but gave me her martyred look and shook her head. 'Good-night,' she said quietly.

As I walked to the car, I thought again of my mother and one of her favourite sayings, 'There is always somebody else worse off than you.'

I headed for home, tired but happy with the way Children's Reading Day had turned out, arriving just as the clock at County Hall chimed nine. The small flat which I rented above The Rumbling Tum café in the High Street would seem very cold and lonely after such an entertaining and eventful day. I parked behind a little green Morris Minor which I recognised immediately and I jumped out of my car like – er, a rabbit with the runs. The side window of the Morris Minor slid down.

'Hello,' said Christine. 'I've just put the cauldron on. I wondered if you would like to join the Wicked Witch of the West for supper?'

7

Valentine Courtnay-Cunninghame, 9th Earl Marrick, Viscount Manston, Baron Brafferton, MC, DL, was a larger than life character, whom I had met for the first time one cold, bright day the previous autumn. I had been driving casually along an empty, twisting road on my way to a small rural school, when a pheasant he had just shot landed on the bonnet of my car. I don't know who was the more surprised, me or the pheasant. Having come to an abrupt halt and whilst contemplating roast pheasant for Saturday supper, a rotund, red-cheeked character had climbed over the drystone wall, shotgun in hand. He had a great walrus moustache and hair shooting up from a square head and was dressed in Norfolk jacket, plus-fours and deerstalker hat. He had come to claim the bird he had bagged. That was Lord Marrick.

I had met him on a number of occasions after that – at school governors' meetings, staff appointments and when I took reports to the Education Committee on which he served as Vice-Chairman. I had also accompanied him round a number of schools to look at aspects of the curriculum and show him good educational practice. I found Lord Marrick to be a plain-spoken, shrewd but extremely warm man with a cheerful good humour and a deep sense of reverence for the land his family had been so much a part of for many generations. He had received the little-awarded Knight of the Order of St Sylvester from the Pope himself the previous year.

On one occasion Lord Marrick had told me how he had

been walking through Nether Brafferton Wood, which formed part of his extensive estate, when he came upon a large hairy individual at the entrance to a shabby tent.

'Who are you?' he had asked abruptly.

'Jack,' the man had replied. 'And who are you?'

'I am Lord Marrick and you are on my land.'

'Am I?'

'Yes, you are. Would you be so good as to de-camp, pack up your things and depart.'

'Why?'

'Because, as I have said, this is my land.'

'I'm not doing any harm,' the man had said amiably.

'That is beside the point. This is my land.'

'Where did you get it from?'

'I got it from my father,' Lord Marrick had explained calmly.

'Well, where did your father get it from?' the man had asked.

'From his father.'

'Well, where did he get it from?'

'He got it from his father who got it from his father who got it from his father, right the way back to the Norman Conquest when Sir Richard de Courtnay acquired it.'

'Well, how did he get it?' the man had asked, making no effort to move.

'He fought for it,' Lord Marrick had replied.

'Well, I'll fight *you* for it!' had come the reply.

'Good story, isn't it?' Lord Marrick had roared. 'The very devil. "I'll fight *you* for it." Of course, I let the fellow stay, told him not to go lighting fires and disturbing the grouse and said there'd be a hot meal up at the house. I mean you can't just throw "a gentleman of the road" off your land, certainly not one who possesses such wonderful impertinence and wit. Well, can you?'

★

The evening before my appointment with Lord Marrick, the snow fell unexpectedly and in bitter earnest. Peering from the window of my small flat which overlooked Fettlesham High Street, I watched the great flakes begin to settle and gradually form a thick carpet along the pavements. Walls, trees, road signs, letter boxes, rooftops were soon shrouded in white. I thought of the farmers. I had seen a Dales winter the previous Christmas. The icy wind had raged, the snow had packed up in great mounds and piled into drifts which froze until the whole landscape had been transformed into one vast ocean of crusted billows. I recalled seeing a farmer, his collie dog leaping at his heels, tramping through the thick snow in a field behind a school, in search of his foundered sheep. I remembered well the grim, determined expression on his face. His was a hard life.

The next morning, 25 November, I was up bright and early. I pulled back the curtains to find the snow had stopped but had settled. The main road out of Fettlesham, however, looked to have been cleared and traffic was moving as usual. The weather forecast said there would be no more snow on the way and that a thaw would likely set in during the day, so I decided to chance it and drive out to Manston Hall.

I called into the office to check if any papers for the meeting had arrived, but apart from a couple of messages, a summary of a policy document from the Ministry of Education and the usual circulars and publishers' catalogues, there was nothing for me.

'You're in very early this morning, Gervase,' said Harold, whom I bumped into at the door to the office as I was on my way out.

'I called in on the off-chance that the papers for the Feoffees meeting would have arrived, but they're not here. Mrs Savage said she'd send them over. So much for liaising.'

'Well, they'll perhaps have them for you when you get

there – if it's still taking place. It's very thick snow this morning and you'll have a tricky drive up to Manston. You have to go over Ribbon Bank. I think this cold spell has caught everyone out and you'll not find any gritting lorries along that road yet. Perhaps you ought to ring through and see if the meeting is still on.'

'Yes, that's a thought,' I said, returning to my desk and picking up the telephone. I looked up the number and dialled. 'I thought you were on inspection this week?' I said to Harold, whilst waiting for someone at the other end of the line to pick up the receiver.

'I was but the school's snowed in and those children who did arrive have been sent home, so we are postponing it. I got a call from the Headteacher very early this morning.'

The telephone was answered by Lord Manston's secretary who confirmed that the meeting was going ahead and looked forward to meeting me later that morning. She reassured me that the weather further up the dale was not too bad and that all roads were passable.

'Well, it's still on,' I said and then had a thought. 'Harold,' I said, 'if you have nothing else on today, why don't you come with me to the meeting or go in my place? You know far more about these Feoffees than I do.'

'No, no,' said Harold, 'it's good experience and they are expecting you anyway. Just be careful on the roads. Oh, and give my regards to Lord Marrick.'

Once I had left the main Fettlesham–West Challerton road, I wondered to myself whether it had been such a good idea after all to risk such a potentially hazardous journey. The fields and hedgerows, hills and fells which surrounded me, merged into one great white expanse, unbroken and shimmering to the horizon's brim. The scene was magnificent but I was too concerned with keeping my eyes fixed on the road ahead and avoiding careering into some ditch to appreciate it on that cold, bright morning.

The car skidded a good few times on the narrow untreated roads and it took three or four attempts to get up Ribbon Bank, but thankfully there were no sharp inclines after that and I was soon, with a great feeling of relief, crawling towards the tall ornate gates and square lodge which marked the entrance to Manston Hall.

Manston Hall was not a large house by stately homes' standards but was a beautifully proportioned building of extraordinary charm and beauty. Built in warm, red brick and with many large rectangular windows, it stood out square and bright and solid in its vast parkland. All around the hall stretched a strange white world stroked in silence. No wind blew the snow into drifts, no birds called, no animal moved and, save for the sporadic soft thud of snow falling from the branches of the towering dark trees which bordered the drive, all was silent. There was a stillness, as if life itself had been suspended.

There were several large saloon cars, a Range Rover, a Rolls-Royce and a shiny black limousine with a small flag on the bonnet, parked in front of the hall. The old Volvo estate which I drove looked very much out of place in such expensive company. I looked at my watch. Ten minutes past ten. I was late. I checked my hair in the rear view mirror, straightened my tie, collected my note pad and climbed out.

The great black door to Manston Hall, flanked by elegant stone pillars, was opened by an ancient retainer. He was a tall man with a long, pale, angular face, dark deep-set eyes, very thick wild white hair and a large nose which curved savagely like a bent bow.

'Good morning, sir,' he intoned sepulchrally and gestured for me to enter.

I walked into a spacious entrance hall which was painted in pale yellow and blue. While the retainer pushed shut the heavy door and re-arranged the draught-excluder in front of it, I gazed round in wonder. The ceiling was a jungle of decorative plasterwork, the intricate twisting designs standing out from the darker background. A series of matching panels was set in the walls, between which were large oil paintings showing different animals: grazing cattle, fat black pigs on stumpy legs, bored-looking sheep, leaping horses, packs of hounds. The floor, of white inlaid marble, matched the huge and magnificently carved chimney-piece, above which a full-length portrait in dark oils depicted a severe-looking man posing in military uniform. An organ case with massive Ionic columns and elaborate carving stood at one side, flanked by a pair of pale, delicate tables with dark marble tops. On the opposite side, the entire wall was covered by a vivid tapestry depicting some classical theme. The central character, a woman with a great tangle of hair and piercing eyes, looked remarkably like Medusa.

'May I have your name, sir?' asked the retainer straightening up. He spoke in a hushed voice and his face was entirely expressionless.

'Gervase Phinn,' I replied.

'Is that Mr Phinn?' he enquired.

'It is,' I replied.

'If you would come this way, Mr Phinn.'

I followed his slow, measured steps down a long corridor. We passed one rather formal-looking room with dark portraits on the walls and porcelain on the antique, highly polished furniture and then a more comfortable lived-in study with rather shabby sofas and armchairs. Our unhurried progress ended at two tall carved wooden columns. The retainer opened the door and I was ushered through it.

'Mr Gervase Phinn,' announced the retainer and then departed without a glance. I was in the library, a panelled room with a ceiling rich in fine plasterwork. One wall had shelving which stretched from floor to ceiling and which was crammed with leather-bound books. A huge Persian carpet covered the dark polished wooden floor. There was a group of men in animated conversation, standing before a great roaring open fire. On hearing of my arrival, Lord Marrick glanced in my direction, waved his hand expansively in the air and strode across to meet me.

'Mr Phinn. Gervase. Good of you to come. Dreadful weather, isn't it?' He did not wait for a response. 'Hope you had no trouble finding us? Come along in and meet everyone.'

Taking my arm he led me towards the group and began introducing me, as the education representative, to the frighteningly august group of individuals. There was Brigadier Lumsden, a big-nosed, big-voiced ex-soldier; Archdeacon Richards, a plump, cheerful-looking little cleric with a round red face; the present Greave of the Feoffees, a stocky man in a loud-checked tweed suit with a face as soft and brown and wrinkled as an over-ripe russet apple. Then there was Dr Coulson-Smith, the High Sheriff, a short, thick-necked individual with a curiously flat face; a tall silver-haired policeman in impressive uniform with a short toothbrush moustache; and finally Judge Plunkett, a painfully thin man with a face full of tragic potential. It sounded like a page from *Who's Who*. I shook hands, smiled fatuously at each one and wondered why I was there. What exactly could an insignificant school inspector contribute to this gathering of the great and the good?

'Gentlemen!' boomed Lord Marrick. 'We appear to be all present and correct so shall we make a start? If you would follow me, I'll lead the way to the morning room.' We followed the peer into another equally magnificent room in the centre of which was a long, highly polished table at one end of which sat a young woman with black lustrous hair and big dark eyes. Carved, balloon-backed rosewood chairs were arranged around it and I was seated between the tweed suit and the policeman.

'Now, gentlemen,' Lord Marrick began, when we were all seated and looking in his direction, 'I've asked Janet, my secretary, to take a few notes.' He indicated the woman by his side who smiled down the table. 'I appreciate your giving up valuable time to join me here this morning,' continued Lord Marrick, 'particularly in this bloody awful weather and I want to assure you that this meeting will be short, sharp and to the point and not ramble on like a lost sheep in a snowstorm.' I glanced to the window and noticed that heavy flakes of snow were beginning to fall. So much for the weather forecast I thought. 'Now I hope you got all the papers that Janet sent out last week.' There were nods and grunts of agreement and the shuffling of various documents. Everyone seemed to have a batch of papers except me. Mine were no doubt sitting on Mrs Savage's desk. 'Now, as I have said in my notes,' went on Lord Marrick, 'I want to mark the five hundred years of the Feoffees by a major event at Manston Hall. I want the general public to know about those traditions which are so much a part of our cultural heritage. Whenever I mention the word Feoffees to people, they look at me as if I am not quite right in the head.'

'It was the same when I became High Sheriff in April,' said the thick-necked individual with the curiously flat face. 'I would mention the word "shrievalty" and people thought I was talking in Polish.' He looked across the table at me. 'You wouldn't credit it, would you? That people had never heard of the word "shrievalty"?'

'You wouldn't,' I said, feigning disbelief. I hadn't a clue what the word meant.

'The number of times I have had to explain that it refers to the office of sheriff –'

'Quite so, quite so,' said Lord Marrick impatiently. 'I am sure we could debate the decline in the English language until the cows come home, a topic which I am sure Mr

Phinn, as something of an English specialist, would love to do, but we must press on. Could we throw a few ideas around regarding how the area for which you have responsibility can play its part in the celebration? The Feoffees, as you know, have existed for five hundred years, helping the unfortunate, supporting the sick, giving bursaries and scholarships to deserving causes and I want to have a really good bash up here at Manston Hall to celebrate our achievements. So come on, colleagues, what can you suggest?'

During the next half-hour the ideas came fast and furious. The brigadier suggested a parade of army vehicles including tanks, and a display by the army motorcycle team; the policeman said he could arrange a march past by the police band, and a demonstration by dog-handlers and mounted police; the archdeacon offered a recital by the abbey choir; other suggestions came forth for exhibitions of local history, craft stalls and information stands of all kinds. Then there was a sudden silence and all eyes seemed to be on me.

'Mr Phinn,' snapped Lord Marrick suddenly. 'You have been unnaturally quiet. What can the Education Department offer?' I was on the point of mumbling something about having to consult Dr Gore, gleaning suggestions from schools and discussing certain ideas with my colleagues when my neighbour, the large russet-cheeked individual in the tweed suit, jerked up in his chair as though he had been stung, twitched madly and exclaimed, 'What the devil!' His head then disappeared beneath the table.

'Is it the bitch?' asked Lord Marrick casually. Along with the others, I peered below the table and saw the ugliest, most vicious-looking dog I had ever seen. It was a barrel-bodied, bow-legged bulldog with pinky-white jowls and pale unfriendly eyes. It had rested its fat, round head between the legs of the man next to me.

'Push her off, Quentin!' commanded Lord Marrick good humouredly. 'She loves the smell of tweeds. She's an old softie at heart. Just wants to be friendly and affectionate.' At this point the monster growled and showed a set of impressive teeth. 'Old softie', 'friendly' and 'affectionate' were not words which readily sprang to my mind. The dog peered up with the grey, watery, button eyes of a shark. It then began rumbling like a distant train. The complexion of the man in tweeds had changed miraculously from the soft brown of the russet apple to an unearthly white.

'Come on out of there, Laetitia,' coaxed Lord Marrick, joining us to peer under the table. The dog continued to stay rooted to the spot, growling and grimacing and eyeing the man in tweeds like some long-lost bone.

'She's a wonderful dog. English bulldog. Nobly born of impeccable pedigree. She'd let anyone walk straight into the house. Wouldn't make a sound. Course, they'd not get out again. Teeth like metal man-traps. One snap of those jaws and she'd not let go. Locks on you, see. Couldn't prise her off with a monkey wrench. Yes, if she grabbed a hand you'd lose a few of your fingers.' The man in tweeds looked as if he had been caught in amber. I don't think he's worrying about his hand, I thought to myself. Not a muscle in his body moved. Everyone in close proximity to the dog crossed his legs.

'Laetitia! Will you come out! Heel!' ordered Lord Marrick. The dog blinked lazily, lifted its fat, round face from between the man's legs, yawned massively, displaying a set of teeth like tank-traps, and plodded off, still rumbling.

'Now then, you were saying, Mr Phinn,' said Lord Marrick to the accompaniment of a great release of breath from the man in the tweeds.

Before the meeting concluded, I agreed to mount a display of children's poetry and stories based on famous characters from history, approach a couple of schools to ask them to perform some short plays on an historical theme, enlist the help of my colleagues to arrange an exhibition on education down the ages, a gymnastics display and a performance by the County Youth Orchestra. Finally I agreed to organise essay and public speaking competitions on the theme of customs and traditions. That little lot would keep Mrs Savage busy, I thought to myself gleefully.

Lord Marrick appeared well pleased with how the meeting had gone. I waited until the others had departed before going over to him. He was explaining something to his secretary but looked up as I approached. 'Quite a successful morning, eh, Mr Phinn?' he said.

'Yes, indeed, Lord Marrick,' I replied. 'I just wanted to apologise for my late arrival but I had a few problems getting up Ribbon Bank. I'm afraid the snow was particularly thick and –'

'Not a problem.'

'And also for arriving without the papers. I didn't want you to think that I hadn't bothered to bring them along. I'm afraid they didn't arrive at the Education Office. I checked this morning but they definitely weren't on my desk.'

'Well, that's strange because I delivered them myself when I was at County Hall last week for the Education Committee. No point wasting money on postage. Gave them to Dr Gore's secretary. The woman with the red nails and the teeth.'

'Mrs Savage,' I said slowly.

'That's the woman. Janet, will you arrange for another set to be sent to Mr Phinn? Thank you.'

Lord Marrick himself escorted me back to the entrance hall. We stopped beneath the vivid tapestry depicting the classical theme and the woman with a great tangle of hair and piercing eyes. I heard the patter of feet behind me on the white inlaid marble floor and, turning, found behind me not only the wretched bulldog but two exact miniature versions of itself. Both puppies had the grey button eyes, the pinky-white jowls, the rows of sharp teeth, the stumpy tails and both growled and grumbled in unison with their mother.

'Those are her pups,' Lord Marrick told me proudly. 'Lucretia and Caesare. She's showing them off, you see. I'm hopeful they will win me a blue ribbon for Best of Breed at the Fettlesham Show in a few years' time.' He bent down and stroked the fat little heads. Both puppies stared up with a lofty disdain. Then Laetitia nosed Lord Marrick's hand away and growled before moving in my direction and rubbing her body against my legs.

'She likes you, Mr Phinn.'

'Really,' I managed to whisper.

'Do you know she can be the most wilful, bad-tempered, moody creature imaginable and certainly not one to lock jaws with, but when she takes a liking to someone, she'll stick to him like glue and be his bosom friend for life.' The dog began to whimper. 'You've made a great impression,' continued Lord Marrick beaming widely. 'You will have a job to get rid of her.'

I don't know why, but at that moment I thought of Mrs Savage and I made a mental note to give her a wide berth in the coming weeks.

Over the summer, when the schools were on holiday, we inspectors had the long and onerous task of analysing all the school reports from the previous academic year and writing an extensive commentary for submission to Dr Gore and the Education Committee. Although this exercise was one of the most tedious and time-consuming aspects of our work, it was invaluable in giving us a clear and detailed picture of how well, or otherwise, schools in the county were doing, what were the issues which needed to be addressed and whether standards, particularly in literacy and numeracy, were rising or falling. The analysis was also useful in helping us plan the in-service training of the teachers and offer a programme of courses, conferences and workshops which focused on their particular needs.

It was with a great sense of relief that my commentary on the state of English teaching in the county turned out to be positive. Most teachers clearly spent a great deal of time and effort teaching children to read and write and encouraging them to turn to books for pleasure and for information. There was, however, one area of the English curriculum which seemed to be neglected. Mrs Peterson and Mrs Dunn at Highcopse Primary School were clearly not alone in spending little time on poetry. In report after report I noted that this subject was often consigned to the margins of the serious business of study and that some children had little experience of appreciating and writing verse. I decided, therefore, to mount a series of weekend courses to help teachers develop their expertise, offer ideas and strategies and give them greater confidence in teaching this important area of English.

The first course was planned to take place in early December. I wanted to get it out of the way before the end of term events, when schools would be immersed in carol concerts, parties, presentation evenings, nativity plays and all the other activities which come with the festival. I knew from my experiences the previous year that this would be my busiest time and I would be out in schools every day and most evenings as well. I was not, however, prepared for the response to attend the poetry course. When the deadline came for final applications, my in-tray was piled high with over fifty requests.

'You should be pleased, instead of pulling a face like a bulldog which has just swallowed a wasp,' commented Sidney, staring at his own meagre pile of applications. 'I've got a miserable ten people for my December art course.'

'I *am* pleased,' I responded, feeling slightly uncomfortable at the mention of bulldogs. 'It's just that it's rather more than I anticipated.'

'Well, there's a simple remedy. Write to half of them saying the course is full and tell them there's space on a really exciting art course planned to take place at the same time.'

I pondered Sidney's suggestion but decided to go ahead with the large number. The various contributors to the course were delighted with the interest from so many teachers and had no worries about working with such a big group. The Staff Development Centre had been booked well in advance but I rang Connie to let her know that there would be more teachers attending than anticipated. Then I steamed ahead and ordered the materials, arranged for the course programme to be printed, and despatched letters of acceptance to the applicants.

Everything was going like clockwork – and then I

received the letter. My heart gave a jump when I came across the frighteningly official envelope with the large royal crest and the heavy black lettering: *The Ministry of Education*. It was from the formidable Miss de la Mare, Her Majesty's Principal Divisional Inspector of Schools. She said she had been impressed with some of the creative writing she had observed in the few schools she had recently visited in the county and mentioned her visit to Backwatersthwaite and the poetry lessons of the 'inspirational Mr Lapping'. She said that, as I was no doubt aware, she was compiling a national report on the teaching of the arts in primary schools and wished to discuss certain matters with me. Then she had noticed, as she was looking through the county in-service handbook for teachers, that I was running a series of weekend poetry courses and thought how useful it would be if she attended one. She concluded her letter: 'I have followed the normal protocol and contacted Dr Gore and he is happy for me to join you. I trust there will be no objection on your part?'

'No objection!' exclaimed Sidney with a hollow laugh, when I read him the letter. '"No objection on your part", she says. As if you are in any position to object. It would be like a prisoner of the Spanish Inquisition saying to his torturer: "I say, senor, I would rather you didn't do that with the old thumbscrews", or a French aristocrat informing the man on the guillotine, "Not today, monsieur, thank you very much". You have no choice in the matter, whatsoever. The question is merely rhetorical. She's cleared it with the CEO, so you've no option. You are well and truly lumbered with her. Fancy having the HMI version of a rottweiler watching you for two days. That will cramp your style and no mistake. And by the description of her provided by poor George Lapping, she makes Mrs Savage sound like Florence Nightingale and Connie like Mother Teresa. She'll be watching your every move with those little beady eyes and noting things down and filing away all this information about you at the Ministry of Education.'

'And everything was going so smoothly,' I sighed. 'I could have well done without this.'

'Oh, that's the way of things,' said David in his Prophet of Doom voice. 'Always something or somebody who goes and has to spoil one's equilibrium. I don't think I've ever run a course without a mishap or a problem. Everything is going fine and then – disaster! You are cycling along the country lane on a bright, balmy day with the sun shining on your face and the fresh wind blowing through your hair and suddenly somebody pushes a thundering great stick through your spokes and you're over the handlebars and flat on your face.' At this point he removed his reading glasses, placed them neatly on the desk in front of him and leaned back in his chair. We knew we were in for one of his monologues. 'No, I have yet to run a course free from some hitch or another. There's the course member who has been sent by the headteacher who doesn't want to be there in the first place and thinks the thing is a total waste of time. She sits there, on the front row – to continue Sidney's metaphor – like Madame Defarge knitting, as if waiting for the great blade to descend and your head to roll into the basket before her.' He brought his hand down in a sharp chopping movement.

'They are the worst,' I agreed, nodding. 'The front row cynic who has nothing to learn.'

'Then there's the teacher who turns out to be verbally aggressive,' continued David, 'because he's been passed over for promotion and, of course, he blames you because you were on his interviewing panel. And the expert who has been on every blessed course and conference in the in-service handbook and knows it all and tells you so.'

'I think I might have a few of those on this poetry course,' I said, glancing through the applications.

'Or the outside speaker who fails to turn up and you are left facing a hostile audience, feeling like the first Christian to be thrown to the lions. Then there's the occasion when you and thirty teachers turn up all bright-eyed and bushy-tailed one Saturday morning to find the Staff Development Centre all locked up and Connie away in Mablethorpe in her caravan for the weekend.'

'Ah, now that won't happen,' I told him, 'I've checked the date with Connie.'

'My goodness, I've had my fair share of disastrous courses,' said David morosely. 'Mind you, I've never been scrutinized by an HMI. Now that is deeply worrying. At least my disasters went unobserved.'

'I am sure that Gervase is greatly heartened and encouraged by all that,' remarked Sidney. 'I should imagine that he won't get a wink of sleep contemplating all the potential calamities.'

'Hang on a minute,' exclaimed David. 'It was you who started all this off with your gloomy predictions about this rottweiler of an HMI cramping his style and watching every move with her little beady eyes. I hardly think your comments are likely to re-assure him.'

'I was going on to say,' said Sidney, 'before you started on your running commentary of all your failed courses, that I will be directing my art course at the very same time as our young colleague and will be there at the Staff Development Centre to give him the benefit of my advice and guidance, as well as my undivided support and succour.'

'Huh!' snapped David. 'You'll not have any time to be giving him any undivided support and succour. You'll be too busy arguing with Connie as you always do.'

Before Sidney could respond, I stood up, walked behind him as he sat at his desk, put my hand on his shoulder and said, 'That is really very kind of you, Sidney. I might just ask Miss de la Mare to pop into a few of your sessions. After all, she is interested in the arts in school which covers your subject as well.'

'Ha, ha!' laughed David, throwing up his hands in the air. 'That's taken the smug expression off his face.'

A week before the course, I double-checked that all the arrangements were in place. Connie was fully briefed, the speakers had the dates in their diaries and all the details, course members and Miss de la Mare had received the programme, and the books and materials I was to use had been delivered. On the Friday evening before the course commenced, a bitterly cold night, I drove out to the Staff Development Centre to set out the tables and chairs, put up the exhibition of children's work and to make certain all the equipment was working. I expected to see a dark and deserted building but, as I pulled into the car park, I noticed that every room seemed to be lit up. Connie, in her predictable pose, with arms folded and the death-mask expression, stood in the entrance like some Eastern statue.

She made a sort of clucking noise as I entered. 'What are *you* doing here?' she asked bluntly.

'I've come to set up the rooms for tomorrow's poetry course,' I replied.

'You'll be lucky. I say you'll be lucky,' she snapped, giving a twisted smile. 'The place is as full as bingo night at the Empire. Everyone, bar the Queen and members of the royal family are in here tonight. It's bedlam. There's the vicar, him with the jeans and the motor bike, rehearsing his pantomime because the church hall's heating's off. There's the Brownies at the back like a hoard of wild dervishes and a whole load of senior citizens in cowboy hats and great big boots line dancing in the reception area because the village hall's boiler's broke down too. Some of them can hardly stand up never mind trying to leap about to cowboy music. I've seen three of them with zimmers. I mean that floor's slippery – I only polished it this morning. But would they listen? They shouldn't be out on a night like this. It's bitter. Do you want a cup of tea?'

'Yes, please, Connie.' I followed her down the corridor to the kitchen and, to be fair to her, there was a great cacophony of noise issuing from every room in the Centre. I took two cups and saucers from the cupboard and watched her as she filled the kettle.

'Mr Clamp has just gone after setting up his artery course for tomorrow, leaving behind him the usual trail of destruction and debris. You might as well get back in your car and have a quiet Friday night in – something which I was intending to do before I got the call from that dreadful Mrs Savage at County Hall telling me to allow all these people in. "As this is a time of peace and goodwill," she says in that posh voice of hers and as if butter wouldn't melt, "we are making the premises available for the church drama group, the Brownies and the senior citizens' dance club, since their pipes are frozen up and they are desperate. I'm sure we can help out." I said to her, "What's with the 'we'? It's all very well making the premises available but it's me what has to stay and supervise and give up my Friday night as well." I said to her, "It's not you who'll be having to deal with the trendy vicar, an unco-operative Brown Owl and a posse of geriatric line dancers – and Mr Clamp to boot." She had no answer to that I can tell you!' She opened a tin of biscuits. 'Mind you, I'm on double time. Do you want a Garibaldi?'

I had a sinking feeling that David's prophecies about doomed courses were about to come true. 'So, I can't set up my rooms for tomorrow, then?' I asked.

'Not unless you want to negotiate with the Brownies and the OAP line dancers, you can't.'

'What time will they be finished, do you think?'

'Well, this place is being locked up at nine, come hell or high water.'

'I'd better leave it until tomorrow then, Connie,' I said. 'I'll be here early to set things up, if that's all right.'

'I'm opening up at seven, as per usual,' she replied as I started to go. 'Don't you want a cup of tea then?'

'No, I'll get off.' I was thinking that I might give Christine a ring and see if she would like to go out for a drink.

Connie followed me out of the main door, as if to see some undesirable off the premises. It was then that I noticed the flower. Outside the entrance to the Centre, in a large wooden tub full of pale spiky grass and the withered remains of summer blooms, was a splash of red. It was a large flower with crimson leaves.

'What do you make of that, Connie?' I asked.

'It's an alopecia.'

'A *what*?'

'I noticed it this evening when Mr Clamp was unloading his stuffed animals for his artery course. I mentioned it to him. I said I had never seen a flower like that growing in December, except winter pansies. He said it was a hardy winter variety of alopecia that flourishes in the frost.'

'I don't know much about flowers, but it looks like a geranium to me.'

'It's a scarlet alopecia,' said Connie. 'Mr Clamp says that they only flower every ten years and that they like the cold. They're quite rare actually. He suggested I write to that gardening programme. What do you think?'

'I think Mr Clamp's got a vivid imagination, Connie, that's what I think.'

'So you don't think it's an alopecia then?'

'As I said, it looks like a geranium to me, but I've never seen one bloom in the winter, not outdoors, at any rate.' I poked the earth surrounding the flower and it was as hard as iron. 'It's very strange, I have to admit.'

To the strains of some very loud twanging country and western song, the shrieks of excited little girls and the picture of Connie in my rear view mirror staring at the flower, I drove home. I hoped I could persuade Christine to come out for that drink. I needed to have my mind taken off the course the next day. As it turned out, I need not have worried so much – but Christine did provide the perfect diversion.

The next morning I arrived at the Centre bright and very early. I checked the equipment, arranged the tables and chairs, set up the exhibition in the large room where the course was to take place and waited nervously for the first teachers to arrive. Even though I had run courses before, I could not help being rather on edge. David's words kept coming back to me. Would my speakers turn up? If they did, would they be well received? What would I do if I got a group of difficult teachers? Was the programme relevant? Suppose the heating went off? To occupy myself, and take my mind off things which might go wrong, I began to write a short poem, taking as a theme the flower which had bloomed miraculously in the cold weather. Very soon I had written a couple of verses which I entitled 'Red Bloom of Winter'. I compared the flower to 'a splash of blood on the dark earth', describing it as 'a crimson cluster hidden in the grass, straight stemmed, defiant'; it was 'a bright life in the midst of death'. I was deep into creating vivid imagery when the door opened and Connie made an entrance, holding a brush like a weapon.

'There's a woman in reception wanting to see you. I thought at first it was one of the geriatric line dancers come back to collect her zimmer but she said you were expecting her. Sounded like "Fella Beware".'

'Miss de la Mare,' I whispered to myself. 'She's the HMI I told you about, Connie,' I said, jumping to my feet and hurrying to the door.

'Well, I hope she's not blocked my entrance,' grumbled Connie, following me down the corridor.

Miss de la Mare was not as I expected her to be. I imagined a solid, ample woman with savagely cropped grey hair, small severe mouth and hard glittery eyes, the kind that make you think that at any moment you are about to be pounced on. I expected her to be dressed, as George Lapping had described her, in thick brown tweeds, heavy brogues and in a hat the shape of a flowerpot. The woman waiting for me in the entrance was very different. She was a plump, cheerful-looking woman with a round face freckled like a good egg, and neatly bobbed silver hair. She was dressed in a coat as bright and as red as a letter box with a long multicoloured scarf draped around her neck.

'Mr Phinn,' she proclaimed, shaking my hand vigorously. 'Winifred de la Mare. Good of you to let me come. Really looking forward to joining you. Now, I know that you will have lots to do, so don't mind me. You just crack on with what you have to do. I'll just tootle off and mingle with the teachers when they begin to arrive. Oh, by the way, I noticed in the course booklet that there's an art course going on at the same time. Do you think your colleague would mind if I popped in this afternoon?'

'He would be delighted, I'm sure,' I replied gleefully.

'Good show!' She peered around her before adding, 'I don't suppose there's a chance of a cup of tea? I've travelled a fair distance this morning.'

'Of course,' I replied turning to Connie, who was loitering in the background. 'I wonder if Miss de la Mare could –'

Before I could complete my request, Connie set off in the direction of the kitchen, announcing that if my visitor would care to follow her, she would put the kettle on. As they strolled off, I caught a snatch of their conversation.

'You keep this Centre very neat and tidy.'

'I try my best and you can't do any more than that.'

I had an idea, from that moment on, that the course would be a success.

To my great relief, my opening lecture and the morning workshops were well received. The teachers were good-humoured and genuinely interested and took part in all the assignments with great enthusiasm. Miss de la Mare, despite her rather overbearing manner and her frequent interruptions, proved to be most amicable and involved herself fully in all the activities, joining the discussions and even tackling the writing tasks.

At lunch-time I introduced the HMI to Sidney. He was holding forth to several young women teachers who had gathered around him in the dining area. They were staring up at him as wide-eyed as infants.

'Miss de la Mare,' I said when Sidney looked up and gave me a surreptitious wink, 'may I introduce my colleague who is the Creative and Visual Arts Inspector?'

'Winifred de la Mare!' she barked.

Sidney's smile stretched from ear to ear and could have been seen a few hundred yards away. 'I am delighted to meet you, Miss de la Mare,' he said. 'I hope you are enjoying the poetry course.'

'Very much,' she said briskly.

'Miss de la Mare is wondering if she might join you for the remainder of the day,' I said with such a wonderfully smug feeling.

The fixed smile waned a little on Sidney's face. 'Join me?' he said. 'You would like to join me?'

'If you have no objection,' said Miss de la Mare.

I recalled my earlier conversation with Sidney. He really had no choice in the matter. The question was merely rhetorical.

'I should be delighted,' he said, with little conviction in his voice.

By the time Sunday afternoon had arrived, I had seen relatively little of Miss de la Mare. She seemed to have been so captivated with the work Sidney was undertaking that she had remained with him for all of Saturday afternoon and Sunday morning. For the last session of the poetry course, however, she re-appeared. The teachers were discussing a selection of verse by known and unknown poets and some of the course members had agreed to read out poems they had written themselves. I decided to chance my arm and read my poem, 'Red Bloom of Winter'. I conveniently failed to mention that it was my own work. When I had finished declaiming to the group there was a rapt silence.

Then one rather pensive-looking woman spoke. 'Beautiful,' she sighed. 'Beautiful. It's such a very tender poem. I just loved the delicate sound formation and the strong sense of the mystic.'

'Did you really?' I cooed.

'I think the poet captures the sense of desolation really well,' added another. 'She's obviously immensely depressed, perhaps on the very brink of taking her own life?'

'Who is?' I ventured.

'The woman in the poem. All the words and images stress her rejection and feeling of emptiness and futility. The mood is one of coldness and frigidity. The relationship has turned sour. It's so very sad.'

'What relationship?' I ventured again.

'Why, the woman's relationship with her partner. She is represented by the red flower,' explained the teacher. 'That is the central symbol of the verse. The man is the hard, cold earth which is freezing the very life out of her. She is the woman of warmth and life, the Earth mother.'

Another teacher entered the discussion. 'Perhaps the flower is more a symbol of the hatred and deep-seated jealousy of the woman who has been betrayed.'

'Betrayed?' I asked.

'There's a great deal of violent imagery in the poem, references to "blood" and "death" and the "frozen stem as rigid as a corpse".'

'It could be more to do with her death,' said the pensive-looking teacher.

'But there isn't a woman in the poem,' I said.

'The poet has obviously suffered,' she continued. 'I think she's quite disturbed.'

'Is the poem about saving the planet?' asked a small man with large glasses. 'Doesn't the dying flower represent the destruction of the environment? All that is bright and beautiful is being choked to death.'

'Or is the poem about life itself?' sighed the woman who had spoken first.

'Or could it just be about a flower?' I hazarded.

'But who would want to write a poem about a flower?' asked the rather intense-looking woman.

Later in the staff room, after all the teachers had made their farewells and thanked me for a stimulating course, I sat with Miss de la Mare. Sidney bobbed in to say goodbye. He looked like the cat which had got the cream. He had whispered to me earlier in the hall that he had got on well with Miss de la Mare who had been highly complimentary about what she had observed.

'He's quite a character, Mr Clamp,' said the HMI. 'An immensely creative man and very innovative and, like many introverts, a man of few words.'

'A man of few words!' I gasped. 'An introvert?'

'Oh yes, I found him a most unassuming and quietly spoken man but very talented. I did so enjoy my time with him and the art teachers and I have a mind to ask him to contribute to a national course on "The Arts in School", which I am directing next summer in Oxford. He might of course be a little shy about speaking to a large group. Do you think he would be interested?'

'I'm sure he would,' I replied. Sidney had made another conquest.

'You may care to come along too,' continued Miss de la Mare. 'I found those parts of the poetry course I attended most interesting. I thought your choice of that final poem quite inspired.'

'Thank you,' I replied.

'You obviously chose the poem about the flower to get the discussion going about the very nature of poetry writing.'

Did I? I thought to myself.

'And it certainly got them to think and to argue,' continued Miss de la Mare, 'but you can see what a lot of work you have to do.'

'I do?'

'Why, yes. It really wasn't as good as all the teachers thought, was it? In fact, the poem was rather overwritten, rather clichéd, don't you think? So many people imagine that a poem *must* have some hidden meaning, some symbolism, something profound to say. It is quite possible for someone to write a simple little poem, however trite it might be, about a flower. I have always been of the opinion that poems can be about anything and that anything you wish it to be can become a poem. You see, the reader brings so much of herself to the poem, very often seeing something in the verse that the poet never intended. I feel sure the poet here never imagined that her poem about a flower would be regarded as a description of life itself.'

'No, I suppose not,' I said, feeling somewhat deflated.

'Did one of the sixth-formers you have come across write it?' she asked.

I shook my head. 'No, it's by a modern poet.'

'I once visited a large primary school in the middle of a dreadfully depressing inner city area,' Miss de la Mare told me, smiling at the memory. 'The work of the children consisted largely of arid exercises on the noun, the verb and the adjective but when questioned the children had not the first idea what the parts of speech were. Page after page was filled with dreary exercise after dreary exercise. There was the occasional story, the odd comprehension but not a sign of a poem. And then I found this nervous little boy in the corner of the classroom. When I asked if I could examine his book he looked at me with such large sad eyes and he said very quietly, "No." I tried to coax him but he was adamant, saying that his work was not worth looking at. He couldn't spell, his writing was untidy and he never got good marks for his work. I eventually persuaded him to let me see his writing. The book was indeed very poor and, like all the rest, crammed with unmarked exercises. There was the occasional comment from his teacher in bright red ink for him to re-write or to take greater care.

'Then, at the very back of the book I came upon a piece of writing in small crabbed print. I asked him if he had written it. He nodded. I asked him if he had received any help with it. He shook his head. Well, it was quite a small masterpiece. He had written, and I remember the words so well:

> Yesterday yesterday yesterday
> Sorrow sorrow sorrow
> Today today today
> Hope hope hope
> Tomorrow tomorrow tomorrow
> Love love love

'"What a wonderful little poem," I told him.

'He thought for a while, stared up at me with those large, sad eyes and announced: "They're mi spelling corrections, miss."'

Connie collared me on my way out later that afternoon. 'It's dead!' she exclaimed.

'What is?'

'My flaming alopecia, that's what! It wilted and then died. I knew I shouldn't have watered it.'

'I shouldn't think it made much difference, Connie,' I reassured her.

'I've never had a flaming alopecia before,' she said sadly.

I learnt from Sidney the next day that he, as I had suspected, had been behind the ruse. He had arrived at the Staff Development Centre on the Friday night to set up for his course. Backwards and forwards, under Connie's eagle eye, he had emptied his car of materials and artefacts for his 'Art for Christmas' weekend. Branches of yew, fronds of holly, ropes of ivy, bunches of mistletoe, stuffed robins and last of all two large poinsettia plants had been carried into the Centre. As he had tried to negotiate the vicar's motor bike, which had been parked precariously near the entrance, Sidney had snapped off the stem of one of the plants. Rather than leave the cluster of red leaves on the floor for Connie to complain about, he had stuck them into the tub and thought no more of it. When later Connie had drawn attention to it, he had informed her that it was a rare flaming alopecia plant.

'I think it was very unkind of you,' I remarked, 'and I've a good mind to tell Connie.'

'Don't do that, old chap,' he replied, leaning back in his chair and placing his hands behind his head. 'Connie is so wonderfully naive, so splendidly gullible, so amazingly ingenuous, that it would be cruel to enlighten her. I do not approve of anything, you know, Gervase, which tampers with natural ignorance. Ignorance is like a delicate exotic flower, touch it, and the bloom is gone for ever.'

'I've read Oscar Wilde as well, Sidney,' I said. 'And it wasn't a delicate exotic flower, it was fruit. "Ignorance is like a delicate exotic fruit," says Lady Bracknell. It's in *The Importance of Being Earnest*.'

'Well, I said it first!' exclaimed Sidney with mock surprise. 'This Lady Bracknell must have heard me say it on one of my courses. Anyway, "flower" is far more appropriate, in the circumstances, don't you think?'

'And what will happen,' I asked him, 'when Connie discovers that alopecia is a scalp condition and not a variety of rare winter-flowering plant?'

'She will probably not speak to me for a long, long time,' smiled Sidney, stretching back even more expansively in his chair. 'Which suits me fine because it will keep her out of my hair. I say, that's rather clever, isn't it? Alopecia? Hair?'

I shook my head. 'You're incorrigible, Sidney.'

'I'm really going to make an effort with Christmas this year,' announced Julie, a week before the schools closed for the holidays.

'And why is that?' asked David, looking up from his papers and peering over his gold-rimmed, half-moon spectacles.

'Because last year,' replied Julie, taking the opportunity to have a break from distributing the early morning mail, 'was so indescribably awful that I'm really going to try not to let it get to me this year. I'm going to go with the flow, just let it all wash over me. Do you know that last year I was *glad* to get *back* to work. I spent ages and ages looking for presents which in the end didn't suit. I wrote hundreds of cards to people I haven't seen for ages and am not likely to ever see again and then, at the very last minute, somebody sent me a card who I hadn't sent one to and I had to rush to catch the last post to send them one. Well, this year I'm not sending any cards and I'm giving all my nephews and nieces money and I've asked everybody else what they want. It's a much better idea, I think.'

'Oh no,' I said, 'I don't agree at all with that. Part of the excitement of Christmas is sending cards and getting surprise presents.'

'Well, I can do without surprise presents, thank you very much,' replied Julie, flicking half-heartedly through the mail. She looked up. 'You know what surprise present I got from Paul last year?'

'I don't,' I said, 'but I guess you are about to tell us.'

'Red underwear! That's what I got. Shocking, skimpy,

red silk underwear. Now who in their right minds – apart from Mrs Savage and a French prostitute – would be seen dead in red underwear?'

'Although I am not an expert on ladies' lingerie,' said David, 'I do think red underwear sounds rather attractive – on a woman that is.'

'There's the typical man speaking,' Julie told him. 'I wouldn't be seen dead in red underwear.'

'It could have been worse,' I ventured. 'Paul could have given you oven gloves.'

'Well, at least I would have worn the oven gloves,' retorted Julie. 'He's certainly not getting me into, red underwear.'

'So what about Christmas Day?' I asked. 'Have you cancelled that?'

'We're going out for dinner. That's the other big improvement. Christmas Day last year was a disaster. Mum put the turkey giblets in a dish and when she came to make the gravy they'd mysteriously disappeared. You would have thought that she'd lost all her life savings the fuss she made. Eventually, Uncle Tom admitted that he had given them to the dog. We had Mum moaning, Uncle Tom apologising, Auntie Pat crying, Dad ignoring it all – and then the dog was sick. Granddad nearly choked on a silver sixpence and Grandma lost an earring so we spent the afternoon playing clean the carpet, find the sixpence and hunt the earring. Then we watched *Chitty, Chitty*, bloody *Bang Bang* for the umpteenth time on the telly until we all fell asleep. It was a nightmare. Four days of living hell.'

'You had a lively time and no mistake,' remarked David, chuckling to himself.

'That's just it, Mr Pritchard, I don't want a lively time. I have enough of a lively time with you inspectors all the year round. At Christmas I want peace and quiet, with no hassle, no noise, no stress.'

'And speaking of hassle, noise and stress,' said David, cupping a hand around his ear, 'I think I can hear the dainty tread of the Inspector for Visual and Creative Arts on the stairs.'

'And that's another thing,' said Julie, pursing her lips before holding up the papers in front of her, 'I've got a mountain of work to finish for Mr Clamp and I was hoping to get off a bit earlier tonight to finish my Christmas shopping.'

A moment later Sidney burst into the office. 'Happy Christmas!' he roared, throwing his briefcase on Harold's chair. 'I just love this time of year. The smell of pine in the air, shop windows crammed with colourful gifts, carols and cribs, fairy lights, holly and mistletoe, and Santa's grotto, ho! ho! ho! It just grabs you by the throat and says, "Peace and goodwill to all men".' He pulled off his coat, hung it up roughly and flopped at his desk. 'Christmas makes you feel so well disposed to others, it's . . . it's . . . what's the word, Gervase? Infectious, yes, that's what it is, infectious. Why, at this time of year I could kiss Connie and hug Mrs Savage.' Sidney suddenly stopped. The three of us were staring at him in bemused silence. 'Is it something I've said?'

'May I remind you, Sidney,' said David, 'that schools have not broken up for the holidays yet and Christmas has not arrived. We all have quite a bit of work to do before the term ends and I believe you, in particular, have a great deal to finish.'

'I've somehow gone back in time,' said Sidney dramatically, talking to no one in particular, 'and found my way into the office of Ebeneezer Scrooge.'

Julie placed the thick pile of papers on his desk. 'Dr Yeats wants the report on Loxley Chase School before the end of the afternoon. He was on the phone twice yesterday. You have six letters to sign, the questionnaire on "Painters in Schools" to complete, your January course applications to check over and you still haven't finished the Arts Council response that Dr Gore asked you to do. In today's mail there are two items marked "very urgent" and two more marked "urgent". And, by the looks of it,' she said, indicating the papers before him, 'you've only got two greetings cards this morning in that little lot. Happy Christmas!'

'Will someone tell me what I have done?' appealed Sidney, watching Julie totter out of the door on her high heels.

'It's what you haven't done,' said David, pointing to the mound on his colleague's desk. 'Julie was not intending to work late tonight. She was wanting to finish her Christmas shopping. If I were you, Sidney, I'd make a start.'

Thereafter, the first part of the day was unusually quiet. Sidney soon settled down to his reports and letters and all that could be heard above the gentle hum of the traffic on Fettlesham High Street were the scratching of pens, the occasional sigh and grunt, and the scraping of a chair on the hard wooden floor. When the clock on the County Hall tower struck eleven o'clock, Sidney's pen bounced off the page in a flourish as he stabbed the final full stop to the Loxley Chase Report. Then he leaned back in his chair, placed his hands behind his head and exhaled heavily. David peered over his glasses and I looked up from my work.

'I take it that our young secretary,' announced Sidney, 'bearing in mind the mood she was in when I arrived, will not be forthcoming with the libations this morning.'

'You know where the mugs are,' murmured David, returning to his report.

'And since you are so full of the Christmas spirit, Sidney,' I told him, 'oozing with goodwill to all men and infected with festive kindness, perhaps you would like to make David and me some coffee at the same time.'

Sidney thought for a moment, smiled dramatically, then jumped up from his chair. 'Of course, dear boy, nothing would give me greater pleasure. I shall take these letters and this completed report through to Julie to placate her as well.'

Over coffee, Sidney began one of his all too familiar interrogations. 'I assume that over Christmas you are taking the blonde love goddess of Winnery Nook to some faraway, exotic location, Gervase?'

'No,' I replied curtly.

'No?' he retorted. 'Is it a wet weekend in Whitby, then?'

'Actually, we are not spending Christmas together. I'm going to my brother's in Retford again. I'm hoping we can have a few days together in the New Year.'

'Barbados, Nice, St Tropez, Paris?'

'Settle.'

'Seattle!' exclaimed Sidney, reaching for his coffee. 'Well, well, Gervase, you are lashing out. This sounds serious. A trip to the States. Seattle will be beautiful at this time of year.'

'No, Sidney, I said Settle, not Seattle.'

'Settle! Settle!' he cried. 'You're taking her to Settle? The pot-holing capital of the Dales. What are you intending doing? Creeping about on all fours underground with lamps on your heads? Hiking over the slippery limestone in driving sleet? Trekking through the snow?'

'Actually, Settle is spectacular in winter,' announced David, taking off his spectacles.

'Don't tell me you're taking him with you as well?' asked Sidney.

'As a matter of fact, it was I who recommended Settle to Gervase. There is a very pleasant little hostelry there called The Traddles. The food is outstanding, the views magnificent and the people who own it very friendly. Also, it's a very romantic place.'

'But it is still Settle,' groaned Sidney. 'And has she agreed to go?'

'I haven't asked her yet,' I said. 'I want it to be a surprise.'

'It'll be a surprise all right!'

'I booked a couple of days back in October and –'

'Well, don't hold your breath,' Sidney told me, 'I think staying at home is preferable to Settle in winter.' He changed the subject. 'And what have you got your inamorata for Christmas?'

'A locket,' I replied.

'Oh dear, oh dear. A locket! A locket is something you give your maiden aunt or a little girl about to make her First Communion.'

'As a matter of fact,' said David again, 'it was I who recommended to Gervase the Mezzo Gallery in Skipton. They design and make the most unusual silver jewellery.'

'But a locket is not a present you give to the woman of your dreams. What he needs for a feisty young beauty of Christine Bentley's obvious charm, attraction and elegance is something particularly feminine, something which expresses his simmering passion, his ardour, something which speaks of his undying devotion, like a mass of red roses, an obscenely large bottle of French perfume, a huge box of Belgian chocolates, a delicate diamond pendant –'

'You mean something tasteful like red silk underwear?' suggested David.

'That's exactly the sort of thing women love,' enthused Sidney. 'They really go for men who are unpredictable and impulsive, who surprise them with unusual gifts. Unlike your other ideas, David, red underwear is an inspired suggestion. Now I will take you to Hoopers of Harrogate, Gervase, and help you select –'

'There is no way I am giving Christine red underwear!' I said emphatically.

'But she will adore it!' cried Sidney, just as Julie appeared with his letters for signing. 'Now what woman could resist red silk underwear? Wouldn't you agree, Julie?'

Julie gave him a long, blistering look before slowly leaving the office.

'You know, I think Christmas brings out the worst in some people,' sighed Sidney shaking his head.

I decided to broach the subject of the couple of days in Settle with Christine that very evening. I had agreed to go with her to the Christmas production at Winnery Nook Junior School and was due to pick her up from her parents' house at seven o'clock.

'Please come with me,' Christine had pleaded earlier that week, 'and give me some moral support with the insufferable Mr Logan.'

To say that Christine did not get on with the self-opinionated Headteacher of the Junior School would be something of an understatement. Mr Logan was a large man with pale watery-blue eyes and heavy jowls. He had the irritating habit of waving his fat freckled hands in front of him as if conducting some invisible orchestra and he spoke at such a speed and in such a strident tone of voice that his listeners were eventually harangued into silence. He was hard-working and managed an excellent staff but it was his patronising attitude to early education which infuriated Christine. For Mr Logan, the Infant School was where 'the little ones' were 'occupied' and 'taught a few basic skills'. It was only when they reached him in the Juniors that the really rigorous work began.

I arrived at Christine's house a little before half-past six. Drops of rain began to fall as I drove up the curved gravel drive leading to the stone-built house. Christine's mother opened the door to me with a warm smile and I was ushered down the long hallway and into the sitting-room.

'What an evening,' she said. 'Come along in, Gervase, Christine won't be long. She arrived back late from school as usual, so she's still getting ready.'

It was a charming, elegant room and about as different as it possibly could be from my dark little flat above The Rumbling Tum café. A large Christmas tree in the corner sparkled with silver tinsel and tiny lights, the mantelpiece was lined with cards, red and gold decorations hung from the walls and a small crib had pride of place on an occasional table. I sat in front of a welcoming log fire which crackled brightly in the grate.

'The room looks splendid,' I said.

'Oh, I just love Christmas,' she replied, echoing Sidney's words. 'It seems to put everyone in such a friendly mood. People smile at one another in the street and strangers talk to you. It really brings out the best in people, don't you think?'

'So you are all prepared for Christmas?' I asked.

'Just about. I told Christine that you would be very welcome to join us but she said you had already agreed to go to your brother's.'

'That's right,' I replied. 'I'm collecting my parents and my sister is coming down and we'll have a family Christmas in Retford. But thank you very much for inviting me.'

'Well, perhaps next year,' she said smiling.

Let's hope I will still be on the scene next year, I thought.

'Ours will be a quiet affair,' Mrs Bentley continued. 'We never see a great deal of Christine at Christmas, to be truthful. She goes off on Boxing Day and –'

'Goes off?' I interrupted.

'Skiing, you know. She's gone skiing every Christmas since she left college. Didn't she tell you?'

'No,' I replied, crestfallen, 'she never mentioned it.'

'Oh dear,' said Mrs Bentley. 'I hope I haven't put my foot in it.'

'You never told me you were going skiing after Christmas,' I remarked as I drove towards Winnery Nook Junior School a short while later.

'Oh didn't I?' she replied innocently.

'No, you didn't.' I realised my voice had a rather petulant edge to it.

'Well, I knew that you were off to your big family get-together in Retford.' When I didn't reply, she continued. 'You didn't want to come, did you?'

'I might have done.'

Christine chuckled and put her hand on my arm. 'But you don't ski, Gervase.'

'I could have watched. Anyway, who are you going with?'

'Oh, just a friend,' she replied, clearly enjoying this little exchange.

'What friend?' I could feel my heart thumping in my chest.

'Someone you don't know.'

'Not Miles, is it?'

'Of course not. I've not seen Miles for ages. Anyway, you know him.'

'Who then?'

'This is getting like the third degree.'

'I think you might have told me.'

'Are you jealous?'

'No,' I said peevishly. 'Well, yes, I am as a matter of fact.'

'Alex. I'm going with Alex, an old college friend. So there. Now you know.'

'And what's this Alex like?'

'Tall, slim, attractive.' She paused and chuckled. 'She's very nice.'

'Oh, it's a she then?' I cried, vastly relieved.

'Of course, it's a she, silly. I'm not likely to be going off skiing with another man, am I?' She moved closer. 'I'm not that sort of woman.'

'Oh well, that's different,' I said. 'I just thought that we might have spent a couple of days together over the Christmas

123

break – the last weekend before schools start again. There's a really nice hotel that David recommended and –'

'I'm only going for a week, and will be back on the second,' said Christine quickly.

'So you'll come?'

'I'd love to.'

'Right then, that's great!' I said, sounding pretty pleased with myself.

'But won't hotels be full up at this time of year?'

'I booked a couple of months ago,' I told her. 'I wanted to surprise you.'

'You were pretty sure of yourself, Gervase Phinn,' she said. 'And where is this hotel?'

'Well, it's not Barbados, Nice, St Tropez or Paris, I'm afraid. It's near Settle.'

'I love Settle,' Christine said. 'I'll really look forward to it.'

'Good, that's settled then,' I said.

We both laughed out loud.

Winnery Nook Junior School was a modern and attractive building constructed in the same honey-coloured brick as the Infant School which was situated a couple of hundred yards away beyond a large square playground. It had the same low-angled roof of red pantiles and large picture windows but was certainly not as warm and welcoming.

I parked the car and Christine and I hurried up the path which was glistening with rain in the light of the street lamps. We passed a series of large black and white notices: 'Property of Yorkshire County Council'; 'Trespassers will be prosecuted'; 'No public right of way'; 'No dogs allowed on these fields'. Attached inside on the glass of the entrance door was a further series of requests and instructions: 'All visitors MUST report to Reception'; 'Parents must wait outside when collecting their children'; 'The car park is strictly for the use of school staff only'.

The place sounded as welcoming as a Ministry of Defence shooting range, and the entrance area of the school had the ambience of a hospital waiting-room. A few anaemic prints hung on a pale yellow wall and three hard-backed chairs had been arranged in a line facing them. On a small table were a couple of magazines and an unhealthy-looking spider plant, its green and white shoots trailing to the floor. As we headed for the school hall, following the throng, a freckly-faced boy of about seven ran up excitedly.

'Hello, Miss Bentley!' he cried, obviously delighted to see her.

'This is John, Mr Phinn,' said Christine, turning to me. 'He came up to the Juniors at the beginning of this term and he was one of my star pupils, weren't you, John?'

'Yes, miss,' nodded the child.

We moved out of everyone's way. 'Are you in the play, John?' asked Christine.

'No, miss, there's only a few parts and they went to the older ones. I'm helping with the programmes and stacking the chairs at the end.'

'Oh well,' said Christine, 'there's time enough. You'll probably be in next year's play.'

'I hope so, miss,' replied the child.

'And how do you like the Juniors?'

'Oh, it's all right, miss,' replied the boy unenthusiastically.

When we had taken our seats, the lights dimmed, the hall fell silent and a fat man with pale, fishy eyes strode to the front. This was Mr Logan, the Headteacher. He waved his hands expansively in front of him, explaining that the evening's performance was a dramatic episode from the well-loved children's classic, *Anne of Green Gables*. He prattled on about there being so few really good Christmas plays suitable for children these days and how he believed in good quality writing, traditional values and high standards. What all this had to do with a school play was beyond me. He then reminded everyone that taking pictures during the perform-ance was prohibited because the flash lights would disturb the actors, that there would be no interval and that there would be a retiring collection to supplement the school fund.

A Christmas production gives a school the opportunity of staging a large-scale dramatic event involving a great many children. It should be a lively, joyous affair, full of colour, music and often dancing, centred on a seasonal theme. I had been in the audience the week before at Willingforth Primary School, and had laughed and cheered with the parents and children at the outstanding perform-ance of 'Scrooge'. All the pupils in the school had been involved in some way.

The evening before I had watched a nativity play at St Bartholomew's Roman Catholic Infant School. The star of the show had been the Innkeeper, played with great gusto by a cheeky-faced little boy of six. In front of the curtains on the makeshift stage there was a bed in which the Innkeeper was sleeping. He was suddenly awoken by Joseph banging loudly on the inn door and asking for a room. Each time the Innkeeper clambered into the bed to go to sleep he was disturbed: by the shepherds looking for the baby, by the Three Kings bearing gifts, by a great flashing star and finally by a host of heavenly angels singing 'Away in a Manger' loudly outside his window. Finally, he had had enough and stamped and stormed across the stage. The curtains had opened to reveal a tableau at the centre of which was a little Mary in blue and Joseph in a dressing-gown, white socks and with a towel over his head, held in place by an elastic belt with a snake clasp.

'What's all this, then?' the Innkeeper had demanded. Mary had held a finger to her lips. 'You'll wake the baby,' she had said. The grumpy Innkeeper had peered angrily into the manger. His face had suddenly changed and a great beaming smile had filled his face. 'Aaaaaahhhhh, he's a bobby-dazzler!' he had exclaimed. 'What a luvverly little baby.'

That evening there were tears in many an eye.

There were only six children in the school production of *Anne of Green Gables*. Five of them struggled through the tedious, wordy and overly-sentimental episode, delivering their lines as if reading from a shopping list. In contrast, the lead part of Anne, played by a plump, red-faced girl with protuberant blue eyes, was undertaken with great enthusiasm and confidence. Dressed in a bright blue and yellow gingham smock (rather unsuitable for the time of year, I thought) and sporting huge bunches of hair tied in red ribbons, she dominated the stage. She declaimed her lines in a dreadful mock-American drawl at the rate of a Gatling gun and had the irritating habit of waving her hands in front of her as if conducting some imaginary orchestra. I had seen something similar to this performance before.

The play thankfully came to an end. Soon Christine was surrounded by a knot of excited pupils eager to talk to her. I was content to sit and watch her as she chattered and laughed and ruffled hair, her blue eyes shining and her beautiful face flushed with pleasure. My reverie was shattered with the appearance of Mr Logan, accompanied by the large girl who had played the part of Anne.

'Good evening, Mr Phinn!' he said. 'I trust you enjoyed our little performance?'

'Yes, the children did very well,' I replied, tactfully.

'Mr Phinn,' the Headteacher informed the girl, 'is a school inspector and he has cast his critical eye over many a school play.' An expectant expression played about the girl's large blue eyes.

'You were very confident,' I said, 'and did very well to remember all those words.'

'I'm auditioning for the lead role in *Annie* next week,' the child informed me. *Annie*, I thought to myself. *Annie* – the musical about the wraith-like orphan.

'She goes to drama school every Saturday,' announced the Headteacher waving his hands in front of him. 'She's my youngest daughter, is Leanne.'

On our way out, Christine and I caught sight of the pale, slight girl who had delivered the opening lines of the play. She would make a perfect Annie, I thought.

'You were excellent,' I told her.

'You were, Cathy,' agreed Christine. 'Really excellent.'

'I only had a few lines, miss,' replied the child, smiling coyly.

'Ah,' I said, 'but you were the first person to speak and it was you who set the scene. We heard every word clearly, didn't we, Miss Bentley, and if I had an Oscar to award – you know, the prizes that very famous actors and actresses sometimes get – well, I would give it to you.'

'That was a lovely thing to do,' said Christine, sliding her arm through mine as we walked down the path. 'And if you only knew what that will do for Cathy's confidence. She was such a shy little thing when she was with me in the Infants.'

'She deserved an Oscar,' I said. 'Anyone who could go on to the stage, before all the other actors, beneath all those bright lights, in front of a hundred people and deliver such ridiculous lines without making one mistake, deserves an Oscar.'

Under a street light, I consulted my programme. 'I wrote down the lines. Do you remember what she had to say?'

'No,' replied Christine, 'I was thinking what an ordeal the whole evening was going to be. What *did* she have to say?'

I read the lines: ' "Is Farmer Hart's farm far from here?"

I can imagine Sidney trying to say those lines after a few Christmas drinks.'

We laughed and laughed all the way to the car.

'So what was Settle like?' asked Sidney. It was the first week back after the Christmas break and a particularly cold and windy morning.

I was certainly not going to elaborate. To do so would have initiated one of his rigorous interrogations about my love life, so I replied curtly, 'Excellent,' and continued to sort through the papers on my desk.

'And was it full of ramblers, scramblers and danglers?'

'Pardon?'

'Hikers, hill walkers and mountain climbers?'

'We didn't go out much,' I replied, putting a file into my briefcase.

'*Really?* Sounds like you had a very intimate time.' I did not reply. 'And the locket?'

'She loved it.'

'Mmmm, and there was I thinking Miss Bentley was a woman of taste. Did she help you choose that frightful attire?'

'Pardon?'

'Gervase, are you going deaf? Have the icy gusts and wintry gales of Settle resulted in a hearing problem? I asked about that horrendous suit which you are wearing and whether Miss Bentley helped you select it.'

'No, I bought it yesterday as a matter of fact,' I replied. 'Sidney, I really do have to get on. I have an appointment.'

'And you are intending going into schools in it, are you?'

'Of course, I am,' I replied, looking up from my papers. 'Why shouldn't I?'

'Because you'll frighten the teachers and terrify the children, that's why.'

'What's wrong with it?'

'It's quite the loudest, ill-fitting and garish piece of apparel I ever did see. You look like a down-at-heel music hall comedian or some impoverished country squire. It's a dreadful suit, outrageously tasteless and flashy and completely out of character for you.'

'I take it you don't like it, then?'

'Wherever did you get it?'

'It was in the January sales.'

'I assumed *that* much,' said Sidney. 'I should imagine that it has been in the January sales since Queen Victoria's time. I asked from where did you purchase the monstrosity?'

'From Fritters of Fettlesham.'

'Fritters of Fettlesham!' exclaimed my colleague. 'Fritters of Fettlesham! Are you aware that the only customers who frequent that antique emporium are decrepit old colonels, elderly clergymen and retired schoolmasters? Why didn't you go to Michael Stewart of Selby or Hoopers of Harrogate and get yourself something more stylish – a tasteful, tailor-made herring-bone, or modest check or pin-stripe?'

I had to admit to myself that the suit was rather unusual. It was a sort of mustardy brown with a dark-red, dog-tooth pattern, wide curved lapels, heavy cuffs and large leather buttons.

'Are you wearing it for a bet?' persisted Sidney.

'Look, this suit may not be at the height of fashion but it is incredibly warm and was remarkably cheap. What's more, the man in Fritters assured me it is the cosiest suit in the shop.'

'Cosiest! Cosiest!' exclaimed Sidney. 'You are not a tea-cosy, Gervase.'

'Look, Sidney, I wanted something which will insulate me against the cold and wet this winter, and on mornings like today, this suit is ideal.' I plucked a label from the large square pocket. ' "This suit," ' I began to read, ' "has a lining treated by a special process to extend the durability of the item. Most people produce approximately 3,000g of perspiration in a standard day and this lining is made to cope with up to 4,000g a day." '

'You'll lose about two stone in weight wearing that outfit,' remarked Sidney, stretching across to feel the cloth.

I continued to read: ' "The lining material contains nine billion microscopic pores per square inch, each one 10,000 times smaller than a rain drop." '

'Wow!' cried Sidney, with mock surprise.

' "These pores will allow perspiration to escape whilst preventing cold from penetrating the material." '

'It would take a harpoon to penetrate that fabric.'

' "This treatment gives a very special feel to the material providing the wearer with protection and comfort –" '

'I get the idea, Gervase,' said Sidney interrupting, 'but it's still the ugliest suit I have ever clapped my eyes on. Anyway, what are you going to be doing this morning? Fell walking, sheep shearing, climbing Pen-y-ghent, exploring the caves at Ingleton, trekking across the Pennines?'

'This morning, if you must know, I am going to Sir Cosmo Cavendish Boys' Grammar School to join the interview panel for the Head of Classics post. The last time I was at that draughty dungeon of a place I was frozen to the bone. The interviews lasted all morning and most of the afternoon with a gang of garrulous governors arguing about everything and nothing. I do not intend to sit in that ice box of a conference room for three or four hours today, slowly freezing to death. This suit may not be particularly stylish, Sidney, but I'll be as snug as a bug in a rug.'

'That's because it very probably was a rug before someone, with a bizarre sense of humour, turned it into a suit.'

'Sidney, I do not intend to spend any more time arguing

with you about what I wear. The last time I visited the school I ended up with the most dreadful running cold and racking cough. I didn't stop sneezing and wheezing for a good week. On this occasion I will be well prepared.'

'Ah,' sighed Sidney, 'but is the school prepared for you?' At this point Julie bustled in with the morning mail. 'And what is *your* opinion of Gervase's attire, Julie, my dear?' he asked.

'He looks like my Uncle Cyril,' she informed us casually, moving from one desk to the other filling the in-trays.

'Was he the doctor?' I asked.

'No, the bookie!' she replied. 'He was the bigamist who ended up in prison.'

'I'm off,' I said, heading for the door, not wishing to prolong the conversation a moment longer.

'And don't go near the cliffs, will you, Gervase?' shouted Sidney after me. 'You'd be a hazard to shipping in that suit!'

Sir Cosmo Cavendish Boys' Grammar School was built at the turn of the century, paid for by the wealthy wool manufacturer and philanthropist from whom the school had taken its name. It was a huge, ornate, ostentatious pile of a building with squat, black turreted towers and mullioned windows, long cold corridors and dark cramped classrooms. I had only been a school inspector for eight weeks when I had been dragooned by Harold into undertaking the inspection of PE and games at the school, in place of David Pritchard who had broken his leg by tripping over a raised paving slab at the Golf Club. The inspection itself had gone pretty well but I had been dragooned a second time – on this occasion by the Head of Department, a broad, solid, hard-looking Scotsman called Mr Auchterloonie – into refereeing a rugby match after school when the official referee had failed to arrive. It had been disastrous.

My second visit had been to attend the interview panel for the appointment of the Head of English, and the day was spent in a refrigerated box euphemistically known as the Conference Room. I had sat there shivering uncontrollably and endeavouring to stop my teeth from chattering. Never again, I had thought.

I now parked the car in the spot reserved for visitors at the front of the school and collected the various papers I would need from my briefcase. I felt beautifully warm as I clambered from the car into the cold morning air and ambled past the great bronze statue of the school's founder which dominated the main entrance. Sir Cosmo stood on a large plinth, hands on hips, legs apart and chin jutting out like a mastiff about to pounce.

'Excuse me, sir.' It was a small boy wrapped up like an Eskimo: thick brown and yellow scarf, leather gloves, fur-trimmed anorak and woollen hat pulled down over his ears. He had a bright, open face. 'Are you here for the interviews, sir?'

'Yes, I am,' I replied.

'Would you like to follow me, sir, and I'll take you to the administration block.'

'Thank you,' I replied.

'Have you travelled far, sir?'

'Just from Fettlesham.'

'Roads icy, sir?'

'Very.'

'You have to take it easy in this sort of weather, don't you, sir?'

'You do indeed.' What joy to find such politeness, I thought to myself.

'I can't say that I like the snow and ice, sir,' said the boy, scuttling along ahead of me.

'Neither can I, and it is particularly bitter this morning, isn't it?'

The round face beneath the thick woolly hat, now pink with cold, smiled, 'Well, sir, never mind, you look pretty warm in your winter coat.' That made me sound distinctly like a sheep.

The foyer of the administration block was spartan and draughty. I pressed the buzzer on the reception desk and, as if on some sort of trigger, the frosted glass slid back immediately and I was confronted with a pinch-faced woman with half-moon glasses perched on the end of her nose. She stared at me for a moment with her small eyes. 'Yes?' she asked sharply. 'May I help you?'

'I am expected.'

'Who are you?' she demanded. This woman, I thought, could take a few lessons in manners and common courtesy from the pupil whom I had just met and who had returned to his vigil by the front door. 'Are you from Fosters Floor Coverings?' she asked, not giving me the chance to reply. 'To fit the carpet in the Drama Studio?'

I was tempted to enquire if I looked like a carpet fitter but resisted the urge. 'No, I'm here for the interviews,' I replied equally coldly. 'My name is Phinn.' She ran a long finger down a sheet in front of her. 'It's spelt with a "ph".'

'What is?'

'My name: P–h–i–n–n.'

'There's no one on the list of that name.'

I sighed heavily. 'There's no "f" in Phinn.'

'I beg your pardon?'

'Has it been spelt with an "f"?'

'Whether it's a "p" or an "f" there is no one called Phinn on this list. Did you receive an invitation from the Chairman of Governors to attend for interview?'

'No.'

'Well, there you are then.'

'That is because I am on the Interview Panel. The Headmaster asked me to join him. I am not one of the candidates. I am from the Education Office.'

'Oh, I see. Well, I do wish you had said so earlier.' She ran her finger down another list. 'Yes, here you are. Jarface Phinn.' I didn't bother correcting her. 'The Panel is convening in the Conference Room. I'll arrange for a pupil to take you down.'

'Please don't bother,' I told her loftily. 'I do know my way. I've been here before.'

The glass abruptly slid shut in front of my eyes.

The Headmaster greeted me at the door of the Conference Room. Dr Trollop was a tall, cadaverous man with unhealthy-looking, greyish skin. He was dressed in a dark suit, dark tie and was draped in a long black gown; his mournful countenance immediately reminded me of an undertaker.

'Good morning, Mr Phinn,' he intoned, surveying me morosely and without a flicker of a smile. 'It's good of you to join us.' To match his appearance, Dr Trollop had the soft, vaguely ecclesiastical-sounding tone of voice of a funeral director about to give his condolences to bereaved relatives. I was ushered into the Conference Room to join the Chairman of Governors, Canon Williams, and the other members of the Panel.

A broad individual with an exceptionally thick neck, vast florid face and sporting a mop of unnaturally shiny, jet black hair was in loud conversation with Canon Williams, a thin cleric wearing steel-rimmed spectacles. Already seated at a long mahogany table was Mr Mortimer, the know-it-all parent-governor, who was flicking eagerly through a pile of papers. On my last visit to the school for the interviews for the Head of English post, he had drawn out the discussions when I had asked a candidate about the importance of students reading the great writers of literature. All he had seemed bothered about was whether the students could spell and punctuate and write 'a decent letter of application'. The final member of the Panel was a quietly spoken and nervous-looking foundation-governor, Mr Wright, who smiled weakly at me as I entered. All were dressed soberly, which made me stand out all the more in my suit of many colours. I surmised that these interviews were going to be as long and as tedious as on the previous occasion.

'I must say,' said the man with the vast florid face when we had taken our seats behind the large table, 'it's a damn sight warmer in 'ere than t'last time I were in t'school. I were frozzen to deeath. It's pretty parky on t'tops where I farm so I know all about bleak weather but, by 'eck, t'room were icy. I were fair starved. It took me a couple o'brandies and a gret rooaring farmhouse fire to thaw me out when I got back.'

'Yes, I agree,' said the canon, 'it was decidedly chilly. Of course, I'm quite used to the cold. I can never get the church heating, such as it is, to work and the rectory rarely gets warm. I often wear a body-warmer under my cassock. I get them from Fritters of Fettlesham, you know.' He smiled in my direction. 'However, I think we will be comfortable enough this morning as the Headmaster has kindly agreed to provide some heating for us.' He gestured to a vast metal box of a heater in the corner of the room, which was blowing out great gusts of hot air noisily and at an incredible rate.

Dr Trollop glanced at the heater with gloomy eyes and rubbed his chin thoughtfully. He looked as if he had recently been exhumed. 'I never seem to feel the cold,' he murmured in a hushed voice.

He's probably cold-blooded, I thought to myself.

'Well, colleagues, shall we make a start?' said the canon brightly. 'I think we all know Mr Phinn from the Education Office in Fettlesham, who is here to give us the benefit of his expert advice – oh, perhaps with the exception of Councillor Peterson.'

'I've not met 'im but I've 'eard of 'im,' said the man with the vast florid face. 'Mornin'.'

'Good morning,' I replied, with a sinking heart. So this was Councillor George Peterson, the most vociferous and tiresome member of the Education Committee, and husband of the formidable Headteacher of Highcopse County Primary School.

'Now, we are gathered here to interview for the position of Head of the Classics Department,' continued Canon Williams removing his steel-rimmed spectacles. 'It is a very important position in the school. Last time we interviewed it was for the Head of English post when, if you may remember, our discussions were a tad prolonged, largely because we departed down a number of diverse avenues, all very lively and interesting but immensely time-consuming. I do hope that these interviews will be rather more focused.' He glanced casually in the direction of Councillor Peterson and Mr Mortimer. I reckoned, as I listened to the well-meaning, cheerful clergyman, that these interviews would be no shorter. 'We have three strong candidates for the post, all well-qualified and experienced –'

'Can I just ask something before we go any further?' interrupted Councillor Peterson. I could see a weary expression cloud the canon's face. 'I'd like someone to tell me what's t'point of kids learnin' Latin and Greek? I mean, I were never taught Latin at school and it's not summat what's held me back.'

'Oh, Councillor Peterson,' responded Canon Williams as if speaking to a naughty schoolchild, 'it's very, very useful for one to know Latin and Greek.'

'Why?' demanded the councillor.

'I beg your pardon?' asked the canon.

'Why is it important?'

'Well, it is. I really do not want to go into the reasons for –'

'I can see it comes in 'andy for someone in your line of business, you being a clergyman an' all and 'aving to use it at your services, but –'

'In actual fact, Councillor, I do not use Latin at my services. It's those of the Romanish persuasion who use Latin. The Church of England services are in English and have been so since the sixteenth century.'

'Well, I wun't know abaat that, Canon, I'm chapel miself and there's no chance of our minister using Latin, not by a long chalk.'

'Having said that,' continued the canon, 'I do feel that a good grounding in the classics stands young people in good stead.'

'Well, I can't see it, miself,' grumbled the fat councillor, shaking his head.

'I feel certain that Mr Phinn here could mount a very eloquent defence of the efficacy of a classical education,' said the canon, looking longingly in my direction but I felt it prudent to say nothing.

'Do you think we might get on?' sighed Dr Trollop.

'I would be very interested to hear from Mr Phinn in what ways Latin and Greek are relevant in the modern world.' The know-it-all parent-governor now joined the discussion. Mr Mortimer clearly was not going to let things lie and launched into a lecture on the futility of classics in the curriculum. 'It seems to me to be a total and utter waste of time to study classics. Latin and Greek are of no practical use. French and German, yes, but a couple of old languages nobody speaks – well, I just can't see the point. In this day and age we want captains of industry not relics of a bygone age. We want young people fluent in Japanese and Chinese, conversant with computers, able to enter the world of commerce, international finance and business. We want mathematicians, linguists, engineers, physicists, chemists, those highly skilled in communications.

I for one – and I've said it to Dr Trollop on more than one occasion – feel that the school would be better off employing a teacher of Information Technology rather than a classics master.'

Canon Williams looked extremely ill-at-ease and turned to Dr Trollop for help. The Headmaster, however, also felt it politic not to enter the debate and continued to stare at the heater with a solemn countenance. He had obviously heard Mr Mortimer's views many times before.

Mr Wright, the foundation-governor, suddenly spoke up. 'I did Latin at school,' he said cheerily. The canon, a great wave of relief suffusing his face, thought he had found an ally and looked to him for some support, but there was none forthcoming. 'We learnt a little poem. I remember it to this day.' He then recited the verse.

> Latin is a dead tongue,
> As dead as dead can be.
> First it killed the Romans,
> And now it's killing me.
> All are dead who spoke it,
> All are dead who wrote it.
> All are dead who learnt it.
> Lucky dead they've earned it.

'That makes my point exactly,' said Mr Mortimer, smugly.

'Oh dear me,' sighed the canon, wiping his brow with the back of his hand.

'And I'll tell thee this, Canon,' boomed the councillor, quite determined to keep the discussion going, 'old Cosmo Cavendish, him who founded this place, could 'ardly string two words together in English, ne'er mind Latin. Only bit o' Latin he knew is the Yorkshireman's motto: "Brasso, in clutcho, intacto." Made his millions in cloth.'

'Our school motto,' piped up the parent-governor, 'was "*Video, Disco, Audio*", and I can remember –'

'My point is —' interrupted the councillor, but he was interrupted himself by the Headmaster.

'Whether we teach Latin and Greek is not an issue here, gentlemen,' said Dr Trollop in a low, wearisome tone of voice. 'The fact of the matter is we teach classical civilisation, we have Latin and Greek on our curriculum, students are examined in these subjects and we require a head of department. We can argue the pros and cons of retaining the classics at the next full governors' meeting if you wish, Mr Mortimer, but this morning we are here to undertake an interview and I would be grateful if we could now proceed.'

'Eminently sensible idea, Dr Trollop,' chortled the cleric. 'So let us move on.'

The first candidate looked like a younger version of Dr Trollop. He stared over his thick spectacles with great gloomy hooded eyes and, in answer to the question why he had applied for the post, breathed out heavily and said that he found the public school where he taught at present a little too demanding and was looking for a quieter life in rural Yorkshire in a school with not so many pupils to teach. When Councillor Peterson tackled him on the relevance of Latin and Greek in the modern world, he nodded sagely and said he sometimes wondered about that himself when faced with a class of adolescent boys more interested in football and pop music. He went on to explain that Latin was a discipline and part of our cultural heritage and helped students with their English.

When it came to my turn to ask a question, I asked the candidate which of the classical scholars had influenced him the most in his own life.

'I don't quite see the pertinence of that question,' he answered wearily. 'Of what significance is it to my position as a teacher who has influenced me or not?'

'I feel it is very relevant,' I replied. 'Were you applying

for the Head of English post I would ask which is your favourite author or poet. It tells me something about you.'

'Well,' he replied dismissively, 'this is not for an English post, so I really cannot say.'

I decided not to pursue the line of questioning any further. There was enough heat in the room already without adding to it. The Conference Room was like a furnace. The huge metal contraption was blowing out great blasts of hot air, mostly in my direction, and I was beginning to feel like a side of beef on a spit.

The next candidate bore an unnerving resemblance to the first: the same thin angular frame, funereal expression, dark doleful eyes and sallow complexion. When asked by the canon why he had applied for the position, he replied that he wanted something more 'pedagogically challenging'. When asked by the parent–governor about his strengths, he replied that he had 'a fertility of intellect' and that he enjoyed mending clocks. In answer to Councillor Peterson's question as to the relevance of Latin and Greek he thought for a moment, crossed his spindly legs, folded his long arms and stared at the ceiling.

'Did you understand t'question?' asked the councillor after an inordinately long pause.

'Oh yes,' replied the candidate still staring heavenwards. 'I was just contemplating the best way of responding.' After another lengthy interlude he enquired, 'Perhaps, rather than answer that question directly, I might be allowed to set up a paradigm.'

'A what?' snapped the councillor.

'A paradigm,' repeated the candidate, pronouncing the word with slow deliberation. 'Would it be acceptable for me to set up a paradigm?'

'It's all right by me,' replied the councillor, 'but is this room going to be big enough?'

'It is quite in order for you to set up your paradigm,' said the canon, his words accompanied by the scraping of chairs as the councillor and the parent-governor moved back to get a better view of what I suspected they imagined to be the erection of some sort of marquee. I was tempted to say that it might prove difficult hammering in the pegs.

The last candidate was a small, middle-aged woman with dark hair scraped back tightly on her head and tied in a neat bun. My heart missed a beat when I saw what she was wearing. She had on a suit made in exactly the same material as my own: mustardy brown with a dark red, dog-tooth pattern. There were no wide curved lapels, heavy cuffs or large leather buttons but it was certainly made from the same cloth. By the look on her face the candidate was as surprised as I when she caught sight of my attire. The other interviewers clearly thought we were related in some way for their eyes flashed backwards and forwards from the candidate to me.

The room was now like a sauna and I could feel the perspiration all over my body and the heavy suit sticking to my body. I wondered how the candidate was feeling, but she answered the questions with great skill and flourish until it came to Councillor Peterson's turn.

''Ave you a family?' he asked.

'No, I'm not married.'

'Do you intend to?'

'Do I intend to what?' she asked sweetly.

'Get married.'

'Councillor Peterson,' the canon interrupted quickly, 'I'm afraid that kind of question cannot be put to the candidate.'

'Well, I just 'ave,' he replied.

'It is entirely irrelevant whether the candidate is married or not.'

'It's very relevant,' he replied aggressively. 'What if this young lady gets married and then 'as a family? She'll 'ave to 'ave time off to 'ave the kiddies and then get somebody to look after them when she's at work. That's not satisfactory at all, is it?'

'You are not allowed to ask that,' joined in Mr Mortimer, 'because it's a non-PC question.'

'A what?' exclaimed the councillor.

'It's not politically correct,' he was informed.

'Well, I think I know more abaat politics than anyone here present,' he spluttered. 'I've been a county councillor for nearly twenty years.'

'Shall we move on, Mr Chairman?' asked the Headmaster, fixing the councillor with a look that brought to mind the Ancient Mariner and his glittering eye.

'I don't have any immediate plans to get married,' said the candidate looking Councillor Peterson in the eye, and with a smile playing about her lips, 'or indeed to have any children.'

'Right then,' he said, leaning back in his chair as if vindicated. 'I'll move on. Do you reckon you'd be able to cope with t'big lads, you bein' a woman an' all?'

The canon breathed out noisily. Dr Trollop shook his head.

'I've never found any difficulty coping with big or indeed little lads.' She smiled and looked directly at him.

'Oh.' Councillor Peterson was lost for words.

'I generally find that they do exactly as I say.'

'Oh.'

'Large boys present no problems for me.'

'No,' muttered the councillor, rather chastened, 'I don't suppose they do, I mean don't, I mean, I'm sure they don't give you any trouble.'

'And your last question, Councillor Peterson, about the relevance of the subjects?' prompted the canon.

'Oh yes. Well, I'm just a simple farmer what scrapes a livin' from t'land and not knowing Latin's not 'eld me back.

A lot of t'lads at t'school will end up running their family farm or mebbe becoming estate managers or land agents or working for t'Ministry of Agriculture and Fisheries. What I'd like to know is, what's t'point of 'em studying Greek and Latin and all this classical stuff?'

The candidate continued to smile sweetly. 'A knowledge of Latin helps us gain a good command of the grammar and vocabulary of our own language. Effective communication is very important in the modern world. It's always impressive to hear English well spoken, don't you think?' She paused and looked Councillor Peterson straight in the eye. 'I also believe that we have so much to learn from studying the Greeks and the Romans. Take Aristotle, for example. He wrote a great deal about logic, metaphysics, physics, astronomy, meteorology, biology, psychology, ethics, politics, philosophy and literary criticism. His philosophy became the foundation for the Islamic religion and was incorporated into Christianity. Then there's Socrates, such a clever, gentle and enigmatic man, very like Jesus.'

'Really?' said the canon suddenly sitting up. 'In what way?'

'Well, their contemporaries found them both difficult to fathom. Neither of them wrote anything down and we have to rely on their disciples to know what they believed and what they said. We do know that they were wonderful communicators, great teachers, that they could use words in such a way that people's lives were changed for the better. Surely learning about such men helps young people to live good, honest lives, to become more compassionate, truthful and humane.'

'Fascinating, fascinating,' murmured the canon. 'I would dearly like to debate this further, but I am afraid that time is of the essence and I will now call upon Mr Phinn, the representative from the Education Office, to put a question.'

'I was going to ask which classical scholar has influenced

you the most,' I said, looking into the candidate's china-blue eyes, 'but I'd guess from what you've said that it's either Aristotle or Socrates.'

'It isn't actually,' she replied. 'It would have to be Seneca.' She turned in the direction of Councillor Peterson. 'He was a Roman playwright and author of many essays and the teacher of Nero, one the most infamous of Roman emperors.'

'T'chap what fiddled when Rome was burnin',' said the councillor.

'The very one,' agreed the candidate. 'Despite teaching the young emperor and forming what he thought was a close relationship with his pupil, Seneca was forced by Nero to take his own life. He told the unvarnished truth, you see. It was a tragic end to a brilliant writer and philosopher. It was through reading Seneca that I decided to come into teaching. You see, he never lost his optimism and enthusiasm and delighted in the company of the young. He said that part of his joy in learning was that it put him in a position to teach, and that nothing, however valuable, would ever give him any pleasure if it were just for his benefit alone. "If wisdom were offered me on the one condition that I should keep it shut away and not divulge it to anyone," he once said, "I should reject it, for there is no enjoying the possession of anything valuable unless one has someone to share it with." Makes good sense, doesn't it?'

There was a silence in the room. The canon nodded, Mr Mortimer shuffled his papers, the foundation-governor stared at the candidate as if she were the Queen herself, Dr Trollop gave a brief smile and nodded, and I knew that this candidate had clinched the job. Indeed, fifteen minutes later, after a surprisingly brief and amiable discussion, Miss Rebecca Barnes was offered the position of Head of Classics.

By this time I was sweltering and near to fainting with the searing heat. The wretched machine was still blasting

146

out fiery hot air, the windows were misted over with condensation, the metal frames of the chairs were scorching, and the wretched suit was sticking to me. The suit's lining containing 'nine billion microscopic pores per square inch, each one 10,000 times smaller than a rain drop' was beginning to steam. I just had to get out.

'Canon Williams,' I panted, 'if you would excuse me, I do have another appointment to get to.'

'Oh yes, of course,' replied the cleric. 'Are you feeling quite all right, Mr Phinn? You look decidedly flushed.'

'I'm fine, thank you, Canon,' I puffed, 'but I must be off.'

'Well, that was a most satisfactory conclusion to the morning, don't you think? I just know that Miss Barnes will be a great success and I can see that Dr Trollop is delighted with such a keen and committed addition to his staff.' The Headmaster nodded his head lugubriously like a tortoise and gave a thin smile. Clearly heat had no more effect upon him than extreme cold.

'She was certainly the best of the three,' the parent-governor said. 'She very nearly convinced me of the usefulness of classics and, of course, when she mentioned Jesus, she certainly had you hooked, Canon Williams.'

'Well, she suited me,' concluded Councillor Peterson, stressing the word 'suited'. 'When I fust clapped eyes on 'er I thowt she'd not be up to t'job but she 'as a lot about her, that young woman, and I reckon she'll do champion.' Then he turned in my direction and his fat face broke into a great smile. 'And I could see that Mester Phinn, here, liked the cut of her cloth, didn't you, Mester Phinn?' I did not say anything but smiled and headed for the door and the fresh air.

As I walked to the car I passed again the great bronze statue of the school's founder which dominated the main entrance. I paused and stared up for a moment at Sir Cosmo, standing proudly on his large plinth, hands on hips, legs apart and chin jutting out like a mastiff about to pounce. Something seemed strangely familiar about the figure. I looked more closely. Yes, it was the suit he was wearing. Sir Cosmo was dressed in a suit with wide curved lapels, heavy cuffs and large buttons. I guess he had done his shopping at Fritters of Fettlesham.

The name, Sunny Grove Secondary Modern School, was singularly inappropriate. It was a grim, towering, blackened building surrounded by high brick walls and set in a depressing inner-city environment of dirt and noise. From the high windows, shabby factory premises and derelict land could be seen by those pupils tall enough to peer through the grimy glass. Row upon row of terraced houses surrounded the school; street after street of grey, gloomy buildings. The few houses that had been built in the last twenty years had acquired a look of drabness and neglect. Even the air had a sooty, dusty taste. It was a depressing scene of litter-strewn roads, graffiti-covered walls, windowless bus shelters – a landscape devoid of trees and empty of colour. The bright morning sunshine did little to make the scene less bleak. The previous term I had marvelled at the awesome view from Hawksrill Primary School – the great craggy fells, steep-sided gorges, trickling silver streams, lustrous pine forests, rolling green pastures and purple moors. It was a world away.

Sunny Grove would have been an ideal setting for a film version of a Dickens' novel. It resembled one of those dark and forbidding institutions described in *Hard Times* or *Nicholas Nickleby*. I could imagine Mr McChoakumchild, the heartless teacher, or Wackford Squeers, the brutal Headmaster of Dotheboys Hall, feeling very much at home here. I was directed across the school playground by a large arrow, following the instructions for all visitors to REPORT TO RECEPTION. It was just after nine o'clock and the school assembly was in full flow. Hearing the boys singing the hymn based on Blake's poem 'Jerusalem', I thought to myself how apt were the lines:

> And was Jerusalem builded here
> Among those dark satanic mills?

As I turned a corner, I bumped into a small, grubby-looking boy of about eleven or twelve who was creeping around the side of the school, as if trying to escape from someone. He had long, lank hair, an unhealthy pallor to his skin and was dressed in a dirty blazer and grey flannel trousers far too big for him. The boy looked up at me with a frightened wide-eyed expression – like that of a rabbit caught in a trap.

'Hello,' I said. He continued to gawp at me. 'Shouldn't you be in school?' He nodded. 'Well, come along then, you can show me the way to the school office.' I motioned him to go before me. Head down and dragging his feet, the boy turned reluctantly towards the school entrance.

The window in the glass-fronted reception desk slid back.

'Good morning, may I help you?' a woman enquired. Then, catching sight of the pupil skulking behind me, she reached for a large, red book which she flicked open. On the cover was written in large letters: PUPILS ARRIVING LATE. 'Excuse me a moment.' She craned her neck to get a better view of the boy. 'Third time late this week, Justin,' she declared, shaking her head and writing down his name.

'Yes, miss.'

'And what's the excuse this time?'

'Miss, I had to run an errand.'

'And where should you be first period?'

'PE, miss,' whispered the pupil.

'Well, you've missed assembly. You had better go straight to your first lesson.' The little boy scurried off. The woman turned her attention back to me. 'I'm sorry about that. Now, may I help you?'

'Yes,' I replied, 'I have an appointment with the Headteacher. My name is Mr Phinn and I'm from the Education Office.'

'If you would like to take a seat, Mr Phinn, I will see if Mr Fenton's available. I think he should be just about out of assembly by now.'

A moment later the Headteacher emerged via the school office and held out a large hand. I had seen his face over many a drystone wall, driving a hundred tractors along the winding country roads, staring stern-faced at sheep auctions, herding sluggish cattle along the farm tracks. It was a Dalesman's face: a thatch of thick, grey hair over a broad, creased brow, weathered features, heavy moustache and brown, good-humoured eyes.

'Good to see you, Mr Phinn,' he said. 'Come along in.'

I followed the Headteacher into a large, comfortable room. The heavy, dark, wooden bookcases lining three walls were crammed with books, and the rest of the room was filled with a large oak desk and leather armchair, two threadbare easy chairs, three ancient-looking filing cabinets and a small table piled high with reports and files.

'Come in, come in,' he said, ushering me ahead of him. He skirted around the two easy chairs and small table and placed himself squarely behind his desk on the large leather chair. 'Were your ears burning this weekend, Mr Phinn, by any chance? I was preaching at Hawksrill Methodist Chapel last Sunday and Mrs Beighton and Mrs Brown – we call them "the merry widows" – were singing your praises. I'm a lay preacher, you know, for my sins. Anyhow, I was chatting to them after the service and your name came up. I believe you visited the school last term. It's a lovely spot up there, isn't it?' How strange, I thought, when I had only been thinking of the place myself five minutes earlier.

Mr Fenton chatted on amiably and inconsequentially for a further five minutes, without stopping for a reply. Then, when a pause came and I endeavoured to respond, he jumped up, negotiated the chairs and the table again and disappeared out of the door. A minute later he was back with a tray of coffee. 'I'd forget my head if it wasn't screwed on. Now then, Mr Phinn, you're not here to talk about Hawksrill and my preaching. Shall we get down to business?'

For the first part of the morning I sat with the Headteacher to look through the examination results and discuss strategies for improvement. The pupils' performance was low compared with the grammar school's across town, but it had been steadily improving over the past few years and Mr Fenton was justifiably proud of this achievement. I soon found that he had strong views which he was not afraid of expressing. When he spoke about his pupils, his dark eyes lit up with a sort of missionary zeal. Then came the sermon.

'The boys arrive here at eleven, Mr Phinn, having failed their eleven-plus examination. Their parents will have received a letter from the Education Office informing them that their son has not reached the required standard to qualify for a place at the grammar school. In effect, these children will have been deemed to be failures. Some parents have promised their son a bike if he passes, a sort of misguided incentive to encourage him to work harder perhaps. The bike is not now forthcoming, of course. Many of the boys arrive here, therefore, under-confident, with low self-esteem. Some have seen their best friends heading up the hill in grammar school blazer and gold badge while they have been heading downhill. Our job, Mr Phinn, first and foremost, is to build up their confidence and self-esteem, continue to have high expectations for them and be sure they know, give them maximum support and encouragement, develop their social skills and qualities of character to enable them to enter the world feeling good about themselves. I want them to use their time at Sunny Grove so they develop into well-rounded young people with courage, tolerance, strong convictions, lively enquiring minds and a sense of humour.' He stopped suddenly. 'I really am sorry, Mr Phinn,' he said, 'I got carried away. I'm sure you don't need to be told all this. I must sound incredibly pompous. I don't mean to be, but I do feel so *passionately* about this and if I have a captive audience . . . It's the Methodist lay preacher in me, I guess.'

'That's quite all right, Mr Fenton,' I replied. 'I really do enjoy listening to someone else holding forth about education.'

'Well, I am sure you are not here for a sermon from me. You'll have to visit Hawksrill Chapel for that. Let's have a tour of the school and then I have arranged for you to join some English and modern language lessons for the remainder of the day. I believe you said in your letter that you would be reporting on the teaching and learning.'

Sunny Grove Secondary Modern School was built at the turn of the century. It was a substantial, three-storey edifice of red brick built around a central quadrangle. Movement about the school was by means of a wide, green-tiled corridor running round this quadrangle. Classrooms, which formed a square around the central paved courtyard on the ground floor, had hard wooden floors and high, beamed ceilings. The windows facing the corridor extended down past waist level, enabling the Headmasters of old to patrol the school each morning, cane in hand, and peer into each classroom to ensure the pupils had their noses to the grindstone. Invariably, they would have been hard men who would impose harsh discipline. Punctuality, silence, obedience and cleanliness would have been their bywords and if they could get the pupils placed in their charge to learn to read and write, add up, fear God and know their station in life, so much the better. The windows facing the street were high, thus preventing any inattentive pupil from staring at the outside world and dreaming.

The school was very different now. Paintwork was in bright blues and greens, and display boards, which stretched the full length of the corridor, were covered in line drawings, paintings, photographs and children's writing. Floors had a clean and polished look, the brass door handles sparkled and there was not a sign of graffiti or litter. Everything looked cheerful and orderly. The quadrangle was now an attractive and informal lawned area with ornamental trees, shrubs and a small pond. There were garden benches and picnic tables and two large modern sculptures.

Following our tour of the building, I headed for the first lesson, to see Mr Armstrong, Head of the Modern Foreign Language Department, with a group of thirty thirteen-year-old boys.

Mr Armstrong was a pink-faced, weak-jawed individual of indeterminate age. As I entered the classroom and took a seat at the back, he surveyed me morosely with the pale grey eyes of a fish glimpsed at the bottom of a pond. He moved to the blackboard, stooping heavily, as though carrying some great invisible weight on his shoulders.

'Now, where were we?' he asked the apparently disinterested and extremely passive group of adolescents, most of whom appeared to be staring vacantly into space or were slumped, as if drugged, over their desks. 'Ah, yes,' he continued, not getting or indeed expecting a response. He then began to chant:

'*Je vais* – I'm going
nous allons – we're going
tu vas – you're going
vous allez – you're going
il va – he's going
ils vont – they're going, masculine
elle va – she's going

elles vont – they're going, feminine
on va – one's going.'

I've only just arrived, I thought to myself, but I wished that this one was going, I really do. The teacher continued to drone on in such a soporific tone of voice that I felt like joining the rest of the drooping listeners. My mind began to wander and my eyelids became heavy. I was brought out of my reverie by a large, thin-faced boy who was sitting next to me.

'Do you speak any foreign languages?' he whispered.

'Yes, I do,' I replied in an undertone.

'Do you speak German?'

'Yes.'

'And do you speak French?'

'Yes, I do.'

He thought for a moment, surveyed the teacher still chanting at the front, and then nodded in his direction. 'Which is this, then?' he asked.

The second visit of the day, to an English lesson with thirty-five eleven-year-old boys, proved to be as tedious as the first and, at times, quite bizarre. The teacher, a Mr Swan, was an extremely frail-looking old man with wild, wiry grey hair and a strangely flat face. He was dressed in a threadbare sports jacket with leather patches, shiny flannel trousers and a mustard-coloured waistcoat. The pupils had been asked to learn a list of collective nouns and were being tested on them. This exercise seemed to me to have very little relevance or value, bearing in mind the low literacy level of the pupils. They would have been much better occupied, in my opinion, developing their skills in reading and in writing clearly and accurately instead of chanting the various collective nouns.

'The collective noun for sheep?' barked the teacher, strutting between the desks.

'Flock,' chorused the class.

'Cattle?'

'Herd.'

'Sailors?'

'Crew.'

This went on for some time until the nouns became rather more esoteric.

'The collective noun for foxes?' cried Mr Swan.

'Skulk,' shouted back the children.

'Cats?'

'Clouder.'

'Leopards?'

'Leap.'

'The collective noun for snipe?' shouted the teacher. There was no response. I had no idea either. 'Wisp,' he informed us, writing the word in large capital letters on the blackboard. 'Skylarks?' There was another silence. 'Exultation.' The word was added to the other. 'What about rhinoceros?' Still no response. 'Crash!' he exclaimed. 'Not a lot of people know that.'

Well, I certainly didn't, I said to myself. 'Crash' would be a very appropriate collective noun to describe a group of bores, I thought. 'A crash of bores'. I imagined with horror a whole school full of Mr Swans. When and how would these youngsters ever apply this knowledge? 'Oh, look, our mam, there's a wisp of snipe and an exultation of skylarks flying over that clouder of cats!'

When the pupils had settled down to tackle a very simple and deeply uninspiring comprehension exercise on glass production in St Helens, I moved around the class examining their books, listening to them read and testing them on their spellings and knowledge of grammar and punctuation. Mr Swan observed me, stony-faced, from behind his desk. Standards were very low indeed.

Justin, the little late-comer I had met earlier that morning, sat in the corner, away from the others, looking nervous and confused. I sat down next to him.

'May I look at your book?' I asked gently.

'Yes, sir,' he whispered, pushing a dog-eared exercise book in my direction. He watched me with that frightened, wide-eyed look on his face. I read from the first page an account entitled 'Myself'.

'Sir, we had to write that for Mr Swan when we came up to this school,' he explained quietly. 'Sir, so he could get to know a bit about us, sir. It's not very good. I'm not much good at writing, sir.' I found the description of himself immensely sad.

> Im not much good at anything really I like art but am not much good. I am in the bottom set for evrything and I've not really got eny friends. I dont really like school, Id like a bike When I leave school, Id like to work in a bread factry. I like the smell of bread baking, you get free bread if you work in a bread factry. The man next door told me that.

The teacher's comment at the bottom read: 'Untidy work. Watch your spellings. Remember full stops.' The boy was given a grade of two out of ten.

'It's not bad at all this, Justin,' I said, staring into his large, wide eyes. 'You just need to do a bit of work on the spellings and put in your full stops.' He nodded slowly. I went through his work with him. 'Now, tonight when you get home, you copy out carefully your next draft of this account. Will you do that?' He nodded. 'You know, I worked in a bread factory once, when I was a student, and you're right about the smell of freshly baked bread. It is a wonderful smell. My job was to take the tins out of a huge oven with a long pole. I wasn't very good at it. And you are right, we did get free bread.'

He smiled. 'Sir, are you learning how to be a teacher?'

'No,' I replied. 'I've been a teacher though.'

'Can you come and teach in this school?' he asked.

'No, I can't do that,' I said. 'I'm a school inspector now.'

'I don't suppose you'd want to teach in a place like this, anyway,' he told me, gazing up with his wide-eyed look.

I gave Mr Swan some rather blunt feedback at the end of the lesson when the pupils had departed for lunch. There was little evidence in the exercise books that his pupils had improved at all in terms of spelling, punctuation and presentation in their writing during the half a term he had been teaching them. There were a few short accounts, an essay, a couple of simple comprehension exercises and no poetry. Whilst there were plenty of critical comments in red biro at the end of the work, there were no suggestions about how the pupils might improve. I explained that I saw little value in teaching the boys about collective nouns when they did not have the first idea what a noun actually was, and many were incapable of spelling the very simplest of words or using the full stop correctly.

'Well, I don't agree,' he said, bristling at the criticism. 'I think that a knowledge of the different collective nouns is very important.'

'Why?'

'It's useful for them to know these things.'

'And when would the pupils be in a position to apply this extensive knowledge of the collective noun?' I was getting irritated by the man's manner.

'That's beside the point. It's part of our cultural heritage. Anyway, Mr Phinn, these boys are very weak academically. I mean, what can you expect?'

'The moon?' I replied.

'I beg your pardon?'

'Sir Alec Clegg, former Chief Education Officer of the West Riding of Yorkshire, once said that "the good teacher expects the moon".'

Mr Swan smiled cynically and there was a long, deep in-drawing of breath. 'Did he indeed?'

'And do you set homework?' I asked.

'Homework? No, I do not set homework. What is the point? These boys would never do homework.'

'Well, I would disagree!'

'Mr Phinn, have you ever taught pupils like this?'

'Yes, I have.'

'Well, I've taught them for rather longer, I think. They're not your grammar school high-fliers, you know. These lads will end up in manual jobs, that's if they're lucky, and not become university professors and brain surgeons. You can't make silk purses out of sows' ears. It's all very well school inspectors coming in telling teachers what they should and shouldn't do, they don't have to do it. Anyway, I'm only here to help the school out.'

'In what way?' I asked.

'I took early retirement a few years ago but was asked to come in to take the classes of Mrs Simkins who is on maternity leave. You just can't get teachers to come in to take this sort of pupil. I'm doing the school a favour, if you must know, and precious little thanks I appear to be getting for it.'

'Really.' Some favour I thought. 'And what is the development of this lesson?'

'How do you mean?' His face was white, his mouth tight with displeasure.

'Having got the pupils to learn the various collective nouns, what do you do next?'

'I teach them that the collective noun always takes the singular form of the verb.' He then launched into a diatribe. 'You hear so much misuse of the English language on the television and radio. People seem incapable of speaking correctly. Newspapers are full of spelling errors. Teachers come out of college these days with no training in grammar.

I blame all those trendy methods teachers have been forced to use. I never took any notice of the hare-brained ideas churned out by lecturers and inspectors.' I could see by his expression that he felt I was part and parcel of this trendy movement.

I sighed. 'But you are dealing with a group of boys, Mr Swan, who have very limited language skills. They need to develop their command of basic reading and writing through clear, structured and appropriate work.'

He seemed undaunted by my comments. 'Well, that's what I've just been saying, isn't it? They are incapable. These boys are very weak academically. In fact, this class are the weakest in the year.'

'Is,' I corrected.

'I beg your pardon?'

'Is,' I repeated. 'This class *is* the weakest in the year, "class" being a collective noun and taking the singular form of the verb.'

'If you will excuse me,' he said, as if he hadn't heard me, 'it is lunch-time.' With that he walked out of the classroom.

12

Towards the end of the lunch break I returned to the Headteacher's room feeling most depressed and wondering how Mr Fenton would react to the damning report I would, no doubt, be presenting to him at the end of the day.

There was a broad, tweed-suited individual with Mr Fenton. I recognised, with a sinking feeling in my stomach, the thick neck, florid face and shiny mop of hair of Councillor George Peterson.

The visitor grinned like a frog on seeing me enter the room. 'Ah, so it's Mester Phinn, is it!' he exclaimed. 'We meet again.'

'Good afternoon, Councillor Peterson,' I said, holding out a hand.

'I see you know each other,' said Mr Fenton, indicating a chair. 'Do sit down, Mr Phinn. I wondered where you had got to. I got you a sandwich. I hope you like ham. Councillor Peterson is one of our governors and also an old boy of the school.'

'He went to see the wife's school last term,' Councillor Peterson told Mr Fenton, 'and then we were interviewing for t'classics job ovver t'town at t'grammar. That were a rum do, and no mistake.' He paused to scratch his mop of hair. 'So what you doing in Sunny Grove today, then?'

'Observing lessons and assessing the quality of the teaching and learning,' I explained before taking a bite of the sandwich.

'My wife were abaat as 'appy as a legless donkey when she got 'ome after your inspection visit to 'er school. I 'ad to get mi own tea, she was in such a state. I don't know what yer said, because she wouldn't tell me, but it dint gu down too well, I can tell thee that.'

'I'm sorry about that, Councillor.'

'Nay, don't thee go apologisin', Mester Phinn. Tha's got nowt to be sorry abaat. Thy 'as a job o' work to do. I said to my wife, I said, that's what inspectors do – pick spots, see what's goin' on, check that everythin's as it should be and find out what's up. That's what they do – go round schools inspectin'. I said to 'er, it's like blamin' traffic wardens for clampin' yer car on a double yella line or a dentist sayin' you need a tooth out. That's what they're paid for, not to tell thee that everythink in t'garden's rosy. That dint gu down too well, neither.'

'I'm sorry that Mrs Peterson took my report so badly,' I told him. 'It really was pretty positive.'

'That's human nature, I'm afraid,' said the Headteacher. 'However much praise is given, it's the niggling little negatives which we tend to remember.'

Again, I wondered how he would respond to my report. There would be no 'niggling little negatives'.

'She soon changed 'er mind after you'd gone in and spent a bit o' time with the children,' continued the councillor. 'Teachin' 'em poetry, wasn't it?'

'That's right.'

'Aye, she come home well pleased after that.'

'I'm very relieved,' I said, and indeed I was.

'Don't see t'point of poetry myself, Mester Phinn. Like Latin and Greek. I don't see the relevance. Never could. Poetry's not going to get these lads a job, is it? They need to be able to write decent letters of application and add up.' I did not respond but saw in Mr Fenton's eyes a weary look of resignation. I prayed that Councillor Peterson would not be remaining in the school to hear my report. 'So, how's this morning gone?'

'It's been very interesting,' I said diplomatically.

'Aye, well it's a good school, this. Course, the lads aren't going to break any records when it comes to exams but they come out of this school a grand set of young men. Don't they, Alfred?'

'I would like to think so, George,' said the Headteacher. 'I'm very proud of them.'

'I've been most impressed with the pupils,' I said.

'So, what teachers 'ave you seen so far?' Councillor Peterson asked, sticking out a formidable bottom jaw and fixing me with his large pale eyes.

'I observed Mr Armstrong and Mr Swan this morning,' I told him.

'He used to teach me, did Mester Swan when I was 'ere, back in t'dim and distant past. By God, is 'e still going?'

'He's filling in for the time being,' explained the Head-teacher, 'doing some supply work during Mrs Simkins' absence. I must say, Mr Swan is finding it rather different from when you were at the school.'

''e must be gettin' a bit long in t'tooth by now,' continued Councillor Peterson. 'I reckon 'e were a fair old age when I was at school because 'is 'air were grey then. He were a good teacher was Mester Swan. One of t'old school.'

'But times have changed, Councillor,' I said and, taking a deep breath, continued, 'and a lot of the old school methods and ideas are inappropriate in this day and age. I'm afraid I did not find Mr Swan a good teacher and shall be describing his very poor lesson in some detail in my report.'

'Oh dear,' I heard Mr Fenton murmur.

Councillor Peterson's jaw dropped. 'By the 'eck, Mester Phinn,' he chuckled, 'tha' dun't mince words. Thar a regular Yorkshireman and no mistake. I can see what mi wife means.'

★

The first lesson of the afternoon was a great improvement on the morning's. The teacher, a bubbly, enthusiastic young woman called Miss Mullane, had prepared a lesson based on a novel set at the time of the Second World War which the second-year pupils were reading. She used well-chosen illustrations and probing questions to develop understanding of ideas and motives. 'What do you think it was like for the evacuee children?' 'How would you react to leaving home to stay in a stranger's house in the country?' 'What would you miss most?' 'How would the parents feel?' 'Can you predict what might happen next?' She encouraged the boys to explore character in greater depth, whilst sensitively supporting the less able, helping them to stay interested and involved by the use of questions matched to their abilities and interests. She required them to justify a point of view, refer to the text, relate to their own experiences and examine the use of language.

The atmosphere in the classroom was warm and support-ive, and the boys responded well to the teacher, clearly enjoying her touches of humour. Miss Mullane had a real empathy with, and respect for, the pupils and, unlike Mr Swan, had high expectations of their success. She encour-aged, directed, suggested, questioned, challenged and developed the pupils' understanding in an atmosphere of good humour and enjoyment.

The classroom environment was wonderfully bright and attractive with appropriate displays of posters, photographs and artefacts which gave the pupils a feel for the period in which the novel was set. Children had talked to their grandmothers and grandfathers about their war memories and there were poems, stories, commentaries, descriptions, letters, diary entries and anecdotes – a whole range of writing related to the Second World War.

As usual, I spent part of the lesson examining the pupils' exercise books. The work was varied and well presented and carefully marked in pencil. One pupil, imagining he had just arrived at his new home, had written his piece in the form of a diary entry. Another was composing a letter home describing his experiences. A third boy was busy with a playscript based on a conversation between the billeting officer and a villager who refused to take an evacuee.

'What are you writing?' I asked a cheerful-looking boy scribbling away at the front desk.

'It's an account based on the novel we're reading. I'm this evacuee, you see, sent from the city into the country to stay with this old couple who are not used to children. I'm writing my story of the journey and my fears and hopes and feelings.' I looked at the neat, clear writing and nodded. 'This is very good,' I said. 'You really describe things well. Some good details in here. You seem to know a lot about the war.'

'Thank you,' said the boy smiling. He stared at me for a moment before asking, 'Were you an evacuee, sir?'

'No, I was born just after the war. My brother was, though, and we have a photograph of him on the station platform at Sheffield in his uniform, with his gas mask in a cardboard box and his little leather suitcase. He looked really sad to be going.'

'Why was he in uniform, sir? Was he a soldier?'

'No, no, but all the children had to wear their uniform. They looked very smart.'

'Was he in the Hitler Youth, then?'

'School uniform,' I said laughing.

Things are looking up, I thought to myself, as I headed for the final lesson of the day. I entered the school hall to find two groups of large, aggressive-looking boys facing each other like street gangs ready for a fight. There was no sign of a teacher. I stood frozen to the spot.

The leader of one group thrust his face forward, curled

his lip and spat out the words, 'So, are ya looking for a fight then? Because if ya are . . .' Those behind him shouted encouragement, gestured and pulled faces. The leader of the other group moved forward slowly and threateningly, maintaining a carefully blank expression on his face.

'No, I'm not looking for a fight,' he mouthed deliberately, stressing each word, 'but, if I was, I could sort you out. I could spit on ya and drown ya. So, if you fancy your chances . . .'

His supporters jumped up and down, jeering and roaring with laughter, taunting the other group with gestures and silly faces. One small boy, with large glasses and wielding a ruler like a sword, tried to intervene.

'Look!' he shouted. 'Stop! You shouldn't be doing this! There's bound to be trouble. We've been told not to fight again. You've got to stop!'

A lad as large as a bear, with close-cropped hair and hands like spades, grabbed him by his coat and pushed him away. He mimicked his voice. 'Oh stop, you'll get into trouble.' He then pulled what looked like a knife from his jacket and waved it in the air, his face ballooning with anger. 'Why waste time with words?' he roared. 'Let's kill 'em!'

That's when I entered the fray. 'Stop!' I yelled. 'Stop immediately! Whatever's going on? What are you boys doing?' I could feel myself trembling. Remarkably, the whole class froze and stared uncomprehendingly in my direction. 'Where's your teacher?' I demanded.

'I'm here,' came a soft, calm voice from behind me. At the back of the hall and out of my view stood a small, prim-looking woman with spectacles on the end of her nose. She observed me over her glasses as if looking at some poor unfortunate sitting on the corner of the street begging for change – a face full of distant pity.

'Whatever's going on?' I asked again. I could feel my heart thudding away in my chest.

'Shakespeare,' she replied smiling and clearly enjoying my discomfort. 'Act 1, Scene 1. The boys are trying to get to grips with the meaning of the text in *Romeo and Juliet* by acting it out in everyday language. It's the part where the servants of the Montagues meet the Capulets in the city square and start facing up to each other for the fight. I'm sure you know it well. All right, boys, relax a moment.' She walked slowly in my direction and extended a small hand. A faint waft of sandalwood soap floated up to me. 'I'm Jan Darlington, the drama teacher, and you must be Mr Phinn.'

'That's right,' I said, attempting a smile. 'I'm most awfully sorry about the interruption. I feel so embarrassed but I really thought –'

'Please don't worry about it.' She turned to her class, laughing. 'Don't just stand there with your mouths open. Sit down for a moment.' The class obeyed instantly. 'If you convinced Mr Phinn that this was the real thing, I think you'll convince your audience next week. There was some real aggression and tension in that scene, your words fair crackled with energy. There was plenty of convincing body language and facial expressions as well. Now, we want that sort of acting when we get back to the text. Remember to keep that deadpan face, Wayne, it really makes you look far more intimidating, and Paul, even more of a dramatic pause before you say that last line. Really space it out to get maximum effect. It's all to do with timing, you see.' The teacher turned to me. 'Do take a seat, Mr Phinn, and we'll try the scene out on you, as Shakespeare wrote it. We would all really appreciate an objective view.'

I sat for half an hour and watched the most gripping opening of *Romeo and Juliet* I had ever seen. Two boys ambled down the side of the hall's stage, chewing and looking bored. Two more boys walked slowly down the opposite side. They eyed each other like fighting dogs.

'My naked weapon is out,' whispered one, standing discreetly behind his companion and drawing a wooden dagger from his belt. 'Quarrel, I will back thee.'

'How – turn and run?' enquired the other, with a cynical curl of the lip.

'Fear me not.'

'No, marry,' sneered the other. 'I fear thee!' The other two boys swaggered forward with their hands in their pockets. Their eyes were like slits and there were cold expressions on their faces.

'I will bite my thumb at them, which is a disgrace to them if they bear it,' whispered one.

'Do you bite your thumb at us, sir?' asked the other, articulating every word.

The verbal confrontation was electric, full of curses and threats, bravado and threatening gestures. And then the fight began. This was mimed and every action was slow and accentuated. When both sides were locked together, their arms and legs knotted in a violent embrace, the small boy playing Benvolio, with large glasses and wielding a ruler like a sword, tried to intervene.

'Part, fools!' he cried. 'Put up your swords; you know not what you do!'

The large lad, Tybalt, gripped him by his coat and pushed him away. 'What, drawn, and talk of peace!' he roared. 'I hate the word as I hate hell, all Montagues, and thee.' He plucked a wooden knife from his jacket and stabbed the air, his face ballooning with anger. 'Have at thee, coward!'

'Let's stop there for a moment,' interrupted the teacher. 'Make the fight scene even slower and more exaggerated. Curve your arm, Simon, in a great arc when you are throwing the punch and, Peter, make that kick slower and more deliberate and show the intense fury in your expression. Remember there should be no physical contact. This part is mimed. You also need to remember that you are thugs spoiling for a fight. It's hot, dusty, you are feeling sticky, there is a tension in the air. Try and capture that. You kept that deadpan face really well, Wayne, well done, and, Paul, even more of a dramatic pause at the end of the line: "Do you bite your thumb at us – sir?" The word "sir" is not a sign of respect. It is said as an insult so stress it.'

Miss Darlington then turned to me. 'Well, let's ask our theatre critic what he thought of the scene.'

I only had one word to offer: 'Superb.'

The bell sounded for the end of school. The pupils, without being told, packed away the props and stacked the chairs before putting on their jackets and shouting their 'goodbyes' to Miss Darlington. I spent ten minutes talking through the lesson with her before setting off, in much better spirits, to deliver an oral report to the Headteacher.

Mr Fenton listened to my preliminary report in silence. I concluded by saying that whilst I had observed some outstanding lessons from Miss Darlington and Miss Mullane, there were significant weaknesses in the teaching of Mr Armstrong. As for Mr Swan, I was of the strongest opinion that he should return to retirement as soon as possible. I referred to the Headteacher's earlier comments about building up the pupils' self-esteem and self-confidence, the need for challenge, pace and strong teacher support and encouragement. 'These pupils are not empty vessels to be filled up with a few arid facts about collective nouns. They deserve better,' I said. 'Now it's my turn to sound pompous. I don't mean to be but, like you, I do feel strongly about pupils who think they are failures.'

'That's quite all right, Mr Phinn,' the Headteacher replied. 'I, too, enjoy listening to someone else holding forth about education. And you are correct, of course. The purpose of education is to change an empty mind into an open one. Mr Armstrong has been with us for a long time and it's very difficult to get a leopard to change its spots. He has attended course after course but with little apparent benefit. His lessons are still exceptionally tedious, I have to admit. He is a well-meaning man and hard working and the boys do have a certain affection for him, but I think the time has come for me to have a stronger word with him about his methods. The other teacher concerned, as you are aware, is covering Mrs Simkins' maternity leave. We had an excellent teacher lined up but she secured a full-time post and pulled out at the last minute. I'm afraid I just could not get anyone else at such short notice. I have to agree, however, the pupils do deserve better. I shall most certainly act on your advice and do everything I can to find a different teacher to fill in before Mrs Simkins returns.'

I nodded, pleased that Mr Fenton was prepared to deal with the problem quickly.

'As for Miss Mullane and Miss Darlington,' he continued, 'your assessment of them comes as no surprise either, and I am delighted that you found their teaching so refreshing. When I was a lad, we plodded through the text in maximum, pleasure-destroying detail. That was the reason, I suppose, that I never took to Shakespeare, not, that is, until I came across Jan Darlington. She brings the words to life, as you quite rightly observe. You know, Mr Phinn, you should pay us another visit for the performance next week. Performing *Romeo and Juliet* in an all boys secondary modern school is quite a challenge, I can tell you.'

'I would very much enjoy that, Mr Fenton.'

'Sadly, Miss Mullane will not be with us much longer. She's joining the English Department at West Challerton High School next term as second in charge. I shall be very sorry to see her leave.'

'I will send a full written report, Mr Fenton,' I said, making ready to go. 'Now, if there is nothing else?'

'It's been a great pleasure to meet you, Mr Phinn,' said

the Headteacher, walking with me to the door. 'It's very reassuring to have inspectors who are so keen about children. I do really believe, you know, that those of us in education can really make a difference, particularly in the lives of less fortunate children, those who are labelled failures.'

'I know that, Mr Fenton,' I said, shaking his hand and looking into the dark, sincere eyes. 'I know that.'

'My father was a miner, Mr Phinn, and I remember him returning from the pit in Maltby where I was brought up, weary and caked in black coal dust but always smiling and good-humoured. He had no degrees or diplomas but he was a well-read and intelligent man and always wanted me to do well at school. He'd never had the chance, you see. My mother was a school cleaner and she too gave me every bit of support and encouragement. She worked hard and long to buy me the grammar school blazer and everything else I had to have, and to keep me on at school. I try to make Sunny Grove like the good home that I was brought up in, a place where there is work and laughter, honesty and fairness. I think I owe it to my parents.'

As I walked across the playground towards the dingy rows of terraced houses, shabby factory premises and derelict land, I looked back at the grim, towering, blackened building with high brick walls. I thought of Mr Fenton and his missionary zeal, and the words of Blake's poem came again to mind:

> I will not cease from mental fight,
> Nor shall my sword sleep in my hand,
> Till we have built Jerusalem,
> In England's green and pleasant land.

'Excellent news, gentlemen!' Harold Yeats crashed through the door making the three of us shoot up from our chairs as if given a sharp electric shock.

'For goodness sake, Harold!' cried Sidney, retrieving the bundle of papers which he had scattered across the office floor in his alarm. 'I wish you wouldn't do that – exploding into the room like some maniacal genie from the magic lamp and nearly giving everyone a heart attack!'

'It's just that I have some really wonderful news!' exclaimed Harold, showing his mouthful of teeth and vigorously rubbing his large hands.

'Is it a pay rise?' asked David lugubriously. 'It's about time we had an increase in our miserable salaries. We ought to get a raise when the teachers do. Four years it is since my income –'

'No, not a pay rise, David, but it is something which will, I have no doubt, bring a smile to that austere Welsh countenance of yours.'

'Mrs Savage has been given the sack?' announced David gleefully. 'Now that *would* bring a smile to my face. When I think of that woman, I genuinely warm to Lucretia Borgia.'

'No, no.' Harold rumpled his hair, frowned, sighed and shook his head.

'We're moving into a new office?' I suggested.

'No, we are not moving into a new office.'

'Connie is retiring?' ventured Sidney, leaning back in his chair, placing his long fingers behind his head and staring at the ceiling. '*That* would bring a smile to *my* lips.'

'If you three would just listen for a moment and let me get a word in, I'll tell you. Dr Gore has agreed, with the Education Committee's approval, for us to expand!'

'Expand!' exclaimed David.

'Appoint another inspector, one to cover science and technology.'

'Oh, be still my dancing feet!' exclaimed David. 'You mean I will no longer be responsible for science and technology?'

'I thought that would please you,' said Harold, again showing his set of tombstone teeth.

'It is absolutely superb news, Harold,' chortled David. 'Of course, it's about time too. I've had to cover science and technology for far too long. It will be a blessed relief to pass on all that work in physics and chemistry to some bright young thing. When will he start?'

'It will be after Easter,' announced Harold pleasantly. 'Some time after the start of the Summer term. The advertisement goes into the *Education Supplement* next Monday, then there will be the usual few weeks to receive applications and references. Then, of course, there will be the interviews and the successful candidate will have to give a couple of months' notice to his employer.'

'He! His!' exclaimed Sidney. 'Don't you two think, in this age of equal opportunities, that it may very well be a woman who is appointed? Why is there an assumption that the new inspector will be a man?'

Harold took a deep, steadying breath. 'Yes, of course,' he replied. 'You are quite right. It was a slip of the tongue. It's just that most science inspectors seem to be men.'

'All the more reason for appointing a woman, I would have thought,' I added.

'It would, of course, be splendid if we were able to appoint a woman,' replied Harold. 'Actually, when we were shortlisting for the English post we all thought that Gervase was —'

'A woman!' exclaimed Sidney.

'Well, er, yes,' Harold stuttered. 'I'm sure Gervase will be the first to admit he has a most unusual name and it does sound . . . oh dear . . . I'm digging in deeper, aren't I?'

'It's all right, Harold,' I laughed, 'I'm used to it. I often get letters addressed to Ms Phinn.'

'But seriously, Harold,' persisted Sidney, 'I think it would be an extremely sensible move to have a woman on the team. The thing is, a woman inspector would offer a very positive role model for all the female science and technology teachers and female students in the county and, of course, an attractive, intelligent, bubbly young woman would add a little verve and colour to this drab cubicle we euphemistically describe as an office. You could go in for a bit of positive discrimination.'

'Now, who's being sexist?' spluttered David. 'Why has she got to be an attractive, intelligent, bubbly young woman? It's not a beauty contest she's competing in, you know.'

'Oh, I don't think there will be any positive discrimination,' said Harold thoughtfully. 'I think not. The CEO and the Education Committee would not go along with that. This is Yorkshire after all. They will want the best candidate for the job, regardless of sex.'

'Gender,' corrected Sidney, 'regardless of gender.'

'Look!' said Harold. 'I came in today really excited about the prospect of another member for our team. I do wish you would stop nit-picking, Sidney. Now, if you could all bear with me for one moment, without interrupting, I shall go through the new procedures.'

'What new procedures?' asked David.

'If you would give me the chance,' cried Harold, 'I will tell you! Thank you. Now, things will be rather different from when Gervase was appointed last year.'

'Did they think they got it wrong, then?' asked Sidney, giving me a wry smile.

'Not at all, it's just that Dr Gore feels we need to refine the process and update it. Mrs Savage –'

David grimaced distastefully. 'I thought she would be lurking in the background somewhere, like the Ghost of Christmas Past,' he growled. 'Is she going to appoint the school inspectors now? It wouldn't surprise me in the least. She has those long, red-nailed fingers in every other pie.'

'Not at all!' said Harold. 'I really do think that you are rather hard on Mrs Savage, David. She's a very industrious and efficient woman, a little on the sharp side with people, maybe, but that's the way with her. Underneath that very steely exterior –'

'There beats a heart of iron?' concluded David.

'The woman is irritating beyond endurance,' agreed Sidney. 'You ask Gervase about the industrious and efficient Mrs Savage.'

'Please don't bring me into this,' I said. 'The last person I wish to talk about is Mrs Savage.'

'She was supposed to send Gervase all the information for another Fee-Fo meeting and, for the second time, deliberately withheld it from him to make him look a fool.'

'No, Sidney,' I began, 'it wasn't exactly like that and I certainly didn't say that I was made to look a fool. In fact –'

'And he had to attend the meeting with all these big-wigs,' continued Sidney obliviously, 'bereft of the necessary papers. For the second time running. When he phoned her up, rather than being apologetic, the vixen said that she had been under the impression he was going to collect them. Furthermore –'

'Sidney,' I interrupted, 'I am quite capable of explaining what happened myself.' I turned to face Harold. 'It was just a misunderstanding, Harold. Mrs Savage said that she would send me the minutes, new agenda and all the accompanying papers for last week's planning meeting just as soon as she received them, but then later denied this and said she had asked me to collect them from her office and –'

'Look, can we hear about the new procedures?' said David in an exasperated voice. 'It has gone six and I was hoping to get home before midnight.'

'Yes, yes, of course,' said Harold. 'But that has just reminded me. I would like to have an update from you sometime, Gervase, about how the Feoffees' event is progressing –'

'The new procedures, Harold,' sighed David, drumming his fingers on his desk.

'Well, as I was about to say, Mrs Savage has recently attended a course on selection procedures and has come back with some ideas which Dr Gore is really taken with. He's going to try out some modern and rigorous techniques. I will be drawing up the shortlist of the final five candidates as usual, but I shall also be attending the interviews myself this time. For the first part of the day, the candidates will sit a short sociometric test before meeting a selection of primary school headteachers in an informal setting. At this point, some preliminary judgements will be made. I thought perhaps Sister Brendan and Miss Pilkington and three others could be invited along. After morning coffee, each candidate will make a fifteen-minute presentation to the interview panel of councillors, Dr Gore and myself. It will be on some topical issue related to science education. Following this, he – or she – will be asked a series of pertinent questions on his or her presentation. Lunch will be with three secondary headteachers and the candidates will again be assessed in an informal setting. In the afternoon they will sit a written paper and this will be followed by the formal interviews. It should all be over by about five-thirty and the successful candidate will be informed at the end of the day.'

'Is that *all* they have to do?' asked Sidney. 'What about hang-gliding from the clock tower at County Hall while singing selections from *Oklahoma* or making a model of Buckingham Palace out of used matchsticks whilst performing a limbo dance beneath the CEO's desk?'

'I have to admit that it does sound like the Spanish Inquisition!' exclaimed David. 'I'm certainly glad I didn't have all that carry-on to go through when I was appointed in the dim and distant past. If you were warm and breathing, then they gave you the job. I was in and out of the interview room in no time at all.'

'When I was interviewed,' Sidney told us, 'I tripped over the carpet going into the Council Chamber, tottered forward, gripped the first hand in sight to get my balance – which happened to belong to a military-looking county councillor with a bright red face – and after that it was all plain sailing. I think he thought I was giving him some kind of Masonic handshake.'

'I'm certainly glad I didn't have to go through all that last year,' I said. 'The single interview was stressful enough.'

'I agree,' said David sadly. 'I don't think I'd get over the first hurdle if I was put through all the things you've planned for these poor souls, Harold.'

'We have to move with the times,' said Harold. 'Now, I would like you all to arrive at the Staff Development Centre at about five-thirty on the day of the interviews on March 1st. Could you just check in your diaries that you are available?'

'St David's Day!' exclaimed our resident Welshman. 'Well, I hope we are not going to be long. We're having a Welsh evening at the Golf Club. Anyway, Harold, why do *we* have to be there? Are the candidates to get a further grilling from us? Do I twist the thumbscrews, turn the rack or pour the boiling oil?'

'Just be a good chap, David, and look in your diary,' said Harold.

'Do you hear that, Gervase?' announced Sidney, smiling

broadly. 'You are to attend another interview and have the opportunity to wear that red and yellow monstrosity you fancifully call a suit.'

'Don't mention the suit,' I warned him, flicking through my diary. 'Why do you want us there, Harold?'

'It's for you three to meet the successful candidate,' Harold told us. 'Gervase, after you were appointed, you mentioned that it would have been rather nice if you had been given the opportunity of meeting your new colleagues, so I intend to put that suggestion into practice. And another thing you mentioned was that you would have welcomed the chance of visiting some schools *prior* to taking up your post. I shall be arranging that for our new colleague as well. Before he – or she – starts, I would like you, David, to take him – or her – into some secondary science lessons and you, Gervase, to spend a day with him – or her – observing some primary design technology work.' Harold bent down to retrieve his briefcase from the floor. 'Well, I think that's everything unless someone has something to ask.'

Julie, who had been standing by the door listening, raised her hand. 'Could I ask something, Dr Yeats?'

'Of course, Julie, what is it?'

'Where is he, she or it going to sit? On top of the bookcase? In a filing cabinet? On the window sill? This office is already overcrowded. You'll never get another desk and cupboard in here. Tom Thumb would have difficulty finding a place to stand.'

'Perhaps you could positively discriminate in favour of the smallest candidate, Harold,' suggested Sidney flippantly. 'Someone about four foot tall and as thin as a rake.'

'And what about all the added typing and filing,' continued Julie, ignoring the interruption, 'and all the extra running about I'll have to do, with another inspector filling up my in-tray? And then there's the coffee –'

'Julie, Julie,' Harold reassured her, 'let's try and be positive. We are in desperate need of someone to take on the extra work. I am certain that all these little internal difficulties can be overcome. I shall have a word with Mrs Savage and see if she can arrange a little extra secretarial help and sort out the room situation.'

'Oh, well, if you have a word with Mrs Savage, the fount of all knowledge,' said David sarcastically, 'all our problems will be solved. She'll just wave her magic wand or, more appropriately, wiggle her witch's broomstick, and everything will be fine. One could not hope for a kinder, more considerate, co-operative, easy-going, invariably cheerful and generally all-round likeable person than the ever-helpful Mrs Savage.'

Harold gave a great heaving sigh. 'I just hope our new colleague has a sense of humour, a thick skin and the patience of a saint.'

The day of the interviews arrived. Harold was in the office early, as were we all that morning to find out who had been shortlisted for the post. Harold was dressed in an extremely smart dark blue suit, a crisp white shirt and college tie, highly polished black shoes, and he carried a leather-backed clipboard.

'My goodness, you look very debonair, Harold,' remarked Sidney.

'You look like a game show host with that clipboard,' added David. 'So, who have you called for interview then?'

'Well, I can't stay long because I need to be at the SDC for eight-thirty to meet the candidates but, briefly, there are five up for the post, including, you will be pleased to hear, Sidney, some women. There's a Mr Carey Price-Williams —'

'Oh, well, he must be all right with a name like that,' interrupted David.

'Can't be doing with folk who adopt double-barrelled

names,' said Sidney. 'In my experience, they are inevitably pompous and self-opinionated people who can't make up their minds. And one Welshman in this team is quite enough. Get two of you lot together and you start singing "Men of Harlech" and talking in Welsh.'

'Welsh is a most mellifluous language,' David told us. 'It ought to be compulsory in schools.'

'The other morning when you were rabbiting on to your wife on the phone, in that guttural, spluttery language of yours, I nearly gave you the kiss of life. I thought you'd got a bone stuck in your throat.'

'Sidney,' said David in a patient tone of voice, 'your analogy about my speaking Welsh has become rather hackneyed now. I have heard that little witticism of yours a good few times now.'

'Gentlemen,' cried Harold, trying to suppress a smile, 'if I may continue. There's a Mr Thomas Wilson, a Miss – er, Ms Jennifer Black, a Dr Gerry Mullarkey –'

'I bet you any money we get the crusty old doctor,' sighed Sidney, leaning back expansively in his chair and putting his hands behind his head. 'I can just picture the old buffer. He'll be a dry, dusty physicist with glasses like the bottoms of milk bottles and grey frizzy hair sticking up like wire wool and he'll have as much conversation as a dead sheep –'

'May I remind you, Sidney,' I said, 'what you thought I would look like. Didn't you have a bet on that, with a name like mine, I would be a huge, red-headed Irishman?'

'Exactly,' began Harold. 'One cannot judge a person by his or her name –'

'Take the name Clamp, for example,' interposed David. 'Now what sort of person does that conjure up? Clamp? Something hard, metallic and with jaws like a shark.'

'And you couldn't be more mistaken about Dr Mullarkey,' Harold continued. 'The application was very impressive. Dr Mullarkey is extremely well qualified, with a range of experience and excellent references.'

'And no sense of humour.'

'Not at all, Sidney,' began Harold, 'Dr Mullarkey sounds extremely lively and enthusiastic –'

'Wasn't Dr Mullarkey a villain in Sherlock Holmes, Gervase?' asked Sidney suddenly, going off on one of his customary tangents.

'No, that was Professor Moriaty,' I said.

'I wonder if he really exists. It's a very strange name is Mullarkey. It sounds a tad suspicious to me. It could be a pseudonym.'

'You said the same thing when Gervase applied, if I remember rightly,' remarked David, 'and, despite his name, he's turned out not too bad.'

'Thank you for those few kind words,' I said.

'Look,' interrupted Harold, 'I came in here for five minutes, not for a detailed analysis of each candidate. I must be off.'

'Hang on a minute, Harold!' cried Sidney. 'You have only mentioned four, only one of whom is a woman. Who's the fifth candidate?'

Harold consulted his clipboard. 'A Miss Gloria Goodwood.'

'Now *that's* more like it!' chortled Sidney. 'Gloria Goodwood. She sounds like the heroine in a romantic novel: young, sylph-like, alluring, with a mass of auburn hair falling like a burnished cascade over her alabaster shoulders. I bet you Gloria would add a little sophistication and glamour to the office. What's she like?'

'If she is successful,' replied Harold, his voice non-committal, 'you will see Miss Goodwood at five-thirty at the Staff Development Centre. I look forward to seeing you all later this afternoon to meet your new colleague.' With that Harold departed.

★

I spent the day working on the plans for those events for which I was responsible at the Feoffees Pageant which was to be held at Manston Hall at the end of May. Schools had provided me with a mountain of children's poetry and stories based on famous characters from history. I sorted out a good selection and at lunch-time took it over to Willingforth Primary School where the Headteacher and staff had agreed to mount the material on display boards. Pupils from three different schools were to perform some short plays on historical themes, and I spent the afternoon calling into each school to see how things were going. Sidney had arranged for an exhibition of children's art, David a gymnastics display and the County Youth Orchestra would give a performance on the lawn at Manston Hall so the Education Department would be well represented.

I was secretly relieved that my efforts to organise the essay and public speaking competitions on the theme of customs and traditions had not been required. I had so much on, I really had not relished organising such a complicated and time-consuming initiative. When headteachers had explained that the students would be up to their eyes in examinations and would not have the time to prepare, I seized the chance to wriggle out of the task.

All communication with Mrs Savage about the Feoffees Pageant had been undertaken by notes and memoranda. I had been very careful to record all the arrangements we had agreed upon and I had made certain Dr Gore had been sent a copy. My promise to liaise had been kept – even if I had ducked meeting with the Snow Queen in person.

As instructed, I arrived at the Centre at the appointed time. Connie, wearing her predictably flat expression, was standing as usual in her familiar pose with arms folded in the centre of the entrance hall like some night-club bouncer. She was facing up to Sidney and David who had obviously arrived only seconds before.

'Top o' the evenin' to you, Connie,' Sidney was saying effusively. 'How are we on this beautiful, mild St David's Day? And here comes Mr Phinn, look you.'

'I'm very well, thank you. I hope you've parked your car well away from the front doors, Mr Clamp, and you as well, Mr Phinn, because it's a health and safety hazard to block my entrance. Wipe your feet, please, Mr Pritchard, I've just done that floor.'

'I would not dream of blocking your entrance, Connie!' exclaimed Sidney.

'I've had to remind you before now. And, if you're expecting something to drink, you're out of luck because there's no milk and I'm all out of biscuits. All those council-lors and candidates have gone through four pints of gold top and two boxes of Garibaldis.'

'It's so good to find you in such a cheerful mood, Connie,' remarked Sidney, 'and for us to receive such a hearty welcome on St David's Day. It warms the cockles of my heart.' With that, he set off at a hearty speed in the direction of the lounge area.

'Speaking of cockles, Mr Clamp,' said Connie pursuing him, 'when are you intending moving them shells, pebbles, dried seaweed and stuffed seagulls you were using on your art course last Christmas? They're taking up room. It's like Blackpool beach in there.'

'I shall remove them this very day,' replied Sidney, swivel-ling round with a great beaming smile on his face. 'Now, what are the candidates like, Connie? Do tell.'

'Well, there's a big, hairy man who has a lot to say for himself.' She dipped her head to the side in Sidney's direction. 'A bit like you, Mr Clamp, but he's Welsh.'

'Ever the flatterer, Connie,' smiled Sidney.

'There's a nicely spoken woman of about forty-five and a very sour-faced individual in a shiny suit.'

'Dr Mullarkey,' added Sidney knowingly.

'I don't know what he's called,' continued Connie, 'but he was very off-hand with me when I asked him to hextinguish his pipe. I can't see how he could make a very good inspector when he couldn't read any of the "No Smoking" signs I have around the Centre. I've even got them on the back of the door in the men's toilets, so he couldn't miss them. I told him he was a health and safety hazard and he gave me such a look – the sort of look my little grandson used to make when he couldn't have an ice cream. "A face like a smacked bottom", as my mother used to say.'

Sidney threw himself into a chair and sighed heavily.

'And the other candidates?' I enquired.

'There was a very friendly young woman. The only one to offer to help me dry the dishes. Very chatty and cheerful, with a lot about her. I took to her.'

'That will be Glorious Goodbody,' purred Sidney.

'And what about the last one?' asked David.

'Look, Mr Pritchard!' snapped Connie. 'I don't spend all day standing about watching people, you know.'

'Of course, you don't, Connie,' sighed Sidney. 'Perish the thought.'

'Anyway, I hope they're not going to be much longer. I've got to do the toilets before I finish. And would you three move into the staff room? I have the carpet to vacuum in here yet. It's those councillors leaving all them crumbs.'

As the hand on the Centre clock ticked towards six, Sidney, David and I were still huddled in the small staff room, getting increasingly impatient.

'You would think that after nine hours of interrogation, they would have picked someone by now,' complained Sidney. 'I have the annual general meeting of the West Challerton Artists' Society at seven-thirty and I need to get home, have a shower, make something to eat and go through my report.'

'And I don't intend staying much longer,' said David. 'I've got a committee meeting at the Golf Club tonight and I want to raise the matter, yet again, of uneven paving slabs. After the meeting – it being St David's Day – I am introducing the Cwmbran Male Voice Choir and I need to be there in good time.'

'And I am speaking to the Parent–Teacher Association at Brindcliffe,' I added.

'The appointment is a foregone conclusion anyway,' remarked Sidney casually. 'I could tell by the way Harold was so depressingly enthusiastic when he got the applications. His little black eyes lit up like a ferret with a cornered rabbit when a certain candidate was mentioned. I bet you a pound to a penny we get the dry old stick with the funny name.'

'I think you may very well be right, Sidney,' agreed David, looking at his watch and shaking his head. 'He said more about that Mullarkey fellow than all the others put together.'

'You don't think you two are pre-judging this poor person a little?' I chimed in. 'He's probably a very decent sort. Just because he's got an unusual name doesn't mean –'

'I suppose so,' agreed Sidney wearily, 'but it would have been rather nice to have Glorious Goodbody at the next desk.'

'It's nearly six o'clock, you know,' David announced. 'I have to get home and change.'

'Well, that settles it then,' exclaimed Sidney. 'We shall depart and find out tomorrow who was appointed.'

As we all stood to go, Harold Yeats crashed through the door, making the three of us jump back as if hit in the stomach.

'For goodness sake, Harold!' cried Sidney. 'I do wish you

wouldn't do that – bursting into the room like some jealous husband in a Whitehall farce.'

'It's just that I have some news!' exclaimed Harold. 'We have appointed.'

'I suppose it's Professor Moriaty?' sighed Sidney.

'As a matter of fact, it *is* Dr Gerry Mullarkey,' replied Harold, 'who is, at this very moment, looking forward to meeting you all. If you would care to make your way down to the lounge area while I de-brief the unsuccessful candidates, you can congratulate Dr Mullarkey and introduce yourselves.'

'I just hope you have picked someone who is going to fit in, Harold,' said David mournfully. 'I hope he has a sense of humour.'

'Oh, I think I can assure you of that on both counts,' replied Harold, showing a mouthful of teeth and vigorously rubbing his large hands together. 'In fact, I think getting on with you lot is almost as important as having the right academic qualifications.'

There was no sign of Dr Mullarkey in the lounge. Behind the kitchen hatch Connie could be heard banging pans with such force that they sounded like the clanging of discordant gongs. The room was empty save for an extremely pretty, slender young woman with short raven-black hair, a pale, delicately boned face and great blue eyes with long lashes.

'Excuse me, we are looking for a Dr Mullarkey,' announced David. 'We were told he was in here.'

'Oh yes,' replied the young woman, turning and smiling broadly at him.

'Are you by any chance Miss Goodwood?' enquired Sidney, approaching her eagerly.

'No, you've just missed her.'

'Have you seen him by any chance?' I asked. 'Dr Mullarkey, that is?'

'Could you describe him?'

'Well, he's middle-aged, I guess, greying hair, serious sort of chap, probably in a dark suit. Smokes a pipe. Actually, I've not even met the man. I'm just going on what others have said.'

'There was a Mr Wilson here for interview, who fits that description, but I think he's speaking to Dr Yeats at the moment,' said the young woman.

'That's very strange,' said Sidney, turning to me and frowning. 'I did say when I first heard the name mentioned that I had serious doubts whether this person existed. I said it sounded suspicious.'

'I wonder if he's already left,' suggested David, 'but it seems odd that he should just up and go.'

'He's a figment of Harold's imagination,' concluded Sidney. 'I don't think there is a Dr Mullarkey.'

'Oh but there is,' said the young woman. We all looked at the beautiful smiling face. 'I'm Dr Mullarkey, Geraldine Mullarkey, but most people call me Gerry. I assume you gentlemen are my new colleagues?'

Our mouths fell open and we stared wide-eyed and speechless.

'Oh, I say,' murmured Sidney, staring into the blue eyes. 'Oh, I say. Good gracious, my goodness. I thought you were a man. I mean I thought Dr Mullarkey was a man, not a woman like you. I mean . . . oh, I don't know what I mean.'

'Good afternoon,' said David formally, stepping forward and offering his hand. 'I'm David Pritchard, Inspector for Mathematics, PE and Games. The hairy, inarticulate, rambling one is Sidney Clamp, the Inspector for Visual and Creative Arts and our self-appointed spokesperson on equal opportunities. The lifeless, open-mouthed colleague, incapable of speech and who looks, at this moment, as if the hamster is dead but the wheel is still turning, is Gervase Phinn, the Inspector for English and Drama. It is good to

187

have you with us, Gerry. May I congratulate you on getting the job. I am sure you will fit in superbly.'

'Oh, I say,' said Sidney, quaveringly. 'Oh, I say.'

'How do you do,' I said, taking her small cold hand in mine. 'It's er . . . splendid to, er . . . have you join us.'

'And if there is anything we can do for you, please ask,' said David.

'There is something, actually,' replied our new colleague. 'I have to catch a train from Fettlesham at just after seven. I wonder if one of you could give me a lift to the station – that's if it's not too far out of your way.'

'No problem,' said David, 'I can easily drop you off.'

'Nonsense!' cried Sidney, who had just about gained his composure. 'You're going in the opposite direction, and anyway, you have your Celtic knees-up this evening, if you remember. I can easily drop Geraldine off at the station.'

'I thought you had your artists' meeting tonight?' responded David tartly.

'It would be much easier for me to drop Gerry off,' I interrupted. 'My talk this evening is at Brindcliffe Primary School, which is directly opposite the station.'

'Well, that's settled,' said Dr Mullarkey, collecting her handbag and briefcase. 'I'm sorry to have to rush. I'm really looking forward to working with you all.' She gave me a stunning smile. 'Shall we go, Gervase?'

14

'Well, I would have thought the idea was to keep them quiet and knuckling down to their reading and writing, and not encouraging them to spend their time talking.'

I was in the kitchen at the Staff Development Centre helping Connie dry the cups and saucers. We were clearing up after the day's course I had been directing on 'Encouraging Talk in the Classroom'. Connie, as was her wont, was giving me the benefit of her views.

'When I was a girl you only spoke when you were spoken to. Youngsters have far too much to say for themselves these days, in my opinion. They've got an answer for everything.' Connie was a woman who did not mince her words and was, as they say in Yorkshire, 'not backwards in coming forwards'.

'Children learn a great deal by talking things through, Connie,' I endeavoured to explain. 'They sort out all the complex ideas they have in their heads, share their views, try out their opinions on others, discuss difficult concepts. Talking is very important in learning.'

'Mm,' she mouthed, entirely unconvinced. 'Well, I think they'd be better off keeping their opinions and ideas to themselves. In my day, children were seen and not heard. If I so much as opened my mouth at school without Miss Pearson's permission, she'd have that leather strap out of her drawer as soon as look at you. And if anyone dared to ask her a question, woe betide them. She didn't encourage children to ask questions. Miss Pearson liked them to listen, keep quiet and get on with their work.'

'Times have changed, Connie,' I said, putting the last of the cups in the cupboard.

'More's the pity,' she replied. 'Now, take my sister's grandson, Robbie. Always in trouble at school, always got something to say for himself, always answering his parents back. They don't know they're born, young people, these days. They want a spell in the army. I said to my sister, I said, "Your grandson wants a damn good hiding, cheeking his parents like that."'

'How old is he?' I asked.

'Fourteen and as broad as a barn door and as thick as a plank of wood.'

'He's a bit old for good hidings, Connie.'

'They should have started when he was small. He was a little demon, he was.'

'Well, a lot of lads go through that stage, you know, when they reach adolescence. It's probably his hormones.'

Connie stopped what she was doing abruptly and turned to face me. 'I beg your pardon?' she snapped.

'It's probably his hormones,' I repeated.

'Excuse me,' she replied curtly. 'There's no history of hormones in our family.'

I quickly changed the subject. 'And how's that little grandson of yours?'

The tight lips relaxed, her eyes began to sparkle with pleasure and a great smile suffused her face. 'Oh, he's a little charmer, he really is. In his second year at school now and on the top table. Bright as a button is our Damien. Wraps his granddad round his little finger he does. Last week he says to Ted: "Granddad, your face needs ironing." The things he says. He's staying with me and Ted at the moment because his sister is poorly. She's off school with sickness and diarrhoea. It's all down her street.'

When I directed my first course at the Staff Development Centre, Connie had watched my every move like some great, hungry vulture. I would glance up from my notes during the lecture to see her peering through the door. At coffee she hovered in the background, tea-cloth in hand, making sure we returned our cups and saucers to the hatch in the kitchen. At the end of the course she watched, arms folded, to make certain I left the room as I had found it. Later, in the cloakroom, I heard the door pushed open and a great booming voice echoed around the tiled walls. 'Have you finished in there yet because I want to do them urinals in a minute!'

'And talking about times changing and taking a turn for the worse,' said Connie, vigorously wiping around the sink, 'what about that nun?'

'Nun?'

'That little nun who was on your course.'

'Oh, Sister Brendan.'

'I had no idea she was a nun. I was talking to her as if she was a normal person. I could have said anything. In the olden days nuns wore big, black outfits right down to the ground and black headgear and wimples that covered up half their faces. I mean, you couldn't tell that she was a nun. She had this blue suit on.' Connie's voice took on an almost affronted tone. 'I mean, her skirt was nearly up to her knees. In my day you never saw so much as a glimpse of ankle. She looked like an air hostess. And she had nothing on her head save for that bit of a scarf. I thought nuns had cropped hair. Well, Julie Andrews did in "The Sound of Music" and Audrey Hepburn certainly had her head shaved in "The Nun's Story". That Sister Brendan had a perm by the looks of it. She'll be having highlights put in and wearing high heels and make-up next. And another thing,' she prattled, and I leant against the kitchen door to listen to her, 'she had three cups of tea *and* most of my Garibaldis. They take vows, don't they? They're supposed to give up all them luxuries. You don't know where you are these days, you really don't. It's just the same with the vicar. He only looks about sixteen and when he came into the Centre to rehearse his pantomime when his pipes had frozen up, he was wearing denim jeans and a leather jacket, and arrived on a thundering great motor bike. He says to me, "Call me Des". I mean, it's not right, is it? No sign of a dog-collar or a hassock. In my day, vicars were vicars and nuns were nuns. You knew where you were. "Call me Des", I ask you! Soon, they'll be letting nuns drive cars and get married.'

'Have you ever thought of taking the veil then, Connie?' I asked mischievously.

'What?'

'Becoming a nun?'

'Me, a nun? Course, I haven't,' she snorted. 'I'm not that religiously inclined and you know full well I can't suffer fools gladly. You must have the patience of Jove to be a nun. I'd find it very difficult to turn the other cheek when I see the mess some people make in the Centre. That Mr Clamp leaves behind a trail of destruction and debris every time he runs a course here, and Mr Pritchard is forever getting his equipment out and forgetting about it. And another thing, don't nuns have this vow of silence? I couldn't keep quiet for more than two minutes. Mind you, that seems to have gone out of the window as well. That Sister Brendan could talk for Britain.'

So could Connie, I thought to myself as I took myself off home, and she would captain the team.

Sister Brendan was Headteacher of St Bartholomew's Roman Catholic Infant School in Crompton, a darkly depressing northern industrial town. She was a slight, fine-featured woman with small, dark eyes and a sharp beak of a nose. When I first met her she reminded me of a hungry blackbird out for the early worm. Her small school was surrounded by tall, blackened chimneys, derelict building sites, dilapidated warehouses and row upon row of red-brick, terraced housing.

The school itself, adjacent to the little church, was a complete contrast. Like the Headteacher, it was bright, cheerful and welcoming and on my first visit I had been immensely impressed by the high quality of the education. The walls were ablaze with children's paintings and poems; posters, pictures and book jackets were on various display tables, while in cabinets were shells, fossils, oddly shaped pebbles, clay figures and other small artefacts. The standard of reading was high and those children I heard, and who came to me in the Reading Corner, one after the other, were obviously keen to demonstrate their skill. All read fluently and with great expression. The number work was also very good, as were the singing and the art work, the history and the geography.

When I was compiling my report, I had had difficulty in finding any issues for the Headteacher and her staff to address. One area I did mention, however, was a greater encouragement of clear speaking and attentive listening. The children spoke with enthusiasm and interest but some had strong accents. I suggested that the staff, whilst not denigrating the children's natural way of talking, might teach the pupils to speak with greater clarity. One means of doing this, I suggested, was through drama. And that was why Sister Brendan had attended my course.

A couple of days after my conversation with Connie, I received a telephone call from the very subject of our discussions. Sister Brendan thanked me for 'a most enjoyable, interesting and useful course' and made a request.

'We would like some more advice on drama, Mr Phinn. Could you come in for an afternoon, do you think?'

'Yes, of course, Sister,' I replied. 'I could drop off some helpful books with ideas for various drama activities and I'll happily talk things through with you and your staff.'

'I was thinking more of a practical demonstration,' she said.

'Pardon?'

'Of you taking the children for a drama lesson and showing us.'

'Well . . .'

'I'm sure, Mr Phinn, that you would be the first to agree that it's one thing telling teachers what to do and it's quite another showing them. I really think we would benefit from seeing you working with the children and putting those ideas you are so keen on into practice.'

What could I say? 'Of course, Sister,' I replied, trying to sound enthusiastic, 'I'd be delighted.' It was like a re-run of Highcopse School when Mrs Peterson had inveigled me into teaching a poetry lesson. Well, that had gone well enough, I thought to myself, and I had no reason to think that a drama lesson at St Bartholomew's would be any less successful.

I soon found out, however, that things were not as I had imagined.

I arrived at St Bartholomew's a couple of weeks later on a cold but bright Friday morning. Sister Brendan saw my car pull up outside the school and was at the entrance to greet me in seconds.

'My goodness, Mr Phinn, you're the early bird,' she said beaming widely. 'Come along in.' I followed her down the bright corridor and into the Headteacher's room. 'It must be over a year since you were last here.'

'That's right,' I agreed. 'I remember it well.'

On my last visit, Sister Brendan had guided or rather 'nunhandled' me in the direction of the school entrance towards the end of the afternoon, pleased, no doubt, to see me on my way. She had been, therefore, somewhat surprised when I had informed her that I intended remaining for the school assembly. I should have left when I had the chance. The assembly had been an ordeal I would not wish to undergo again. I had been used as a sort of visual aid with Sister Brendan constantly referring to me. I had not known the prayers or the hymns and had tried unsuccessfully to mouth my way through, much to everyone's amusement. Yes, it had been a memorable visit.

I was brought out of my reverie by Sister Brendan's voice. 'Now, the plan this morning, Mr Phinn, if it is acceptable to you, is that we will have our assembly and then you can have the two top infant classes for the morning for drama.'

'Two whole classes!' I exclaimed. 'And for the whole morning?'

'Well, I thought we ought to take full advantage of your kind offer to work with the children. Is there a problem with that?'

'No, no problem, Sister,' I replied, feeling a nervous churning in my stomach at the thought of controlling sixty or so lively six- and seven-year-olds for the morning.

'Assembly this morning will be taken by Monsignor Leonard. He comes in every Friday to spend a little time with us. I believe you know Monsignor Leonard, Mr Phinn?' Sister Brendan's small, dark eyes twinkled.

'Yes, we've met a few times, Sister,' I replied.

I had come across Monsignor Leonard on a number of occasions on my travels around the county's schools. He was a gentle and unassuming man who loved the company of children and took a deep and active interest in education. I had not seen him for some time. In fact, the last occasion had been just before the Christmas holidays the previous year and he had watched me struggling to tell the story of the nativity to a group of very lively infants in the small Roman Catholic school at Netherfoot. One child in particular, a massively freckled little boy with spiky ginger hair, had constantly interrupted my account with the most searching questions. On my way out that morning, Monsignor Leonard had smiled benignly, placed his hand gently on my arm and reminded me of an old proverb: 'Here's to the child and all he has to teach us.'

'He's particularly looking forward to meeting you again,' continued Sister Brendan. 'When I told him you would be in school he got quite animated and wondered if he might stay to watch the drama session?'

'Yes, of course,' I replied.

'He'll be bringing with him Miss Fenoughty who is his housekeeper and the church organist. She has stepped into the breach to accompany the children's singing during Mrs Webb's absence. Of course, she just comes in with Monsignor Leonard for his weekly assembly and we make do with a tape the remaining days. I know it sounds a little uncharitable but I don't think I could cope with Miss Fenoughty every day of the week.'

'Is Mrs Webb not well?' I asked.

'She's off school at the moment after her unfortunate accident in the Holy Land.'

'Oh dear. What happened?'

Sister Brendan sighed audibly. 'Just before Christmas she went with the UCM – the Union of Catholic Mothers – on a pilgrimage to Jerusalem. It was called "Walking in the Footsteps of Jesus". Anyhow, she set off walking in the footsteps of Jesus and fell down a pothole and broke a leg.' Sister Brendan studied my expression for a moment before continuing. 'You are one of the few people, Mr Phinn, who has not found that amusing. Why, even Monsignor Leonard, Mrs Webb's parish priest, remarked that had she worn more appropriate footwear, such as the kind of sandals worn by Our Lord, instead of high-heeled shoes, she might not have ended up in a Jerusalem hospital with her leg in plaster.'

'Well, give her my very best. I do hope she is back at school soon.'

'I am on my knees every night praying for that, Mr Phinn,' sighed the nun. 'The sooner Mrs Webb is back at the piano and Miss Fenoughty back to her housekeeping the better will be my state of mind. She hammers on the keys as if there is no tomorrow. The piano fairly shudders when she starts banging away. She's rather deaf, you see, and, despite my efforts to get her to play more quietly, she will insist on crashing along the keyboard as if she's cracking nuts with a hammer. It's the same in church on Sunday. People have taken to wearing ear muffs, it's that bad. Last week the Ave Maria sounded like the "1812 Overture". And, of course,' Sister Brendan continued, 'her memory is not all that good either and she gets the hymns mixed up. Last year at the Easter Mass I asked for "All in an April Evening" and we were treated to a slow, ear-splitting ren-dering of "Through this Night of Dread and Darkness". At one wedding she played at, the couple wanted "Hills of the North Rejoice" but came down the aisle to a thunderous rendition of "Climb Every Mountain".'

'It could have been worse,' I said. 'She could have played "Fight the Good Fight".' By now, I just could not stop myself from smiling.

'I can see you find it funny, Mr Phinn, but let me assure you Miss Fenoughty would try the patience of a saint.' Sister Brendan peered through the window. 'And speaking of saints, here comes Monsignor Leonard, who has to put up with Miss Fenoughty, morning, noon and night.'

Down the path to the school came the priest, a tall stick of a man in a shabby-looking, ill-fitting cassock, and a small, rotund bundle of a woman of indeterminate age. She could have been sixty, she could have been eighty. I followed Sister Brendan to the school entrance to meet them.

'Good morning, Sister. Good morning, Mr Phinn,'

boomed the priest before stooping and shouting in his companion's ear: 'This is Mr Phinn, Miss Fenoughty. Do you remember, I mentioned him this morning at breakfast?'

'I knew a Bernadette Flynn who used to go to Notre Dame High School,' remarked the old lady, scrutinizing me. 'Very talented girl.'

'It's Phinn, Miss Fenoughty, Mr Phinn,' corrected the priest.

'I also knew a Father Flynn, parish priest at St Hilda's. He was a lovely man. I spent hours in the confessional box with him. A wonderful listener was Father Flynn.' She looked up at me with small bright eyes. 'Are you any relation?'

Monsignor Leonard shook his head and smiled and Sister Brendan gave me a look of noble resignation.

'It's Phinn, not Flynn, Miss Fenoughty!' roared the priest.

'Monsignor Leonard,' said his companion quietly, 'there's no need to shout in my ear. It's enough to deafen me.'

'I do apologise,' said the priest in a much more restrained voice. 'This is Mr Phinn, he's an inspector of schools. His name is Phinn, Miss Fenoughty, not Flynn.'

'Pardon?' asked Miss Fenoughty.

Sister Brendan, like the statue of the Virgin Mary which dominated the entrance hall, raised her eyes saint-like to heaven.

Sister Brendan had not exaggerated. Miss Fenoughty's rendition of 'All Things Bright and Beautiful' made the ground shake and the windows tremble. I thought of another set of lyrics for the hymn, beginning 'All Things Loud and Voluble' as she banged away on the keys. Quite a number of the children covered their ears. Monsignor Leonard gave a small homily about kindness to others, loving your neighbour and showing charity to those less fortunate. I noticed Sister Brendan giving Miss Fenoughty a sideways glance. A prayer was said and the assembly was over. While Sister Brendan explained to the children what was to happen that morning and organised them for my drama session, I approached Miss Fenoughty and thought I'd show a little kindness to the less fortunate.

'You certainly play with gusto, Miss Fenoughty,' I said cheerfully.

'Who must go?' she snapped. 'I thought I was going to stay and watch the drama. Monsignor Leonard said he was staying to watch the drama. I have no transport so I shall have to wait until he goes.'

'No, I meant your playing,' I said. 'It was very rousing.' I had raised my voice an octave.

'Oh, well, I can't be doing with these whispery little modern hymns, Mr Flynn. I like a good old stirring, robust tune. You should hear me when I play "When the Saints Go Marching In". Sister says I'm a bit heavy-handed on the piano, you know, and the children think I'm a bit loud.'

'Really?'

'I overheard one little boy last week refer to "that old plonker on the piano".'

'Really?'

'I do tend to plonk, I have to admit.' She chuckled to herself.

At this point Sister Brendan approached and rescued me. 'Miss Fenoughty,' she said slowly and loudly, 'would you like to sit in the staff room while you wait for Monsignor Leonard? He's going to watch the drama.'

'I know he is, Sister Brendan,' she replied. 'Mr Flynn said it would be all right if I watched too.'

'Wouldn't you rather wait in the staff room?'

'No thank you, Sister,' she said firmly.

The nun pulled a face. 'Well, will you take a seat at the back of the hall? Mr Phinn is about ready to start.'

15

The two top infant groups remained seated while the rest of the children returned to their classrooms. Monsignor Leonard and the supply teacher joined Miss Fenoughty who had ensconced herself at the rear of the hall on the only chair with arms. The three of them sat in a row like the judges in a talent contest.

'Now, children,' said Sister Brendan, facing the sea of smiling faces, 'we have with us this morning Mr Phinn. We are very fortunate, because Mr Phinn has taken time out of his very busy life as an inspector to teach a drama lesson.'

'Sister Brendan,' asked a small fair-haired boy, 'what does Mr Phinn collect?'

'Mr Phinn doesn't collect anything, Sean,' replied the nun smiling. 'He's not a collector, he's an inspector. He inspects things.'

'Sister Brendan,' persisted the child, 'what does Mr Phinn inspect?'

'Oh, lots of things to do with school, but he's not here this morning to inspect. Mr Phinn's here to take you for drama.'

'Could he inspect the gerbil, Sister?'

'Of course not, Sean. Now be a good boy, sit up straight and leave the questions until later.' The nun swivelled round and gave me a disarming smile. 'We have a poorly gerbil, Mr Phinn. We think he's eaten a piece of orange peel somebody put in his cage.' She moved closer and whispered, 'Keep an eye on Sean.' She then joined the audience at the back of the hall.

'Good morning, children,' I said.

'Good morning, Mr Phinn,' they chorused. Before me was a sea of bright-eyed, eager infants ready for action.

'People who perform drama are actors and they take on acting parts,' I explained. 'They pretend to be other people and use their bodies, faces and voices to make up a story for other people to watch, just like in a theatre or in the cinema or on the television. Later this morning we shall be acting out a story but first we are going to do a few warm-up activities to get us in the right frame of mind. In a moment, I want everyone to find a space in the hall and then look this way. All right, everyone find a space.' The children did as I asked quietly and without any fuss.

'Good,' I said. 'Now, for a start, let's see if you can all listen really, really well. Some of you might have played "Simon Says" at your birthday party.' A number of the children nodded excitedly. 'Well, this exercise is a bit like that. You just have to do exactly as I say. So, let me see. Everyone ready? Hands on heads.' All the children placed their hands on their heads. 'Good. Hands on shoulders.' Two children hugged each other. 'No,' I said, 'your own shoulders. Don't put your hands on anyone else's. Hands on elbows. Hands on knees.' This continued for a few minutes. The children followed my instructions and things were going really well until I said, 'Hands on thighs,' and all the children covered their eyes.

I decided to move on. 'In a moment I will be asking you to walk around in the hall using all the space, but whenever I say the word "Freeze!" I want you to stop what you are doing immediately and imagine you are frozen. You must remain as silent and as still as the statue of St Bartholomew who looks down on you from the front of the hall.' All eyes examined the large, olive-wood figure of the benign-looking man, with arms outstretched, who stood on a plinth. 'Then, when I say "Relax!" I want you to return to normal.

All right, is everybody ready?' The children stood to attention. 'You are walking through the woods on a bright, sunny day. The sun is streaming through the trees and you can hear the birds singing and the rustling of the leaves and the crackling of the branches underfoot. Freeze!' Most children stood stock still but a few shuffled their feet, others scratched their heads and one large girl began to suck her thumb.

'That was good for a first attempt, but let's see if, when we do it again, we can *all* remain perfectly still.' I repeated the commentary of the walk through the woods and this time all the children froze. 'Very good. Relax!'

'Mr Phinn, when we freeze, can we breathe?' asked the small fair-haired boy who had enquired earlier if I could 'inspect' the gerbil.

'Yes, Sean, you can breathe, but you mustn't move. Now, this time we are on a cold, cold street. The crisp snow crunches under our feet and the icy wind makes our ears and cheeks tingle. We start to shiver and we rub our hands to make ourselves warm. Cars and lorries are whooshing along the road and you are splashed by a big bus. Freeze!' The children froze. 'Relax!' All the children relaxed with the exception of Sean who remained inert, as if caught in amber. 'You can relax now, Sean,' I told him.

'I can't,' he replied through tight lips. 'My feet are frozen in a snowdrift.'

'He might have got frostbite,' chirped up a small girl. 'My grandpa says you can get frostbite in snow.'

'No, he hasn't got frostbite,' I explained, 'because the snow has now melted and that's why Sean can move.' The little boy relaxed and began to rub his feet dramatically.

'This time we are in a far-off desert,' I continued. 'The hot, hot sun is burning down on our heads. We wipe the perspiration from our foreheads and we start to pant. Our mouths are as dry as the sand and we feel faint with the heat. Freeze!' Every child froze except fair-haired Sean.

'But, Mr Phinn, you wouldn't freeze in a desert. You'd burn up or melt.'

'And might get sunburn,' piped up the small girl for a second time. 'My grandpa says you can get burnt in the sun.'

'Yes, that's true, Sean, but this is a magic desert and we are freezing. So freeze, please. Right everyone, relax!'

'My Auntie June came out in blisters in Majorca,' the small girl informed me, nodding seriously.

'Freeze!' I barked and she turned to stone.

Until morning playtime I took the children through a series of different activities and they responded really well. We visited dark dungeons and dusty attics, braved storms and swam rivers, climbed mountains and crawled through caves, dug gardens and threaded needles – a whole range of mimed performances which they clearly enjoyed undertaking. At break-time in the staff room, Sister Brendan seemed happy at the way things were going, as did Monsignor Leonard.

'The children are doing very well,' commented the priest, taking a sip from a large mug of coffee. 'I wonder if I might remain for the rest of the morning to see how the work develops? I just need to drop Miss Fenoughty off in town but I'll be back, if that is all right.'

Before I could answer, Miss Fenoughty, whose hearing seemed to have undergone a remarkable improvement, placed her cup down carefully before saying, 'I think I might stay, if that's all the same to you, Monsignor. I'm certainly enjoying this morning. It's better than the bingo.' Sister Brendan raised her eyes to heaven. 'Is there a biscuit to go with the coffee, Sister?' asked Miss Fenoughty sweetly.

I was feeling a great deal more confident after playtime. The children had been exemplary and taken part in the activities with genuine interest and excitement. I explained to them that we had used our bodies to mime various actions, our faces to express our feelings and now we were going to add some words. As the focus of our drama I picked the poem by Robert Browning, 'The Pied Piper of Hamelin'. The poem has fifteen long verses and, as I was limited for time and the text is sometimes quite difficult, I decided that I would read a little of the original to give the children a feel for the richness of the language but re-tell the story to move things along. The children gathered around me in a half-circle and I began.

> Hamelin Town's in Brunswick,
> By famous Hanover city;
> The river Weser, deep and wide,
> Washes its wall on the southern side;
> A pleasanter spot you never spied;
> But, when begins my ditty,
> Almost five hundred years ago,
> To see the townsfolk suffer so
> From vermin, was a pity.
>
> Rats!
> They fought the dogs, and killed the cats,
> And bit the babies in their cradles,
> And ate the cheeses out of vats,
> And licked the soup from the cooks' own ladles,
> Split open kegs of salted sprats,
> Made nests inside men's Sunday hats,
> And even spoiled the women's chats,
> By drowning their speaking
> With shrieking and squeaking
> In fifty different sharps and flats.

At this point I saw Father Leonard give Sister Brendan a knowing look before staring at Miss Fenoughty, who was sublimely oblivious to the unintended reference to her –

'drowning their speaking in fifty different sharps and flats'.

I then related the exciting story to my hushed and fascinated little audience: how the people crowded into the Council Chamber demanding action from the Mayor and Corporation, how the strange, tall figure with 'the sharp blue eyes and light loose hair', draped in his coat of yellow and red, agreed to rid the town of the rats for the sum of a thousand guilders, how he blew his pipe until his lips 'wrinkled' and the rats emerged.

> And ere three shrill notes the pipe uttered,
> You heard as if an army muttered;
> And the muttering grew to a grumbling;
> And the grumbling grew to a mighty rumbling:
> And out of the houses the rats came tumbling.
> Great rats, small rats, lean rats, brawny rats,
> Brown rats, black rats, great rats, tawny rats,
> Grave old plodders, gay young friskers,
> Fathers, mothers, uncles, cousins,
> Cocking tails and pricking whiskers . . .

I then told the children how the people rejoiced and how the piper danced on and on, playing his shrill notes, through the narrow streets and across the square, followed by a sea of squealing rats. I told them how he took the rats to the river's edge and described how the creatures desperately, blindly, hurled themselves into the murky waters. I told them how the Pied Piper came for his money and how the Mayor laughed in his face.

The children listened with wide eyes and open mouths when I related how the Pied Piper's face had darkened with anger and how he shook his fist at the city and the skies clouded over and an icy wind began to blow.

And so we came to the dramatic conclusion to the tale: how the Pied Piper lifted his pipe to his lips and blew three long clear notes. Then the children came out of the houses, laughing and chattering, lifting their little feet, skipping and running and dancing and clapping their hands. You could have heard a pin drop when I concluded the story of how the little children followed the strange man in his coat of yellow and red up to the mountainside where a great door opened and swallowed them all, all except for the little lame boy who was left behind.

> Alas, alas for Hamelin!
> There came into many a burgher's pate
> A text which says that heaven's gate
> Opes to the rich as at easy rate
> As the needle's eye takes a camel in!

'Now, there's a couple of difficult words in this verse,' I explained. '"Pate" is the old word for head and a "burgher" is –'

A boy with large, round eyes and equally large round glasses waved his hand madly in the air. 'Mr Phinn! Mr Phinn!' he cried. 'I know that. It's something you eat with chips. You can have chickenburgers, beefburgers and hamburgers.'

Another child, with more interest in the impending lunch-time than the Pied Piper, enquired loudly if they were having burgers for dinner.

'That's another kind of burger,' I told her. 'In "The Pied Piper", a burgher is a sort of council official, a bit like a mayor, a very important person who makes all the laws. It was the burghers who refused to give the Pied Piper his thousand guilders.'

The children did not look as if they were any the wiser but I pressed on. I organised the children into various groups to act out scenes from the story: the scurrying, squeaking rats, the mothers and children, cooks and councillors, shop-keepers and chattering women, the Mayor and, of course, the Pied Piper. Everything seemed to be going smoothly.

Even the rather sad-looking girl, who asked me if she could be a cow rather than a rat, went away appeased when I explained that there were no cows in the story and she could be a cat. I asked several of the groups to perform their part of the poem for the others to watch. The children came out to the front of the hall just as the dinner ladies entered to set the tables out for dinner, the caretaker to help them, the crossing patrol warden to collect her 'Stop!' sign and a number of parents to wait for their children. The rear of the hall was full of interested adults who were obviously greatly entertained by the children's performances.

The last group was to act out that part of the story when the Mayor refuses to give the Pied Piper his thousand guilders. The little boy playing the Pied Piper was the child with the great, round eyes and enormous pair of glasses, who had volunteered the answer about the burghers earlier. Now, with all eyes upon him, he looked extremely shy and nervous. The Mayor was none other than Sean, and if he was nervous he certainly did not show it.

'Well, Pied Piper, what do you want?' he called confidently from the centre of the hall.

'I have come for my money,' mumbled the Pied Piper who had sidled nervously across the floor towards him.

'Well, you're not having it!' shouted the Mayor.

'OK,' said the Pied Piper and walked quickly away.

'No! No! No!' shouted the other child. 'That's not what you do!' He appealed to me. 'Mr Phinn! Mr Phinn! That's not right, is it? He wouldn't just say "OK" and walk off, would he? He'd go barmy!' The little boy was getting into a real state himself, his face red with rage.

'Freeze!' I commanded. It was as if a magic spell had been put on him. The child was transformed and became completely motionless. 'Relax!' I turned to the child with the large glasses. 'You would get quite angry, you know,' I said. 'You have got rid of all the rats and the Mayor promised you the thousand guilders. Now he has refused to pay so you would not be very happy about that, would you?' The child shook his head. 'Let's try it again.'

For the second time the Mayor stood confidently in the centre of the hall. 'Well, Pied Piper, what do you want?' he demanded.

The Pied Piper moved across the hall to him. 'I have come for my money,' he said with not much more conviction than the previous effort.

'Well, you're not having it!' shouted the Mayor.

'Why?'

'Because you're not, that's why. I've changed my mind.'

'Go on, give me my money. You said you would.'

'Well, you're not having it!'

'But that's not fair.'

'Tough luck!'

'I'll blow my pipe then.'

'You can blow your pipe until you burst but you're not having any money and that's that!'

'OK then,' sighed the Pied Piper walking away, 'but you'll be sorry.'

Sean's face went crimson with fury. 'No! No! No!' he shouted again. 'That's not what you do!' He appealed to me for a second time. 'Mr Phinn! Mr Phinn! That's not right, is it? He's still saying "OK" and walking away! He'd go bonkers!'

'Freeze!' I cried again. It was as if the child had been turned to stone. 'Relax! Now look, Pied Piper,' I said to the child with the large glasses, 'it was a lot better than last time but you do need to show how annoyed you are with the Mayor. Try again, and this time when you leave the Council Chamber, you must show how angry you are.'

The child stared up at me vacantly through the large glasses. 'Try and think of a time when you were mad with someone. Can you do that?' He nodded. 'Last go then, because it's nearly dinner-time.'

All faces were turned to the Pied Piper as he stamped into the Council Chamber. His eyes were now slits behind the large glasses, his lips were pressed tightly together, his little body looked stiff and he held up a fist threateningly.

'Well, Pied Piper, what do you want?' demanded the Mayor for the third time.

'I have come for my money,' shouted the Pied Piper.

'Well, you're not having it!' retorted the Mayor.

'Go on, give me my money. You said you would.'

'Well, I've changed my mind. You're not having it!'

'But that's not fair.'

'Tough luck!'

'I'll blow my pipe then.'

'You can blow your pipe until you burst, pal, you're not having any money and that's that!'

'Give me my money!'

'No!'

'You said you would.'

'Well, you're not having it!'

'I want my money!'

'Clear off!' boomed the Mayor.

'Well, you can stuff your thousand guilders!' roared the Pied Piper. 'You're a tight-fisted old bugger!'

I did not need to say 'Freeze!' Everyone in the hall had already fallen into a stunned, frozen silence. Monsignor Leonard, Sister Brendan, the supply teacher and Miss Fenoughty were like a tableau at the back. None of them moved a muscle.

Then, into the deathly silence, the small boy with the large glasses and a smile like a Cheshire cat, piped up. 'Is that better, Mr Phinn?' he asked.

Later, as I said my farewells in the school hall, I attempted to direct the conversation away from the morning's drama but without success. Miss Fenoughty was determined to discuss proceedings.

'Drama is like singing, isn't it, Mr Flynn? It gives the children a chance to express themselves through their voices. I did enjoy this morning. I do so love that poem. I thought the little ones did very well, didn't you?'

'I did,' I replied, smiling weakly.

'And that little boy who played the part of the Pied Piper, he was a natural little actor. My goodness he really did sound the part, didn't you think?'

'I did,' I replied again.

'Fancy remembering that word.'

'Word?' I repeated.

'The word he asked you about.'

'I'm sorry, Miss Fenoughty . . .'

'"Burgher". He remembered the word "burgher". Don't you recall at the end, didn't he shout at the Mayor, "Give me my money, you mean old burgher"?'

I heard Monsignor Leonard splutter beside me, hastily plucking a handkerchief from his pocket and burying his face in it. Even Sister Brendan had to suppress a smile. Their obvious enjoyment, however, was very short lived.

'You know, Sister,' exclaimed Miss Fenoughty, with a wild gleam in her eye, 'I've been thinking. I've got the score somewhere for the musical version of "The Pied Piper". Wouldn't it be a good idea to perform it for the parents? I would, of course, be pleased to act as musical director and perhaps Mr Flynn here could deal with the acting. What do you all think?'

We were as motionless as the statue of St Bartholmew of Whitby, who looked down upon us sympathetically from his plinth at the front of the hall. It was the same St Bartholomew, the hermit, who betook himself to the

Farne Islands in the twelfth century to escape the strident noises of the world and to spend his life in complete peace and quiet meditation. I surmise we all envied him at that moment.

Harold and Sidney were in animated conversation when I walked into the office one mild, misty morning a week before the end of the Spring term. They were facing each other across Sidney's desk like aggressive chess players.

'I'm afraid not, Harold,' Sidney was saying. 'I have got more than enough work to keep me fully occupied for the rest of the year without taking all that on.' He paused to wish me 'Good morning' before continuing in a loud and combative voice, 'There's the inspections, three courses to direct, the "Arts in School Project", the Fe-Fo exhibition of children's art to organise, adjudicating that wretched Art Competition at Fettlesham Show yet again. I could go on and on.'

'You *are* going on and on,' replied Harold, quietly. He gave me a toothy smile and wished me 'Good morning' before returning to Sidney. 'Now look, Sidney, we all have to take on extra responsibilities from time to time.' He opened his large hands like the Pope about to give a blessing. 'Gervase and David have the core subjects to deal with. It would be unfair to ask them. Without denigrating your curriculum area, I am sure you will agree that mathematics and English do take up far more time than art and design.'

'I would be absolutely hopeless,' retorted Sidney, shaking his head vigorously. 'I'd be about as successful as a garlic salesman at a vampires' convention. I am temperamentally unsuited and I have no intention whatsoever of agreeing.'

'What is it you are asking him to do, Harold?' I enquired, hanging up my coat.

'To completely redefine my role, that's what!' cried Sidney. 'Well, I'm not doing it.'

'What nonsense, Sidney!' said Harold. 'I am merely asking you to take on a little extra work.'

'A little extra work? A little extra work? Is that how you would describe it? You are asking me to pick up all the hot potatoes on the curriculum, all the complex, vexatious, troublesome, tricky and controversial subjects of which I have no experience and in which I have no expertise. There is simply no question of –'

'I wish one of you would tell me what it is Sidney has been asked to do,' I said.

'Harold,' Sidney told me, scowling in the direction of the Senior Inspector, 'has asked me, in addition to creative and visual arts and all the other multifarious jobs I have to do, to be responsible for sex education, drugs awareness and anti-bullying.' I was unable to suppress a smile. 'I am sure you find this highly amusing, Gervase, but –'

'Look, Sidney,' interrupted Harold, rubbing his heavy bulldog jaw, 'I can't waste any more time arguing with you. I'm seeing Dr Gore at half-past eight and I need to sort out the briefing papers. Someone has got to do it and you are best placed.'

'Best placed!' exclaimed Sidney. 'Oh, I am best placed all right. With my head beneath the guillotine, you mean? Up against a wall facing a firing squad? On the scaffold waiting for the trap to open? Sitting on a bloody land-mine!'

'You would think I was asking him to sell his soul,' said Harold wearily, turning in my direction. He stood up to go and peered at Sidney with his large pale eyes. 'The fact is, Sidney, there is no one else.'

'Why can't our new colleague, the multi-talented and massively qualified Dr Mullarkey, take it on? I am sure she knows far more than I do about sex, drugs and violence.'

At that very moment a head appeared around the door. 'Did I hear my name mentioned?'

Dr Mullarkey was due to take up her post as County Inspector for Science in early June and Harold had organised some school visits before she started so she could get a feel for things and meet a few people. At present, she was a lecturer in education and had asked if this preliminary visit could be before the end of the Spring term rather than early next term when she would be frantically busy preparing her students for their end-of-year examinations.

That morning it was my turn to accompany Gerry, and I had arranged to take her into three primary schools to observe some design and technology work.

'You'll get used to Sidney,' I said as we walked towards the car park. 'He's a sort of extravagant, larger-than-life character, but a marvellous colleague. Everything is a drama with Sidney. The one thing about our office is that it's never dull.'

'I'm really looking forward to starting,' said Gerry, as we skirted the grey exterior of County Hall and headed across the narrow gravel path through the formal gardens. I gave her a quizzical look. 'Really,' she said, laughing. 'Of course, I've got to find somewhere to live, so could do with a bit of advice about location and houses.'

'I'm the last one to ask. I began searching for a place when I started eighteen months ago but am still in my rented bachelor flat on the High Street. I just don't seem to have found the time for house hunting.'

'So you're not married?'

'No.'

'I'll probably do that at the outset,' she said. 'Rent a flat or a little cottage, I mean. I suppose a place in Fettlesham is the most convenient?'

'Yes, it's pretty central.' We walked in silence for a while. 'So, you've no family?'

A smile came to the delicately boned face. 'No, just me. Footloose and fancy free.'

'Really?' I said.

The clock on the County Hall tower struck eight o'clock as I drove down Fettlesham High Street which was just becoming busy with early morning traffic. I was soon on a twisting, empty road, bordered by craggy grey limestone walls and verges fringed by last year's dead, murky-brown bracken and tussocky grass. Beyond the walls was an austere, still scene, a vast undulating world of dark fields covered in a light, fleecy mist, empty save for the small cluster of barns and square farmhouses, and the occasional twisted hawthorn tree. The shadowy green foreground lay ahead of us, backed in the distance by the sombre, pale blue peaks. Bars of purple cloud stretched across the sky. Gerry didn't speak until the pale sun, shining through the clouds with an almost luminous warmth, made the whole landscape before us glisten with the splendour of a gemstone.

'It's magnificent,' she said quietly.

'It is, isn't it? I can never get used to it.'

The small stone primary school we were to visit first was nestled in the very heart of the village of Tarncliffe. It was sandwiched between the post office-cum-general store and the squat, grey Primitive Methodist chapel and looked like a private dwelling at first glance. From the pavement the door opened directly into the one large classroom and passers-by could peer through the leaded windows to see the pupils at work. We were given a warm welcome by the Headteacher, Miss Drayton, and her assistant, Mrs Standish, who both shook our hands vigorously and ushered us into the classroom.

Gerry and I started with the junior-aged children who were behind a large partition, working industriously on various models and construction work. In the corner of the amazingly cluttered and busy classroom were two girls of

216

about ten or eleven, their school clothes shrouded by large men's shirts. They explained to us that they had been asked to design and produce a labour-saving device for use in the home. They had come up with the idea for a gadget which would tell the milkman the number of pints required each day. Their first, not very novel idea had been to design a clockface with numbers from one to eight around the rim and a hand which could be adjusted to point to the number of pints needed that particular day.

'But then,' explained one of the girls enthusiastically, 'what if you wanted some cream as well as milk?'

'Or orange juice?' added the other.

'Or eggs or yoghurt?'

'And some milkmen sell potatoes as well.'

'So the problem has become very complicated,' observed Gerry, looking at their plans. 'Have you managed to resolve it?'

'One solution would be to have six different faces, each one for a different thing – milk, cream, eggs, orange juice, yoghurt and potatoes – but Mrs Standish said our design has to be simple, clear, easy to use and cheap to produce.'

'This is a real problem, isn't it?' said Gerry. 'Have you found the solution?'

'Oh, yes!' exclaimed one of the girls. 'Tessa had a brainwave.' She plucked a piece of paper from her folder and pushed it in Gerry's direction with a triumphant look on her face. Gerry examined the sketch, smiled, nodded and observed, 'Ingenious' before passing it to me. The design was for a small square of thin plywood on which was written in bright capital letters: 'MILKMAN! SEE NOTE IN BOTTLE.'

In another corner of the room a large boy was humming quietly and contentedly to himself, his body moving backwards and forwards in time to the tune as he filed away at a long piece of wood.

'And what are you doing?' asked Gerry cheerfully.

He looked up for a moment. 'Oh, I'm just raspin', miss,' he replied simply, before returning to his work.

I left Gerry with the 'rasper' and moved into the infant section of the classroom.

'Would you like me to read to you?' asked a small girl, with wide, cornflower-blue eyes and a mass of blonde hair which was gathered in two large candyfloss bunches.

'Yes,' I replied, 'I would like that very much.'

'I'm a very good reader, you know,' she confided in me, while she searched in her bag for her book.

'Are you?'

'I read with expression.'

'Do you?'

'And I can do different voices.'

'Really? I expect you use dramatic pauses as well,' I said mischievously.

She looked up for a moment and then added seriously, 'I don't know what they are, but I probably can.'

She was indeed a very accomplished little reader and sailed through her book confidently and fluently. 'I *am* good, aren't I?' she announced when she had completed three pages.

'Very good,' I said.

'I'm good at writing as well.'

'I imagined you would be.'

'Would you like to see my writing?'

'I'd love to.'

'Poetry or prose?'

'Poetry, please.'

'I keep my poems in a portfolio.'

'I guessed you would,' I said, smiling.

Her writing was neat, imaginative and accurate. 'I *am* good at writing, aren't I?'

'Very good,' I agreed.

'I'm good at talking as well.'

'I can tell that. I think your mummy's got a little chatter-box at home.'

'Oh, no!' exclaimed the child. 'My granny has asthma and I'm not allowed to keep pets.'

'I see,' I said chuckling. I couldn't imagine what sort of animal she thought 'a little chatterbox' was.

'My granny calls me her "bright little button".'

'That's a lovely name,' I told her. 'They're very special are grannies and we must really look after them.'

'My granny wobbles, you know,' the little chatterbox continued.

'Does she?'

'She has a special disease which makes her wobble and forget things.'

'I'm sorry to hear that.'

'Yes,' said the little girl, nodding sagely. 'It's called "Old Timers' Disease".'

Gerry, who had joined me a few moments before, just in time to hear the end of my interesting exchange with the 'bright little button', whispered in my ear. 'You know, Gervase, if I get Alzheimer's Disease when I'm feeble, old and grey, I think I would like my children to say that I have got "Old Timers' Disease". It sounds much more friendly and humane, don't you think?'

'I thought you said you didn't have a family?' I replied, surprised at the revelation.

'I don't – yet,' she told me, throwing her head back and laughing, 'but I intend to one day.'

'Excuse me,' said the 'bright little button', patting my arm, 'would your girlfriend like to hear me read?'

At the second school, Sheepcote Primary, Gerry looked through the children's work and discussed the science cur-riculum with the teacher while I moved around the classroom talking to the children about the tasks they were undertaking that morning. On the table, tucked in a corner, were two boys busy sewing. One looked as if he had been dragged through a hedge backwards. He had spiky hair, a round red face and large ears. His nose was running and a front tooth was missing. His shirt was hanging out, his socks were concertinaed around his ankles, his legs were covered in cuts and bruises, and his shoes were so scuffed I could not tell whether they were originally black or brown. His hands and face were both entirely innocent of soap and water. His companion looked as healthy as a prize-winning bull. He was a very large, amiable-looking boy with a round moon of a face, great dimpled elbows and knees, and fingers as fat as sausages. Both boys were surrounded by threads, cottons, fabrics, an assortment of needles, boxes of pins and scissors and both were sewing furiously, their arms rising and falling like pistons.

'Hello,' I said brightly.

'Hello,' replied the larger boy. His companion continued to sew with a vengeance, his eyes narrowed in concentration.

'And how are you?'

'Middlin' well,' replied the large boy.

'And what are you two up to?' I asked amiably.

'Samplers,' he answered.

'Samplers?'

'Victorian embroidery,' the toothless one informed me, still vigorously sewing.

'For Mother's Day on Sunday,' added the other.

'I see,' I said, bending over them to get a closer look at their work. 'May I see?'

'Can't be stopping,' said the toothless one, continuing to sew with great determination, forcing the needle savagely through the canvas. 'Got to get it finished.' He turned to his friend. 'Pass us t'pink will tha, Dean?'

His companion searched through the assortment of coloured threads. 'All gone,' he replied bluntly.

'All gone!' exclaimed the toothless boy. 'All gone! Tha's gone and used all t'pink?'

'I needed it for mi roses.'

'And tha's used all t'purple, an all?'

'That were for mi lilac.'

'And t'yella?'

'That were for mi daffs,' said the large boy apologetically.

'And tha's left me wi all t'blacks and t'browns and t'greys. Thanks very much, Dean!'

The boys, entirely oblivious of my presence, resumed pushing the large needles through the fabric as if their lives depended upon it.

'Just stop a moment, will you, please,' I told them.

The toothless one paused, looked up, wiped the dewdrop from his nose with the back of his hand and then returned to his sewing as if he had not heard me.

'I can't stop,' he told me. 'I've got to gerrit done.'

His companion, clearly very pleased with his effort, held up a pale square of cream fabric. In large, uneven letters were the words: A MOTHER'S LOVE IS A BLESSING. The border was ablaze with a whole host of large, unrecognisable but extremely vivid flowers.

'I've just got mi name to put at t'bottom and I'm all done,' he announced proudly.

'And tha's used up all t'pink,' grumbled his companion, who was still stitching away madly.

The large boy straightened his sampler with a fat, pink hand and admired his handiwork before asking, 'Are you one of these school inspectors Miss was on about?'

'I am,' I replied.

'What do you reckon to mi sampler, then?'

'Well, it's very bright and original but, you know, if I

had come into your school a hundred years ago, you'd have been in real trouble.'

'How old are you, then?' asked the toothless boy.

'What I meant is that if a school inspector had visited your school at the time it was built, you would have been in trouble.'

'Why's that then?'

'Because your stitches are too big. If you look at the Victorian samplers, you will notice that the lettering and designs are very delicate and very carefully stitched.'

The toothless boy stopped sewing abruptly, examined his sampler and carefully put down his needle and thread, before turning to look me straight in the face. 'Aye, well, if I did 'em all small and delicate like what you say, mi mum'd nivver gerrit, would she? I've been on this for four week and I'll be lucky to get it done for next year's Mother's Day, way things stand.'

'I'll get mine done,' Dean chimed in smugly.

'Aye!' snapped the toothless one. 'And we know why, don't we?'

'Why?' I asked.

'Because, when Miss give out all these different Victorian sayings and proverbs, I was off poorly and when I got back I was stuck wi' t'one nob'dy wanted. Dean got shortest – A MOTHER'S LOVE IS A BLESSING – and I got t'longest!' He displayed his piece of fabric with a grubby finger. It read:

> THERE IS NOTHING SO PURE,
> THERE IS NOTHING SO HIGH,
> AS THE LOVE YOU WILL SEE
> IN YOUR MOTHER'S EYE.

'I've only just started mi border,' he moaned. 'And Dean's used all t'pinks and t'yellas and t'purples and I'm stuck wi t'blacks, t'browns and t'greys!'

'You could do animals instead of flowers,' suggested his companion with a self-satisfied smirk on his round red face. 'You don't need colours for sheep and cows and goats . . .'

'I'd need summat for t'pigs, though, wouldn't I?' cried the toothless one. 'And tha's used all t'pink!'

'I'm sure that, however it turns out, your mother will love your sampler,' I reassured him.

'If she gets it!' he barked.

'Well, I may see you boys later,' I said moving away.

'Later?' they exclaimed in unison.

'I thought I'd pop into the Singing class during the lunch-hour,' I told them.

'Singing!' the toothless one exclaimed. 'Singing! We don't gu to no Singing class! That's for t'cissies!' The other boy, putting the finishing touches to his large pink rose, nodded in agreement before echoing his companion's sentiments: 'Aye, choir's for t'cissies and t'lasses. You wunt catch us theer.'

As I headed to another desk, I heard a plaintive cry from the corner table, 'Miss, miss, can I have some pink thread, please? We're clean out ovver 'ere!'

After lunch, on our way to the Headteacher's room, Gerry and I paused for a moment at the door of the school hall to watch a little of the Singing class. There was no sign of the two embroiderers. The juniors, conducted by a very expressive young man in a red corduroy suit, great spotted bow-tie and mustard-coloured waistcoat, were singing with great gusto.

> There was an old lady who swallowed a fly.
> I don't know why she swallowed a fly.
> Perhaps she'll die.

On our way out of the school a little later, we came across a very distressed-looking girl standing crying in the corridor.

Great tears rolled down her cheeks and her small body was shaking piteously.

'What is it?' asked Gerry quietly, squatting in front of the weeping child and gently touching her arm.

'I'm going to die!' wailed the little girl. 'I'm going to die.'

'No, no,' comforted Gerry, giving her a cuddle. 'Whatever makes you think that?'

'I just know it! I'm going to die!' The child wiped her tears away with small round fists, leaving long streaks across her red cheeks.

'Who says you are going to die?' asked Gerry gently.

'Everyone!' exclaimed the child. 'Everyone! I know I am. I'm going to die!'

'How do you know?'

'Because I swallowed a fly, that's why. On the campsite last year in France. I swallowed a fly!' moaned the child. 'They were singing in the hall. They said I'd die!'

Gerry finally managed to reassure the little girl that what she had heard was just a funny song and that she was not going to die. The child departed down the corridor with the mournful words, 'And I need to swallow a spider to get the fly.'

We left Sheepcote School, both smiling, and headed further up the dale. My companion said very little, she just stared in wonderment out of the car window at the sweeping panorama, clumps of early primroses sheltering under the hedgerows bright in the afternoon sun, the dark, far-off wooded fells, rough moorland, great stone outcrops and hazy peaks. Gerry was certainly going to fit in well, I thought to myself. She had an easy natural way with children, related well to teachers and was good-humoured and friendly. I just wondered what she would make of the three of us in the Inspectors' Office, and whether she would be able to cope with the constant verbal badminton between David and Sidney. My leisurely drive was brought to an abrupt halt.

'Stop!' Gerry suddenly cried.

'Whatever is it?' I exclaimed, skidding the car to a halt.

'Look.'

I had seen many animals and birds in my first year travelling around the dales: squirrels dashing suicidally across the road in front of the car to find safety in the trees, the white scuts of rabbits rushing for their burrows, covies of partridges zinging down the headlands, pheasants ambling by the side of the road, so fat one wondered how they could ever get off the ground, the red brush of a fox slipping shadow-like into the bracken, herons flying lazily over wide, rose-grey rivers, and, once, a family of stoats playing in the quiet sunlit lane. Sometimes I would stop the car and lean against a gate to watch the scene in the fields falling away below me: a tractor chugging along a track, lambs twitching their tails and jumping high in spring sunshine, crested lapwings wheeling and plunging in a great empty sky and sometimes, best of all, I would listen to the call of the curlew.

I had never witnessed, however, what I saw then on that March day. In the field to the side of the road two hares, with long, lean bodies and great erect ears, squared up to each other and began boxing. We watched fascinated as they punched and pummelled each other. The sparring continued until the tired and defeated animal was chased away and the victor rose high on his hind legs, observed us with indifference, and loped away triumphant and unafraid.

Cragside Primary, our third and final port of call, sat in the shadow of the massive sphinx-like Cawthorne Crag. There was a mouth-watering aroma of baking pastry permeating the building.

'The children learn to cook in this school, Mr Phinn,'

explained the Headteacher. 'I feel it is important that all children, and particularly boys, should know how to bake a loaf, make a pie, even cook a whole meal. They won't always have their mothers looking after them. Of course, it used to be called baking-time when I started teaching, then it was cookery class, then home economics and now, I believe, it's called food technology. It's all the same in my book. Today, we are trying our hand at pastry and our school cook, or catering manager as the Education Office will insist on calling her, is overseeing our efforts.'

The school kitchen was a hive of activity. Two boys, smart in white aprons, were helping a large woman with floury hands take their culinary efforts out of the oven. One boy had such a dusting of flour on his face that he looked like Marley's ghost.

'Do you like tarts?' he asked as I approached.

'Pardon?'

'Tarts. Do you like tarts?'

'Jam tarts,' added the woman with the floury hands, winking at me.

'Oh, I'm very partial to tarts.'

'Do you want one of mine?'

'I think our visitor might enjoy one of your tarts, Richard, at afternoon break with his cup of tea.' There was a look on the woman's face which recommended me not to eat one of the tarts on offer.

'But I want to know what he thinks,' the boy told her.

'You have to wait until they are cool, Richard.'

'Tarts are better when they're hot, miss,' persisted the boy. He then looked at me with a shining, innocent face. 'Don't *you* think hot tarts are better than cold ones?'

'I do,' I agreed, 'and I will have one of your tarts now.' The cook's face took on an expression which told me that I had been warned.

The boy selected the biggest on the baking tray – a large,

crusty-looking, misshapen lump of pastry. In the centre was a blob of dark red which I supposed was jam. It looked the most unappetising piece of pastry I had ever seen, but I could not go back now. The boy watched keenly as I took a massive bite.

'What do you think?' asked the boy eagerly.

It was extremely difficult to speak as the dried-up confection coated the inside of my mouth. I coughed and sprayed the air with bits of pastry and dried jam. 'I have never tasted a tart like this in my life,' I assured him honestly, between splutters.

A great smile spread across the boy's face. 'Really?'

'Really.'

'Would you like another?'

'No, thank you,' I replied quickly, 'one is quite enough.'

'Does your wife want one?'

'No, thank you, Richard,' replied Gerry, trying to suppress her laughter. 'I've just had my lunch.'

At the end of the afternoon, as we were heading for the door, the little chef appeared with a brown paper bag in his hand. 'I've put one of my tarts in here for you, miss,' he said to Gerry, 'to have with your tea tonight.'

'That's very kind,' she said. 'Thank you very much.'

'And another one for you, sir,' he added.

'Thank you,' I replied.

'Funny thing is baking, isn't it?' the boy pondered, holding out his hands in front of him the better to examine them. 'You know, my hands were dead mucky before I started making my tarts and just look how clean they are now.'

Gerry placed the brown paper bag carefully in her briefcase and smiled.

A mile or so from the school I pulled off the road. My intention was to discuss the day with Gerry, share our observations and for me to explain a little of what I considered the job of school inspector involved, but she was silent and once more awe-struck by the view, now softened in the late afternoon sun.

'It's like sitting on the roof of the world,' she murmured.

In front of us stretched a grim, primitive, endless land. Nothing broke the silence: no complaining sheep or yapping collie dog, no lusty cock crow or curlew's fitful cry, no roar or babble of falling water or sighing wind. All was still. Then, high above, a pair of circling buzzards, their great wings outstretched, soared alone in an empty sky.

'I'm going to love this job,' Gerry said quietly.

'I'm sure you will,' I replied.

She looked at me with her dark blue eyes. 'Do you think I'll fit in?'

'Oh, yes, definitely.' She stared out of the window and sighed. 'However, there's something very important I've got to ask you,' I said seriously.

'Yes?' her brow furrowed slightly.

'Would you like your tart now or save it for later?'

The first school I visited in the Summer term was Ugglemat-tersby County Junior School where I had agreed to take the assembly and spend the day visiting classes. The school was situated in the very centre of a dark, brooding village, sandwiched between the Masonic Hall, a square and solid box of a building in rusty-red brick, and the public house, built of a slaty limestone turned a greasy grey, with windows like black cold eyes. The overcast sky and slanting April rain made the school and its surroundings even more bleak and unwelcoming. The area circling the village was a strange and desolate land of sweeping grey moors. It was a wet and barren landscape, naked save for a few ancient oaks and a couple of centuries-old farmsteads. A few hardy sheep, nibbling at the wiry grasses as thin as the whistling wind, were watched by a pair of hooded crows perched in the gaunt arms of a dead tree like vultures awaiting a death.

There were two women in the drab entrance hall of the school. One was large, with a pale, perfectly spherical face, crimson adhesive lipstick and heavy rounded shoulders. The other was a stern, disagreeable-looking woman with small deep-set eyes, a tight little mouth and bright peroxide hair which stuck up like a brush – not an agreeable combination. They stopped talking when I entered and eyed me sus-piciously.

'Good morning,' I greeted them cheerfully.

'Mornin',' they replied in unison.

'Dreadful weather, isn't it?'

'Dreadful,' they replied together.

I was about to press the buzzer on the small reception desk when the larger of the two addressed me. 'If you're 'ere to complain, get to t'back o' t'queue.'

'No, I'm not here to complain. I have an appointment with the Headteacher.' I pressed the buzzer and a moment later a small, harassed-looking woman scurried out. Before she could ask who I was and what I wanted, the large woman pushed forward menacingly.

'Have you told 'im we're 'ere?' she barked.

'I have, Mrs Wilmott. Mr Sharples will be with you in one moment.'

'I've been stood 'ere the best part o' ten minutes.'

'And me, an' all,' added the smaller of the two women.

'I'll be purrin roots down if I wait 'ere much longer.'

'I appreciate that, Mrs Wilmott, but it is always very hectic on a Monday, and it is always best to make an appointment to be certain that the Headteacher is available. Mr Sharples is busy at the moment –'

'He's *always* busy when I come into school. Well, I'm not goin' until I've seen 'im.'

'If you could just bear with me for one moment, Mrs Wilmott, until I find out what this gentleman wants –'

'He wants to see Mr Sharples,' announced the large woman.

'He's got an appointment with 'im,' added the other.

'Mr Phinn,' I said, smiling at the small receptionist. 'I think the Headteacher is expecting me.'

'Are you the book representative?'

'No. Mr Sharples will know who I am when you tell him.' I thought it best to keep my identity secret from my two aggressive companions. The receptionist hurried away without a word and was back in quick time, accompanied by an exceptionally thin and sallow-complexioned man in a shiny suit and highly polished shoes. When he caught sight of the large woman and her companion with the bright hair, the Headteacher smiled the resigned smile of a martyr about to face the stake.

'Good morning, Mr Phinn. I will be with you in one moment.' He turned to the women. 'Now then, Mrs Wilmott, Mrs Leech, what can I do for you both?'

'It's our Mandy!' snapped the large woman.

'I guessed it would be,' replied the Headteacher wearily. 'What is it this time?'

'She come home Friday with nits – and they're not 'ers!'

'Not hers?' repeated the Headteacher.

'Not 'ers! She must 'ave gor 'em from somebody in this school because there's no nits in our 'ouse.'

'Well, I am most grateful that you have pointed that out to me, Mrs Wilmott. I will alert the other parents.'

'She shouldn't be comin' 'ome with nits which aren't 'ers,' continued the large woman.

'Indeed no,' replied Mr Sharples, retaining his concerned countenance.

'I've brought 'er in this mornin' and I don't want 'er comin' 'ome with another 'eadful of nits tonight!'

'I take it you have been to the chemist for a specially treated shampoo for head lice?' asked the Headteacher.

'Yes, I 'ave! She's 'ad three good dousin's.'

'Very wise. I will write to all parents asking them to check their children's hair and ensure that they send them to school with clean scalps.'

'Well, I 'opes that's the end of it! She shouldn't be comin' 'ome with nits what aren't 'ers.'

'I did send a copy of the leaflet concerning the prevention and treatment of head lice to each parent or guardian last term, if you recall, Mrs Wilmott. It recommended the use of a fine-tooth comb on wet hair and specially prepared lotions or rinses obtainable from the pharmacist.'

'I know all that!' snapped the woman. 'But my Mandy has short 'air and it's kept clean and combed regular.'

'Head lice are not fussy about hair length or condition of the hair, Mrs Wilmott,' explained Mr Sharples. 'Clean hair is no protection.' The Headteacher then turned his attention to the other woman. 'And have you come about head lice, Mrs Leech?' he asked the smaller woman in an excessively patient tone of voice. 'Or is it something else?'

'I've come about knickers!'

'I beg your pardon?'

'Crystal's come home wearing knickers what aren't 'ers!'

'I see,' sighed the Headteacher. He turned to me and displayed his martyr's smile. 'Do go on into my room, Mr Phinn.' He gestured before him. 'I have a feeling this will take a little time.'

Through the open door I heard him attempting to pacify the two mothers. Ten minutes later he entered the room, lowered himself into his chair, sighed heavily, stared at me for a moment with great doleful eyes and then remarked, 'I became a headteacher, Mr Phinn, to educate the young, to teach children, but what do I have to deal with, day in and day out? Nits and knickers, that's what. Those two women are the very bane of my life. They spend more time in the school than the teachers whom they pursue with the relentless fervour of two hungry foxhounds. When I sent the forms out for the new intake of children, under the section where she had to write her husband's name, Mrs Wilmott entered: "Father not yet known". I had a dreadful premonition when I read it that Mandy's mother would not be the easiest of parents to deal with.' He shook his head and grimaced. 'And as for Mrs Leech –'

'Mr Sharples,' I interrupted, glancing at my watch, 'I think it may be about time for the assembly.'

'Oh, good gracious me, so it is, so it is. Do come this way, Mr Phinn.'

The junior children were all waiting quietly in a plain, dark school hall with heavy brown drapes framing long windows which looked out upon the cold and lonely moor. Row after row of children, with serious faces, sat quietly, cross-legged on the hard wooden floor, watched by their serious-faced teachers who stood, arms folded, around the sides.

'Good morning, children,' said the Headteacher.

'Good morning, Mr Sharples, good morning, everyone,' they replied with little enthusiasm.

'We will start with the hymn "All things bright and beautiful, All creatures great and small",' the Headteacher told them solemnly. The tired-looking teacher at the piano, who had been watching him with a glum expression on her long pale face, struck up the tune in such a slow and laboured way that the joyous hymn sounded like a funeral dirge. There was little verve or volume in the singing and no effort on the part of the teachers to encourage the pupils by singing themselves. I thought of the children at St Bartholomew's who had sung so lustily and in such a heartfelt way, almost competing with the booming rhythms of Miss Fenoughty plonking away on the piano.

'This morning,' said Mr Sharples, when the hymn had finally ground to a halt, 'we have a guest in school. I am sure it will not have escaped your notice that there is a gentleman with us.' All eyes focused upon me. 'Mr Phinn is a school inspector and he is going to take our assembly before joining you in the classrooms for the day. If Mr Phinn asks you anything, answer him in your usual polite manner and should he look lost I am sure you will be able to tell him where to go.' With that, the Headteacher joined his colleagues at the side of the hall and folded his arms.

'Good morning,' I said and began the assembly. I attempted to get a response by asking the children about Easter – what had they done over the holidays, had they been anywhere interesting, had they received any Easter eggs? – questions which usually stimulate lively responses.

In this case little was forthcoming. Clearly, assemblies in this school involved listening and not contributing. The only movement I noticed amongst the solemn rows of children was random scratchings at scalps. Rows of serious faces observed me quietly as if waiting for a performance to begin so I pressed on. I read them the very poignant children's story, *The Selfish Giant* by Oscar Wilde, which concerns the mean-minded Giant who owns a large and lovely garden with soft green grass, beautiful flowers like stars, and peach trees covered in delicate blossoms of pink and pearl. One day he finds small children playing in his garden and angrily chases them away. 'My own garden is my own garden,' he says and he builds a high wall so none can enter. When spring arrives, the Giant's garden is empty of birds, the trees have forgotten to blossom, snow covers the grass with a great white cloak, and frost paints the trees silver. The Giant sits sadly at his window and looks down on his garden which is in perpetual winter and he wonders why the spring did not return.

Then, one morning, he hears the birds singing and sees the most wonderful sight. Through a little hole in the wall, the children have crept in and they are sitting in the branches of the trees which are now covered in blossoms. Only in one corner is it still winter. There stands a little boy weeping bitterly for he is too small to reach up to the branches of the tree. The Giant's heart melts. 'How selfish I have been,' he says. So he creeps downstairs and into his garden. He takes the little child gently in his hands and puts him in the tree. And the tree bursts into blossom and the birds come and sing in it. The Giant takes a great axe and knocks down the high wall so all the children can come to play in his garden. Every day they come to play but the little boy the Giant loves more than any other, the one he put into the tree, is never with them.

Years pass and the Giant grows very old and feeble. One

winter morning he looks from his window to see in the farthest corner of the garden a tree covered in lovely white blossoms. Its branches are golden and silver fruit hangs from them. Underneath stands the little boy he loves. Downstairs runs the Giant with great joy. Across the grass he runs until he comes close to the child. And then his face grows red with anger. 'Who hath dared to wound thee?' he cries, for on the palms of the child's hands are the prints of two nails and the prints of two nails are on the little feet. 'Tell me,' roars the Giant, 'and I will take my big sword and slay him.'

'Nay,' answers the child, 'these are the wounds of love.'

'Who art thou?' asks the Giant, and a strange awe falls on him and he kneels before that little child. And the child smiles.

'You let me play once in your garden. Today you shall come to my garden, which is Paradise.' And when the children ran into the garden that afternoon to play, they found the Giant lying dead under the tree, covered in white blossoms.

I had barely finished the story when a number of hands shot up. This is more like it, I thought. The children are beginning to respond and I can now talk about the story and relate it to the theme of being kind and considerate to others. The owner of one of the hands waving at me was a large, red-cheeked boy with hair the colour of straw.

'Yes?' I said, pointing in his direction.

'I'm a Methodist,' he announced loudly.

'Really?' I replied.

'And I'm going to Paradise!'

'I'm sure you are.'

'Mr Phinn!' Another boy almost identical to the first in size and colouring shouted from the back, 'I'm Church of England and I'm goin' to Paradise an' all!'

'I'm certain you will get in as well,' I replied.

Then a large girl with a chubby face, rounded shoulders

and wild, woolly hair rose to her feet and announced dramatically, 'I'm nowt – but I'm still gerrin' in!'

'I'm sure you'll be the first in the queue, Mandy,' the Headteacher told her before instructing the children not to call out.

I met Mandy later in her classroom. She was sitting next to a small, sad-looking girl of about ten or eleven with a tight little mouth and bright blonde hair. I guessed that I had met her mother earlier that morning. The two girls stopped talking when I approached and eyed me suspiciously.

'Would you like to tell me what you're doing?' I asked pleasantly.

'Why?' demanded the larger child.

'Well, I would like you to.'

'But why?'

'I'm a school inspector,' I said. 'Don't you remember? Mr Sharples mentioned in assembly that I would be coming into classrooms. I'm here to look at your work.'

The girl shrugged, scratched her scalp and pushed her book across the desk. 'We're writing,' she explained.

'About what?'

'What we did ovver t'weekend.'

'I see. Would you like to tell me what you did?'

'Not particularly,' she replied, scratching her scalp again.

'She been weshing her 'air all weekend cos she 'ad nits,' announced the smaller girl.

'Shurrup, Crystal!' cried the larger girl, elbowing her. 'You don't 'ave to tell everybody, tha knaws.'

'Everybody knaws,' said the other casually. 'Yer mam broadcast it.'

At the next table sat the youthful Methodist with two other large boys.

'Could I have a look at what you're doing?'

'Aye tha can, if tha likes.' He pushed his book across the

236

desk in my direction. In large untidy writing was an account of his visit to a Saturday sheep auction with his grandfather.

'So you live on a farm, do you?' I asked.

'Aye, that's reight.'

'And you have sheep?'

'Well, I reckon we wunt be goin' to a sheep auction if we kept pigs, now would we?'

'No, I suppose you wouldn't.' I had learnt quite a bit about farming in my first year travelling around the Dales' schools and found that, by engaging children in a discussion about the things they were interested and often expert in, I could break the ice and very soon get them talking. From there I would move on to ask them what they liked doing best in school, talk about their writing, listen to them read and test their spelling. 'So what breed of sheep do you have?' I asked.

'Mostly Swaledales but we're thinkin' o' diversifyin'.'

'Really?'

'That's why we were at Fettlesham market. Granfether were lookin' at t'Texels.'

'I see. So what do Swaledale sheep look like?'

'Tha dun't know owt abaat sheep then?'

'Not a lot.'

He shifted in his chair the better to face me. 'Well, tha can allus spot a Swaledale. It 'as curly 'orns on its 'ead, sort of a black face wi' a white snout, sometimes wi' a bit o' specklin' on and it 'as a fairly light carcass. Now yer Dales-bred sheep are an 'ardy breed and fare well on this sort o' land and in this sort o' weather. It can ger a bit parky up 'ere and rain fair teems dahn so you need summat wi' a bit o' gumption. Sometimes we cross 'em wi' Blue-faced Leicesters to produce a mule breeding sheep. Anyroad, we've 'ad a bit o' trouble wi' sheep dip flu and blow fly this year and we're looking at Texels to see what they can do.'

'And what do Texels look like?'

'They're not much to look at – bit like a bull terrier, fat white bodies, short wool, legs wide spaced but they're pretty docile and give a lot o' milk. They give extra lean meat an' all and there's more fat on t'carcass. They're easy to maintain are Texels. Mi granfether reckons there'll be a sight more of a profit in 'em. Tha sees they have higher kill-out percentage and better conformation and grading than yer Swaledales.'

'Do they really?' I had not the first idea what the boy was talking about. I changed the subject. 'And you are a Methodist?'

'Aye. Mi granfether's a lay preeacher at t'chapel in Uggle-mattersby. His sarmons is famous, tha knaws. People cum for miles to 'ear 'im speyk. He says he gives Divil a reight run for his money when he gets gooin. I might ger 'im that book what yer were reading. Astagorritwithi?'

'Pardon?'

'Book. Astagorritwithi, so's I can mek a note on t'title?'

I took the book from my briefcase and watched as he copied down the title in his large, untidy writing. 'Cham-pion,' he said when he had finished. 'It'll do fer Granfether for 'is birthday.' Then he inclined his head in the direction of Mandy who was busy scratching away at her scalp on the next table, and whispered, 'See that lass, 'er wi' gob on 'er, well she's 'ad nits, tha knaws. By looks in it she's still gorrem. Tha wants to keep a fair distance, otherwise tha'll be teckin' 'ome summat tha nivver bargained fer.'

Mr Sharples heard my critical preliminary report at the end of the day with the sort of impassive expression a professional mourner would have spent a lifetime perfecting.

'Firstly, Mr Sharples, I have to tell you that the quality of teaching and learning and the standards of attainment in the school are just not high enough. Reading and writing standards are low in relation to the children's ages and the basic skills of spelling are unsatisfactory. The children arrive from the Infants with a reasonable command of language and read soundly enough but their progress from then on is slow.' I referred to my notes. 'I have seen no enthusiastic and optimistic teachers today and no lesson which I could judge to be good. Indeed, there was no purpose to two of the lessons I observed, no clear objectives or careful planning, and the range of teaching strategies was very narrow. Do you wish to comment on that?'

'No,' replied the Headteacher bluntly.

'The exterior of the building is very drab and uninviting – something you cannot do much about – but the inside is little better.'

'What's the state of the building got to do with education?' he asked. 'Provided the place is clean and warm, we don't need to turn the place into some exotic showcase.'

'Do you not think children work better in a bright, attractive and welcoming environment where their efforts are displayed around them rather than in a series of drab classrooms containing little to interest or challenge them?'

'I don't place much importance on that sort of thing,' he replied dismissively.

'The book stock is poor, there are very few dictionaries in the building and the work as a whole needs to be far better directed. I really feel there needs to be more enjoyment, more excitement and fun in the curriculum, to get the children interested and wanting to learn.'

Mr Sharples sighed heavily when I had finished, stared at me for a moment with his great doleful eyes, and then remarked: 'I became a headteacher, Mr Phinn, as I mentioned to you when you arrived, to educate the young, to teach children, but what do I have to deal with, day in, day out?'

Nits and knickers, I thought to myself, recalling the earlier conversation.

'Difficult parents, interfering governors and critical school inspectors, that's what. They are the very bane of my life. I'm just not allowed to get on with my job in peace and quiet. It's very easy to sit in judgement for a day, Mr Phinn, but I have to be here day in and day out.' He made his chosen profession sound like a prison sentence. 'This job gets more and more difficult. The stresses and strains, the pressures and problems I have to cope with. People just don't realise. They have no idea. You've seen the children who attend this school. If I had the raw material then I might be able to get the results you say I should be getting. But look at where these children come from. I mean, what can you expect?'

'Mr Sharples,' I said slowly, 'surely that is what good teachers do – they have high expectations. They expect the moon. Now I appreciate the many pressures and stresses in education at the moment, but anyone who becomes a headteacher must realise that dealing with difficult parents, interfering governors and critical school inspectors is part and parcel of the job. I will, of course, be sending a detailed written report to the school, outlining the issues you need to address and giving suggestions on how you might improve. I shall also be arranging to make a further series of visits.'

'So I take it you are not entirely happy with what you have seen?' said the Headteacher wearily, studying his fingernails.

'No, Mr Sharples, I am not. I would not be doing my job if I told you that everything in the garden was rosy.'

The Headteacher looked up at this point and glowered. 'Well, speaking of gardens, Mr Phinn, that story you read to us at assembly about a giant who dropped dead under a tree did not exactly put us all in a good-humoured mood, did it? It certainly didn't bring a smile to my face.' He got to his feet. 'I don't have to listen to any more of this,' he said. 'Just put in your official report. And now, if you don't mind, I've had a very hard day.'

With that, he walked across his office and held open the door, clearly indicating that the inspection was over.

Cold wind and slanting rain swept about the car as I left the dark, brooding village. The overcast sky, dark desolate moors and great looming fells made me feel extraordinarily depressed. I never liked giving a poor report but sometimes it was needed. A few sheep were still nibbling at the wiry grass, and the hooded crows perched in the branches of the dead oak did not look as though they had moved all day. One of the sheep looked up as I drove slowly past. It was a fat ram with curly horns, a black face with a white snout and great doleful eyes. It stared impassively and reminded me so much of the Headteacher of Ugglemattersby County Junior School.

Mrs Savage appeared very much at home in the entrance hall of Lord Marrick's stately home and blended in beautifully with the pale colours of the room. She was dressed in an elegant cream coat beneath which she wore a flowing blue chiffon dress and her fingers, wrists, ears and neck had a generous assortment of showy gold jewellery. Standing before the huge and magnificently carved chimney-piece and below the oil painting of some military ancestor of Lord Marrick's, she looked like the Lady of the Manor waiting for a photograph to be taken, with her imperious expression and hands clasped formally before her.

'Ah, Mr Phinn,' she said, advancing and clicking noisily with her heels on the white inlaid marble floor. 'You are here at last.'

I glanced at my watch. 'It's only just gone eight,' I replied. 'I didn't want to get here too early.'

'As you know,' she replied haughtily, 'I like things to be done efficiently and thoroughly and not leave anything to chance. I want to make certain that every final detail has been taken on board.'

It was the Saturday of the Feoffees Pageant and the weather was perfect, the sky a cloudless blue and it was warm for the end of May. Marquees and multi-coloured tents were scattered on the green sward of parkland to the front of Manston Hall. The event was to start at 11.00 am when the Feoffees would process in full regalia and Lord Marrick would officially open proceedings. Already the area around the hall was a hive of activity. The police bandsmen had arrived and were busy setting up their chairs and music stands near a small stone obelisk, an officious army sergeant with a bristling moustache was berating a squad of young soldiers beside three huge, shiny tanks and assorted army vehicles, and an RAF dog handler was putting his savage-looking beasts through their paces. A juggler, in a colourful patchwork outfit, was entertaining a knot of little boys in surplices, red cassocks and stiff white collars. Stallholders were busy arranging their wares, jewellery, pottery, cakes, books, brassware and all manner of items on long trestle tables.

I had spent the previous morning with Mrs Savage, no longer being able to avoid a face-to-face meeting. Her brief had been merely to deal with the administration but, true to form, she had expanded her role and had insisted on marching around the park, checking items off against a large clipboard of notes held officiously in front of her. She had made certain that the Exhibition marquee was absolutely as ordered, that the staging had been correctly assembled for the drama productions, that the covered area for the gymnastics area conformed to all the safety regulations, and that the Orangery was properly set up for the Youth Orchestra. The various group organisers were obviously well in control and regarded Mrs Savage with a mixture of irritation and amusement.

'I may be something of a stickler, Mr Phinn,' said Mrs Savage now, 'but I do like everything to be –' She stopped mid-sentence when a barrel-bodied, bow-legged bulldog with pinky-white jowls and pale unfriendly eyes appeared from the direction of the library. 'What a remarkably ugly-looking creature,' she said. The dog made a low rumbling noise and displayed a set of sharp teeth. Mrs Savage strode towards it. 'Shoo!' she snapped. The dog stared at her with its cold grey button eyes. 'Shoo!' she repeated, smacking her hands together sharply, her heavy jewellery jangling.

The dog hesitated for a moment in disbelief, then slunk away whining. Laetitia had met her match.

I followed Mrs Savage's rapid progress down the stone steps of the hall and towards a large marquee, outside which was a big sign announcing EDUCATION EXHIBITION. We were just about to enter the tent when a small man in a blue boiler suit approached. He addressed Mrs Savage. 'I've been looking for you.'

She gave him one of her famous condescending looks. 'Really?'

'Where do you want it, love?'

'I *beg* your pardon?'

'Your tent?'

'Tent?' She arched an eyebrow.

'Your tent,' he repeated. 'Where do you want it putting?'

'What *are* you talking about?' she said irritably. 'I don't know anything about a tent.'

'Where you're doing your fortune-telling.'

'Do I look remotely like a fortune teller?' she asked in a sharp and strident tone of voice, her eyes shining with intensity.

'I was told to look for a woman in blue and yella wi' lots o' bangles and beads.'

With a clash of bracelets, she pointed in the opposite direction. 'Well, I suggest you look elsewhere. I am certainly not Gypsy Rose Lee.'

'Sorry, I'm sure,' said the man as Mrs Savage disappeared into the marquee.

The art exhibition was magnificent. Sidney had worked hard the afternoon before and produced a dazzling display of work. There were delicate watercolours, bold oil paintings, detailed line drawings, portraits in chalk and charcoals, rural scenes in inks, sculptures, embroideries, tapestries and collages. It was a mass of colour. On large boards a range of poetry and tidy handwritten accounts of historical events had been displayed. Behind the Education marquee, teachers were preparing for the drama production, going over final details with their young charges, while a troop of junior gymnasts was practising on large blue mats. In the Orangery members of the Youth Orchestra were rehearsing for their performance which would take place later that morning.

'Well,' said Mrs Savage, smiling uncharacteristically, as we headed back towards the hall, 'I think everything is in order.'

I had to hand it to the woman. Things had been organised extremely well. She had contacted schools and arranged for the children's work to be collected for my exhibition. I had done very little, apart from suggesting the various activities and inviting teachers to take part.

'Yes,' I said. 'You've worked very hard.'

She stared at me for a moment. 'Thank you,' she said. 'I think we both deserve a cup of coffee.' She gestured in the direction of the Refreshment Tent. 'Shall we?'

The Feoffees Pageant went like clockwork. At eleven o'clock on the dot, Lord Marrick, as Greave and Chief Lord of the Feoffees, dressed in a long scarlet gown and heavy gold chain, followed the Mace Bearer and led a line of largely elderly men in dark suits and bowler hats. They processed up the steps of Manston Hall where Lord Marrick made a speech and officially opened the pageant to celebrate the Feoffees' five hundredth anniversary.

The police band struck up a rousing tune and the park was soon full of people, pushing and jostling through the exhibitions, watching the performances, listening to the music or just sitting relaxing in the warm sunshine.

'Splendid! Splendid!' said Dr Gore later that morning as he entered the marquee where the children's work was displayed. He was dressed in a charcoal grey suit with his bowler hat perched rakishly on the side of his head. I suppressed a smile. 'It really does look impressive in here. Wonderful work. Quite delightful. The Youth Orchestra are going great guns in the Orangery and the gymnastics are about to begin so I must pop back and see those. I just wanted to call in to say how well everyone has done. I think we can say that the Education Department has held its own, eh?' Before I could respond, he strode off, rubbing his hands and repeating enthusiastically, 'Splendid! Splendid!'

'I think the old man's pleased,' remarked Sidney phlegmatically.

Mrs Savage stood at the door to the office, dressed in a wildly striped multi-coloured smock, long cream silk scarf, pale grey boots and the usual assortment of heavy clanking jewellery. Her hair was curled up in long tendrils on her head and held in place by a great silver clasp in the shape of a spider. It was well before nine o'clock on the first morning of the following week. Mrs Savage rarely ventured into the Inspectors' Office at the best of times and to see her at the crack of dawn was entirely unexpected, not to say disconcerting.

'I could hear the noise from the bottom of the stairs,' she said to no one in particular, in that sharp, disapproving voice of hers.

'We were laughing,' said Sidney, smiling in such an exaggerated fashion that he looked quite manic. 'We were sharing an amusing story, a funny little anecdote, a whimsical moment, an engaging little account.' He was rather labouring the point. 'Schools are funny places, you know, my dear Mrs Savage.'

'Really?' replied our visitor, retaining her sour expression and clearly irritated by Sidney's exaggerated good humour.

'Mr Pritchard was telling us about his recent visit to an

infant school,' Harold told her. 'Weren't you, David?' His colleague nodded slightly and it was clear he was not going to relate the story for the benefit of Mrs Savage, of whom he had an abiding dislike. 'Yes,' continued Harold amiably, 'it was a most entertaining little tale. Mr Pritchard had asked this small boy if he had been anywhere interesting over the Easter holiday and the little chap told him he had been to Scarborough for the day. "And did you go on a donkey?" Mr Pritchard asked him. "Oh no," the child replied, "I went in my dad's car." ' Harold chuckled. 'The things children say nowadays.'

'Yes, well I'm sure that's all very amusing, Dr Yeats,' said Mrs Savage, without the trace of a smile.

'And how may we help you?' enquired Harold.

'I have called over for two reasons. Firstly, Dr Gore, to whom I spoke on Sunday, was very pleased with everyone's efforts with regard to the Feoffees Pageant and asked me to convey his appreciation. He will be writing to you formally to express his thanks. Things went extremely well and Lord Marrick was particularly grateful for all the hard work that had been expended.'

'That is very good to hear, Mrs Savage,' Harold told her.

Mrs Savage turned in my direction. 'I would appreciate it, Mr Phinn, if you could come across and see me some time.' I heard Sidney stifle a laugh. She gave him a quick glance. 'We need to put our heads together to compile a report on the Feoffees Pageant for Dr Gore's annual report to the Education Committee.'

'Yes,' I said, 'I'll give you a ring.'

'It would be more convenient for me if we could do it now. Have you a window in your diary?'

'I'll have a look,' I said.

While I was flicking through the pages in my diary, she turned her attention to Harold. 'The second and more important reason for my visit, Dr Yeats, concerns a much less pleasant matter.' David rolled his eyes and Sidney adopted his usual pose, placing his hands behind his head, leaning back in his chair and fixing his gaze on the ceiling. Mrs Savage continued undeterred. 'I've come up especially early before you all disappear off on school visits. I need to talk to you all together.'

David drew in a long weary breath, sighed dramatically and shook his head. Sidney continued to look heavenwards. Mrs Savage fixed them with a venomous stare.

'That sounds ominous,' said Harold in the most pleasant of voices and no doubt hoping to defuse a potentially explosive situation. 'Do enlighten us, Mrs Savage.'

David looked abstractedly out of the window, Sidney didn't move a muscle and I feigned interest in a diary entry, so she had no one except Harold on whom to focus her icy stare.

'As you will be aware, Dr Yeats, part of my remit is to record all the weekly forecasts that the inspectors complete when they are sent to me each Friday afternoon. This procedure is so Dr Gore knows where all the inspectors are during the following week. I'm sure I don't have to tell you that.'

'No, Mrs Savage, you do not have to tell us that,' echoed David in a weary voice. 'I have been filling in those engagement sheets for time immemorial.'

'Well,' she continued, unperturbed by the interruption, 'I have to say that some of the weekly programmes from this office, sent to me last term, were of times incomplete, sometimes inaccurate, frequently illegible and, on a growing number of occasions' – she paused and tried to gain Sidney's attention by glaring pointedly in his direction – 'I have received no programmes at all. Now, it is essential that Dr Gore knows exactly where all the inspectors are during the week.'

'Why?' asked David, suddenly turning from the window.

'I beg your pardon, Mr Pritchard?'

'Why exactly does Dr Gore need to know where we all are every minute of the day?'

'Because he may wish to contact you in an emergency.'

Sidney suppressed a snort rather ineffectually. 'We are school inspectors, Mrs Savage, not the air-sea rescue.'

'Nevertheless, he needs to know where you are.'

'In all my twenty-odd years as a school inspector,' David said, 'there has been not one, single occasion when any sort of emergency has arisen which demanded my immediate and undivided attention and there has been nothing so very important that it could not wait until the next day.'

'Suppose a member of the Education Committee requires an urgent answer to a query?' She was certainly persistent.

'He or she should be able to wait until the following morning, surely,' stated Harold with amused detachment.

'It is our business to respond promptly and effectively,' continued Mrs Savage with lofty disdain, 'and to make the system more efficient, I have, with Dr Gore's full approval, decided on a new procedure.'

'Oh dear, oh dear,' groaned David, 'not another mass of paperwork and more wretched forms to fill in?'

'What about next Thursday?' I suggested, hoping to curtail the lively and increasingly belligerent exchange.

'Pardon?' asked Mrs Savage.

'For me to come across to see you. At about five o'clock?'

'Yes, yes, that sounds fine. Now about these new procedures. Dr Gore has asked me to get you up to speed,' announced Mrs Savage, adjusting the silk scarf as she caught sight of her reflection in the glass of the door.

'Get us up to what?' demanded Sidney.

'Up to speed,' repeated Mrs Savage, slowly and deliberately. 'Fully conversant with the changes.'

Over the past few months Mrs Savage had been attending a course for education officers. Returning from her weekly lectures and seminars and filled with new ideas and concepts, she had initiated a number of changes in the administration of the Education Department. The module she had undertaken on selection procedures, for example, had resulted in new and complicated procedures for appointing staff. Gerry Mullarkey had been the first on the receiving end of that. Another transformation was in Mrs Savage's vocabulary. She had adopted a completely new language, a language full of jargon, psychobabble and gobbledygook. A foreigner with a good grasp of English, on meeting Mrs Savage, would assume that she was from another planet, such was the incomprehensible nature of her language. David had entertained us one afternoon with an account of the recent meeting of the standing committee concerned with pupils who had been expelled from school, which he chaired. Mrs Savage had been 'deputed', as she informed him, 'to act as rapporteur'.

'She managed to translate perfectly clear, readable and succinct comments into the most meaningless twaddle that I have ever heard. There was one lad, who had been expelled from school for answering back and shouting at the teachers. He was a damn nuisance, that's what he was, and needed a few days off school to cool off – or more likely, "a good, tidy slap", as my old Welsh grandmother used to say. In the minutes, Mrs Savage, who is now, after her DIY education course, something of an expert on difficult children, as well as every other blessed thing, had it recorded in a sort of gibberish.' He had reached across his desk and plucked a piece of paper from his out-tray. 'Here, listen to this for complete and utter nonsense: "One behaviourally challenged student with ADHD (attention-deficit-hyperactive-disorder) and ODS (oppositional-defiance-syndrome) came from a multi-delinquent family with siblings high on the incarceration index." In simple English it means he was loud-mouthed and troublesome and his brothers were behind bars. When I enquired of our "rapporteur" if she were now our resident psychologist, she gave me that look which would turn you to stone. The woman's going off the rails or, as she might term it, she has "manic episode stress-inducing disorder" or, as I might describe it, "pain in the neck syndrome".'

'As I was saying,' continued Mrs Savage now, 'I am here at the behest of Dr Gore to explain the new procedures and to get you all up to speed. We do not want anyone off-message, do we? I would like, starting now, for all the inspectors to complete a blue Form IMF.'

'A what?' snapped David.

'International Monetary Fund,' explained Sidney.

'The Inspectors' Monthly Forecast form!' exclaimed Mrs Savage. 'This will replace the green Form IWF, the Inspectors' Weekly Forecast form, which you send to me at present. I will now know well in advance where you are during the days and evenings and then –'

'Evenings?' interrupted David. 'What's this about evenings? You want to know what we are doing in the evenings? Good gracious me, this gets worse and worse.'

Mrs Savage gave a twisted little smile. 'Only if it's official County business, Mr Pritchard. I am not the slightest bit interested in what you get up to in your own time.'

'Just as well,' said Sidney, looking in my direction. 'I am sure Gervase would not wish to record the many assignations he has with a certain young headteacher.'

'Now, should there be any changes you wish to make,' continued Mrs Savage, ignoring him, 'you will need to complete a yellow Form AIMF, an Amendment to the Inspectors' Monthly Forecast form. All visits to schools need to be recorded accurately and clearly and, should there be any changes, the amendments noted. Both the IMF and the AIMF should be sent to me directly so I can make the necessary alterations and adjustments to your programmes.'

'In triplicate?' asked Sidney sarcastically.

'I have brought over a batch of the new forms,' she continued undeterred, 'which I have left in your secretary's office and I would like them returned to me completed, ASAP.' She stared pointedly again in Sidney's direction. 'Now, it is important that we all come aboard on this.'

'Mrs Savage –' began David rising to his feet.

'Well, we will see how it goes, Mrs Savage,' interrupted Harold with the unruffled gentleness of the peacemaker. Then, without conviction, he added, 'It sounds very reasonable to me.'

'No, Harold!' cried David. 'It does not sound at all reasonable. I have better things to do than complete a lot of silly forms. I do not wish to "get up to speed", to be frank, nor to "come aboard". I am quite content working at my own steady pace. I am not on a running track nor in a racing car. I well recall some of Mrs Savage's other hair-brained ideas and wonderful initiatives, such as wearing those idiotic luminous identity badges, putting ridiculously complicated codes on the photocopier or making us park in remote areas of the County Hall miles away from this office. All abandoned, as I recall. I have no intention whatsoever of spending my time on forecasts or filling in amendment sheets whether they be blue, green, red or psychedelic pink! I have more bumf on my desk than a Belgian bureaucrat. Now, if you will excuse me, I have a school to visit because that is what I do for a job – inspect schools and *not* sit around pushing coloured paper backwards and forwards!' With that David snatched up his briefcase and departed.

'And much as I would like to debate the efficacy of your forms, Mrs Savage,' Sidney told her, maintaining his carefully blank expression, and heading for the door at the same time, 'I too have an appointment at nine o'clock in the far distant Dales.'

Mrs Savage looked like a startled ostrich. 'Well . . .' was

all she could muster to say in a strangled sort of voice.

'I will have a word with them, Mrs Savage,' Harold told her gently, 'and, as I said, we will see how it goes. I feel certain –'

'I have to say I find your two colleagues very offhand, Dr Yeats,' said Mrs Savage, regaining some composure and readjusting the chiffon. 'I am only endeavouring to make the system more efficient, that's all. I do have a job to do and it makes it exceedingly difficult if the people who –'

'I'm sure you are only doing what you feel is for the best,' reassured Harold, showing his set of tombstone teeth.

'And I shall be mentioning their opposition to Dr Gore.' She looked in my direction. 'Have you anything to say, Mr Phinn?' she asked curtly.

'Well, now you ask, Mrs Savage, I really do think that we have quite enough paper arriving on our desks. The present system seems to me to work well and –'

'I am sure there will be no problems,' interposed Harold, rubbing his large hands together. 'It shouldn't take all that long to complete your forecasts. Julie can check through my colleagues' desk diaries, fill in the details and bring the forms over later today or tomorrow.'

'Where is your secretary, by the way, Dr Yeats?' asked Mrs Savage suddenly.

'I asked her to take our new colleague over to the main building and show her where everything is – post room, resources area, library, that sort of thing.'

'I see.'

There was a clattering of shoes on the stairs and a few moments later Julie arrived accompanied by the new science inspector who had arrived that morning.

'Ah, I see you have arrived,' said Mrs Savage, ignoring Julie and addressing herself directly to Gerry Mullarkey. She did not wait for any response. 'I was expecting you this afternoon, but since you are here, I'll explain a few things if you would like to accompany me over to my office.'

Gerry smiled an easy smile. 'And who are you?' she enquired.

'I am Mrs Savage, Dr Gore's personal assistant,' she responded tartly.

'I'm pleased to meet you, Mrs Savage,' said Gerry in a quite charming voice.

'What is your shorthand like?' asked Mrs Savage.

'Non-existent.'

'Your typing speed?'

'About a word a minute, I should think.'

'Well, this does not sound at all encouraging. Can you use a dictaphone?'

'No.'

'Have you any qualifications at all?'

'Well, I have a degree in physics, a masters degree in microbiology, a Ph.D., and I'm a Fellow of the Royal Institute of Chemists.'

'Oh!' exclaimed Mrs Savage. 'I thought you were the temporary clerical assistant, from the agency in Fettlesham.'

'No, no,' interposed Harold, 'this is Dr Mullarkey, the new science inspector, who has just started. I believe you were on one of your courses at the time of the interviews.'

'Oh, I see. Someone might have said something earlier, Dr Yeats. I assumed that Dr Mullarkey was a man.'

'Most people do,' replied Gerry.

Mrs Savage looked, for once, distinctly uncomfortable and I could not wait to recount the episode to Sidney and David.

'Well, perhaps when you have a moment, Dr Mullarkey,' said Mrs Savage, 'you could call up and see me in my office. It's in the Annexe to the rear of County Hall. Well, I have work to do,' she told us with stiff finality, as though we were wilfully detaining her, and with that she swept in the direction of the stairs. She reappeared a second later. 'And

I would appreciate those forms, Dr Yeats, as soon as possible.'

'She is the most objectionable, unpleasant, ill-mannered, sour-faced old trout I have ever met!' exclaimed Julie when Mrs Savage had finally made her grand exit. 'Swanning about in that ridiculous coloured tent of a dress like Florence of Arabia, treating everybody like yesterday's left-overs. Never said one word to me. Did you notice that? Not a word. And did you see the hair? She looks like she's been frightened by a firework. And as for that plastic surgery she's had, it didn't work, I can tell you that. When you get close up, the skin that's been stretched right back off her face is tucked under her chin like a gerbil's pouch. I reckon the surgeon must have been left-handed.'

'Julie,' I said, 'don't hold back. Tell us what you really think about Mrs Savage.' Laughter returned to the office.

'You never told me she was beautiful.'

Christine and I were walking down the drive to Castlesnelling High School on a warm Friday evening on our way to the final performance of the staff and students' production of the musical *Oliver!*. Christine looked stunning. Her hair shone golden, her blue eyes sparkled like ice in the moonlight and the light-coloured, close-fitting coat showed off perfectly her slim figure. She looked like a movie star. I felt so proud to be with her.

'I didn't think it was important,' I replied casually.

'You just said she was very clever, you never mentioned that she had looks as well as brains.' Our conversation had got around to Dr Gerry Mullarkey, who had visited Winnery Nook School that day. 'She was certainly singing your praises. She said how helpful you had been.'

'Really?' I replied in a non-committal tone of voice.

'Taken her around schools, introduced her to all the important people, helped her settle in, even shown her some of the wonderful scenery. You must have seen quite a lot of her.'

'Well, it's the least I can do. After all, she is a new colleague and everyone was really friendly when *I* started.' By this time we had arrived at the entrance and a good opportunity for me, I thought, to change the subject. 'I hope this production is going to be all right,' I said, opening the door for Christine. 'The last play I saw here was awful.'

'Is she married?'

'Who?'

'Geraldine Mullarkey.'

'No, she's not married.' I tried again to change the subject. 'It was a gruesome production of *Hamlet* they did here last year. The stage at the end looked like a scene from the First World War, full of people wounded and bleeding and dying and dead –'

'And is she coming tonight?' she asked, walking ahead of me.

'Christine, will you stop going on about Gerry. No, of course she isn't coming tonight. She's the science inspector. What would she be doing at a school play? If I didn't know you better I'd say you were jealous.'

'Well, she *is* very attractive.'

'So you keep telling me.'

'And you've been spending a great deal of time with her. She said you had been particularly helpful by attending a difficult meeting with her a week ago. Was that when you cancelled our night out at the theatre?'

'Yes, it was, as a matter of fact.'

'Mmmm.'

'What's "Mmmm" supposed to mean? Christine, there is nothing going on between me and Gerry Mullarkey. She's just a colleague.'

'But a *very* attractive colleague with whom you have been out quite a few times now.'

'I've not been going out with her, as you put it. Ours is a purely professional relationship.'

'Has she got a boyfriend?'

'No, I don't think she has.'

'Mmmm.'

'There you go again.'

We found our seats, smack in the centre of the front row and Christine continued the conversation.

'You seem to be surrounded by good-looking women.'

'Christine, most of my time is spent with small children,

spotty adolescents, ageing women teachers, married men, crusty county councillors and nuns. I don't know where you get this idea that I spend my whole day with the contestants for Miss World. You make me sound like some sort of Casanova. And, as for the Education Office, it's like a men's club. There's hardly a woman in sight.'

'There's your secretary.'

'She's not much more than a teenager and she's engaged.'

'There's that very attractive woman with the expensive clothes.'

'Which very attractive woman with the expensive clothes?'

'She was with Dr Gore earlier this week when he came to speak to the infant school headteachers. She was wearing this incredible silk sari affair with masses of silver jewellery.'

'You mean Mrs Savage!' I exclaimed.

'*She's* very unusual and striking.'

'Christine, the limestone caverns beneath Malham Tarn are very unusual and striking, Pen-y-ghent in winter is very unusual and striking, Hopton Crags are very unusual and striking, but I don't want to spend all my time down a cave, up a mountain, or hanging off a cliff. Mrs Savage would be the last woman on earth I would have any designs on. I'd sooner play postman's knock with the bride of Frankenstein. Mrs Savage is the most disagreeable person I have ever met. And,' I added hotly, 'she's *old*.'

'Mmmm,' hummed Christine, smiling, 'I do seem to have touched a raw nerve.'

I had been hoping for a pleasant, stress-free evening and a chance to forget about the hectic couple of weeks I'd just had, but things were not turning out like that.

Following my visit to Ugglemattersby County Junior School, I had taken great care over my written critical report and then shown it to Harold. He had sighed, shaken his head and told me to take a copy over to Dr Gore, who he felt needed to see it. I had arrived at the CEO's office first thing the next morning, despite knowing full well that there would be very little possibility of getting a direct audience with the great man himself. Mrs Savage, no doubt, would be keeping vigil. Sure enough, she had spotted me creeping down the top corridor, had shot out of her room like a keen-eyed guard dog and had impeded my progress, insisting that Dr Gore was very busy. I had then been asked to complete one of her wretched pieces of paper – Form SIN 1: Schools in Need – and I had spent a tedious ten minutes ticking a series of little boxes, while she hovered over me like a malign presence.

Later that day I had been called to the telephone and informed by Mrs Savage that the CEO, having read my report, was very concerned about the obvious weaknesses at Ugglemattersby School and a full inspection was to be organised and that I should get on with it.

I emerged from my reverie about the tiresome day when the man who had just come to sit on the next seat engaged me in conversation. 'Good evening, Mr Phinn.'

I turned to face the florid countenance and great walrus moustache of Lord Marrick.

'Oh, good evening, Lord Marrick,' I replied.

'I'm a governor here, you know,' he said, explaining his presence at the school play. 'Like to show the flag, support the school and all that. Actually, I'm glad I've bumped into you. Just this week sent a letter off to Dr Gore thanking you and your colleagues for all the help with the Feoffees Pageant. Went off really well.'

'Yes, it seemed to be a great success,' I said.

'Cracking day!' he exclaimed.

I put my arm around Christine's shoulders and nudged her forward. 'Lord Marrick, may I introduce you to Christine Bentley, Headteacher of Winnery Nook Infant and Nursery School?'

Lord Marrick leaned across me, took Christine's hand in his, patted it gently and smiled warmly. 'Very pleased to meet you, Miss Bentley.'

At this point we both caught sight of a large figure ambling towards the front of the hall. I recognised the thick neck, vast red face, purple pitted nose and mop of unnaturally shiny, jet black hair. It was Councillor Peterson.

'Good God!' exclaimed Lord Marrick, turning towards me. 'I hope George Peterson isn't going to inflict himself on us. I've never met a man who can talk like him. Case of verbal diarrhoea. Pain in the proverbials, he is.' The councillor spotted us, waved and headed in our direction. 'He's seen us! He's coming over. Brace yourself, Mr Phinn.'

Just at that moment the lights began to fade, the orchestra stopped tuning up and the conductor, a dapper little man in a dinner jacket, made his entrance. Councillor Peterson thought better of coming over to us and found a seat further along the row. Both Lord Marrick and I sighed with relief.

'Have you met Councillor Peterson?' Lord Marrick whispered.

'Yes,' I replied, 'I've met him.'

I had seen umpteen school productions of *Oliver!* but this was the first where live animals formed part of the cast. I had advised the Head of Drama, when he telephoned me before Easter to invite me to the performance, that it was extremely risky to have animals on stage. Children were unpredictable enough, but animals! He told me that the cat and dog he planned to use were very well trained and that he wanted this production to be as authentic, different and memorable as possible. He ignored my advice.

All went well in the first half of the show. In Act I, Widow Corney's cat behaved impeccably, purring and mewing at just the right moments to the delight of the audience. When Mr Bumble stroked its head, it meowed and yawned widely as if it had rehearsed this very movement;

it received a well-deserved flutter of applause. The fat, bow-legged bull terrier, Bullseye, pulled on to the stage by the fearsome-looking Head of the PE Department playing the part of the villain, Bill Sikes, also behaved remarkably well. It sat obediently when commanded, growling on cue and even snarling when Fagin appeared. It was a vicious-looking creature with a body like a small white barrel and when it yawned it displayed a set of serrated teeth of frightening proportions. The Head of PE really took on the part of the bullying thief with a vengeance. He was a huge, hairy, swarthy complexioned individual with a great booming voice and a twisted sneer. He roared and threat-ened, banging his cudgel so hard on tables, chairs and anything in his path that the very stage set shook. The children in Fagin's gang looked genuinely terrified of him.

It happened in the very last act. Nancy (the Head of the Food Technology Department) had just finished a rousing rendering of 'As Long As He Needs Me'. She had put her heart and soul into the singing because it was the last night and all her family and friends occupied a large block of seats in the middle of the hall. They had shown loud appreciation every time she had made an appearance on stage. It was the *dénouement* of the drama. Nancy had brought Oliver to the meeting place on London Bridge to return him to his family but she had been followed by Bill Sikes. He entered a darkened stage dragging the fat, snarling brute behind him. The stumpy little tail was tucked down (not a good sign, I learned later), the barrel body was quivering and the small, grey, shark eyes looked distinctly sinister.

'What you doin' on London Bridge at this time o' night, Nancy, my gel?' growled Bill Sikes. The dog made a deep, low, rumbling sound.

'Bill!' cried the Head of the Food Technology Depart-ment in a plaintive voice. 'Why do you look at me like that?'

The Head of PE glowered, curled his top lip, shook his cudgel menacingly and moved towards his victim. The dog snarled, as if on cue. 'It's dark 'ere under the arches, aint it, Nancy, my gel, but there's light enough for wot I got to do.'

'Whadaya mean, Bill?'

'You've opened them pretty red lips of yours, Nancy, once too often but you'll not be opening 'em again . . . hever.' He then gave a great tug on the piece of rope attached to the dog. Bullseye had planted his bow legs firmly on the boards, however, and did not move an inch.

'Come on, Bullseye!' commanded the Head of PE in a voice as rough as gravel and gave the rope another great tug. The dog lifted its fat, round head slightly and fixed him with its cold button eyes. Then it shot like a cannonball straight for him, snarling and slavering.

'Bloody hell!' shrieked the Head of PE and, dropping his cudgel, shot off stage right, leaving the dog centre stage and Nancy frozen at the other side. The animal eyed her viciously and began to move slowly in her direction. The conductor, with great presence of mind, took charge of the situation and, tapping his baton on his music stand, led the orchestra into a reprise of 'As Long As He Needs Me'. The Head of the Food Technology Department, in a frightened little voice, quavered the song to a hushed audience. The dog ambled across the stage, surveyed her for a moment, growled and then displayed his magnificent set of teeth.

There was a voice offstage. 'Here, Daisy, here, girl! Daisy, come on, Daisy, here, girl!' The dog remained rooted to the spot, snarling and snapping its jaws. The Head of the Food Technology Department stopped singing and, terri-fied, stared at the beast as it edged closer.

'This is no bloody good at all!' Lord Marrick said loudly, rising to his feet. He strode to the side of the stage, mounted the steps, skirted round the trembling Nancy and took hold of the dog's collar. 'Now then, Daisy!' he commanded staring down into the animal's shimmering eyes. 'Sit! Down!' The dog returned the gaze for a moment, then flopped flat to the floor. 'Come to heel!' ordered Lord Marrick. The dog scrabbled to its feet obediently and was led off stage to loud, appreciative clapping. A rather shame-faced Bill Sikes reappeared, quickly despatched Nancy by strangulation and made an embarrassed exit.

'Well, that were a rum do,' observed Councillor Peterson, scratching his head as we headed for the exit at the end of the performance.

'They just need to know who's the master,' said Lord Marrick, looking pretty pleased with himself.

Following the play, Christine and I went out to dinner in Fettlesham. By the time we reached the restaurant we were both in high spirits. Re-living the play's unusual climax, we laughed until we cried. Over coffee, I looked across the table at her. She looked so beautiful. Perhaps this was the moment to tell her that I had fallen for her in a big way.

'Gervase,' she said suddenly, 'there's something I feel I have to tell you.'

'Oh,' I said. This sounded horribly ominous.

'Well, it's rather embarrassing, but I really do have to tell you.'

'What?' My heart sank. She was going to tell me she did not want to see me again, that she was not prepared to share me with Gerry, that she'd heard about office affairs, that there were other fish in the sea, that she had met someone else. 'What?' I asked again. 'What is it?'

'Well,' she paused and glanced away from my piercing gaze. It looked to me as if there was a slight smile on her lips. 'It's really very difficult but someone has to tell you.'

'Tell me, tell me,' I insisted.

'Now it's not something you should feel at all ashamed about.'

'For goodness sake, Christine, put me out of my misery.'

'It is quite embarrassing but –'

'Christine! *Will you tell me?*'

'You have some little lodgers.'

'Lodgers?' I was utterly perplexed.

'In your hair.'

'In my hair?'

'Please stop repeating me,' she said. 'It's difficult enough as it is.' She took a deep breath before whispering, 'You've got nits.'

'Nits!' I cried. Several heads turned in our direction.

'You've been, um, scratching all night. It's quite common for those who work with children to get head lice. You've probably been in a school where a child has them. I see lots of cases. Now, tomorrow you must go straight to the chemist and get some medicated shampoo and a very thin metal comb.'

'Yes, miss,' I said quietly. 'Is there anything else you wish to tell me?'

'Well, I think you're free of scabies,' she replied laughing.

'Will you still go out with me?'

'When you have got rid of the little lodgers,' she said smiling warmly.

I was outside the chemist's bright and early the next morning. While I waited for the shop to open, I considered where I might have picked up the nasty nits. It could not have been from my first visit to Ugglemattersby School because that had been over a month before. However, I had recently paid the school a second visit and now remembered that the self-same Mandy Wilmott had been scratching away at her wild and woolly hair when I had sat in on her class to see if any improvements had been made.

A young woman in a bright white nylon overall opened the door at nine o'clock, and smiled at me as I entered. This is oh so embarrassing, I thought to myself.

'May I help you, sir?' she asked brightly.

'Yes, I'd like . . . something . . . for . . . for . . .'

She detected my embarrassment. 'Something for the weekend?'

'No, no!' I exclaimed. 'I'd like . . . er . . .'

'Would you prefer a male assistant to help you, sir?'

'Pardon?'

'Is the item you wish to purchase of a personal and intimate nature? Would you prefer the manager to serve you?' She smiled knowingly.

'Oh, well yes, it is of a personal nature. I want something for lice.'

'Is that for head lice?' she asked.

'Oh yes, definitely head lice.'

'Right,' she said and dipped down behind the counter. 'There's this very good shampoo and you need a fine metal comb as well. Is it for your little girl? Long hair often proves very attractive.' I nodded. 'Poor thing. You need to put plenty of conditioner on her hair and comb it thoroughly when it's wet. Nits can't stick to hair with conditioner on.'

'I see.'

'Is there anything else?'

'No, no, that's all,' I said, paying for the items before beating a hasty retreat.

Most of the weekend was spent washing and showering and scrubbing and combing and by Monday my visitors had gone. I arrived at the office to find my colleagues in very high spirits.

'I could hear the noise from the bottom of the stairs,' I said as I entered.

'You sound just like Mrs Savage,' Sidney told me with

tears in his eyes, and that set everybody off into paroxysms of laughter.

'Don't come in!' shouted David. 'Stay at the door.'

'Oh no, no, you can't come in yet, Gervase,' commanded Sidney.

'Whatever is going on?' I asked from the doorway.

'Oh, do tell him, Sidney!' cried David. 'Do tell him!'

'Tell me what?' I demanded.

'They couldn't have found a more deserving home,' chuckled David.

'What *are* you talking about?' I asked, getting irritated.

'For goodness sake, let him in,' said Harold.

'I think you should tell him, David, and savour the moment,' said Sidney.

There was a great gasping in-drawing of breath and then David, trying to keep a straight face, announced: 'Mrs Savage has got nits!'

'*What?*' I cried.

'She sent over one of her bits of coloured paper this morning,' explained Julie with smears of mascara down her cheeks.

'Known from this day on as Form NIT 1,' said David. 'And on it she says –'

'No! No, wait a minute, let me read it!' cried Sidney, plucking a pink sheet of paper from his in-tray. Then he read the memo in a mock-serious tone. '"Members of staff should note that there has been an outbreak of head lice in the Education Department at County Hall. Employees should take the necessary precautions, check their hair and scalp and, should they discover any infestation, remain off work, use the appropriate medicated hair treatment from a chemist and only return to duty when clear. Head lice, *Pedicus humanus*, are small insects and feed by sucking blood through the scalp." Julie, will you stop laughing, I'm trying to read this. "Lice find it difficult to escape wet hair when

266

combed because it is slippery and they can't get a grip so —" '
By now everyone was bent double in paroxysms of laughter.
'Oh, I give up!' roared Sidney.

'Julie phoned Mavis on the main switchboard,' spluttered
David, 'and found out that Mrs Savage has been infested
along with most of the top corridor. Everyone reckons she's
the carrier. She was seen scratching her way into the CEO's
room first thing this morning. Evidently Dr Gore has now
banished her until she's got rid of them.'

'I do think you are all being a little unkind to Mrs Savage,'
said Harold, attempting to suppress his laughter. 'I'm sure
that she is not as bad as she is painted. She can be quite
charming and it can't be nice to have lice.'

'I must remember that little phrase the next time she
comes over here with her silly bits of paper,' said David. 'It
can't be nice to have lice.'

'And before you can enter here, dear boy,' said Sidney
to me, holding up his hand like a crossing patrol warden,
'you have to be thoroughly checked. We have our own
resident expert on insects, minibeasts, parasites and wildlife.
I give you Dr Geraldine Mullarkey.'

Gerry jumped up from her desk, directed me to a chair,
tilted back my head and peered at my scalp. She moved a
few strands of hair with her long fingers. 'All clear,' she
announced. 'Cleanest hair I've seen in months.'

'Ah, Gervase,' sighed Sidney, leaning back in his chair
and putting his hands behind his head. 'What a way to start
the week — to have a beautiful young woman run her soft
fingers through your hair. It's worth having nits for.'

I turned very very red — and prayed that my colleagues
would think the blush emanated from being so close to the
enchanting Dr Mullarkey rather than for the real reason.
As I fiddled with some papers on my desk, I recalled that
in the middle of the previous week I had been across to the
Annexe to discuss my second visit to Ugglemattersby with

Dr Gore and that I had had to wait for some time in Mrs Savage's office until he could see me. I now had a very nasty suspicion that I had been the original carrier of the little lodgers to the top floor.

There was a sharp rap on the glass. A large, round, red-faced policeman peered into the car and gestured for me to wind down the window.

'May I help you, officer?' I asked.

'Yes, sir, I think you can,' was the reply. 'What exactly are you doing?'

'Pardon?' I was quite taken aback by the sharpness of his manner.

'I asked you what exactly are you doing?'

'Nothing,' I replied. Help! Was my tax disc out of date or were my tyres worn down to an illegal state? 'Is there something wrong?'

'We have had a number of calls from several concerned residents in this vicinity, and from a teacher reporting a suspicious-looking character parked outside the school and watching the children as they enter. And, furthermore,' he emphasised the words, 'making notes in a black book.'

'Oh, I see.' I sighed with relief. 'I can explain.'

'I hope you can, sir. Would you mind stepping out of the car?'

'Yes, yes, of course.'

'I have been observing you for the last five minutes and your behaviour does give rise to a number of questions.' He took out his notebook and flicked it open. 'Now, sir . . .'

'I'm a school inspector,' I explained.

'I see,' he said, looking decidedly unconvinced. 'School inspector.' He wrote it down. 'And you have some means of identification, do you, sir?'

'Of course,' I replied, reaching for my wallet and producing my County Hall identity card which was promptly plucked from my hand. He then carefully scrutinized the photograph, looked earnestly at me, copied down the details and snapped the book shut.

'Is everything in order, officer?' I asked.

'It appears to be, sir, but if I may say so, it is unwise to sit outside a school watching the children go in and out. It does lend itself to speculation. Much better to go in and make your presence known to the Headteacher.'

'Yes, officer, quite right,' I answered sheepishly. 'It won't happen again. It's just that I arrived rather early for my appointment. I shall, of course, take your advice in future. It just never occurred to me.' The policeman nodded seriously but made no effort to move. 'So, if that's all –?'

'I'll accompany you on to the premises, sir, if I may.'

So I was escorted across the road, down the school path and to the entrance of Tupton Road Primary School, watched with interest by assorted children, a gaggle of whispering parents and a large, solemn-faced crossing patrol warden who held her STOP! CHILDREN CROSSING! sign like some Wagnerian operatic heroine wielding a spear.

I was greeted at the door of the school by a lean middle-aged woman with a pale, indrawn face. Behind her stood her small, nervous-looking companion who clutched an umbrella like a defensive weapon. The taller of the two had large dark eyes which looked even darker nestling as they were in heavy black make-up. The pale face and black eyes gave her the appearance of a racoon.

'Is there something wrong, officer?' she exclaimed.

'Are you the Headteacher?' asked the policeman.

'Yes, I am,' she replied in an anxious voice. 'Mrs Daphne Wilson. Has there been an accident?'

The policeman ignored the question. 'Do you know this gentleman, madam?'

'Never seen him before in my life,' she said, staring intently at me.

'He was the man in the car outside the school, Mrs Wilson. The one I telephoned the police about,' added the small woman with the umbrella.

'Oh, was he?' said the Headteacher.

My heart sank. The school secretary emerged from her office and scrutinized me as if trying to put a name to a familiar face. A moment later the caretaker appeared from the school hall, armed with a sweeping brush, and glared at me as if I had walked across his wet floor. 'I'm Gervase Phinn!' I announced to the knot of observers. 'The school inspector.' My audience continued to gape. 'From the Education Office in Fettlesham. I have an appointment.'

'Oh yes, of course,' said the Headteacher, reddening with embarrassment. She turned to the policeman, who was flicking open his notebook again, and said, 'It's quite all right, officer. I *am* expecting an inspector, but I never imagined that he would come with a police escort.'

The secretary and the caretaker disappeared and the policeman, having satisfied himself of my identity, departed, pausing at the gates of the school to reassure the group of anxious onlookers.

'Mr Phinn,' said Mrs Wilson holding out her hand and smiling to cover her discomfiture, 'I'm pleased to meet you.'

'I am terribly sorry, Mrs Wilson . . .' I began and then attempted to explain that I always gave myself plenty of time to find the schools I visited and that if I arrived early I sat in the car – but that this was something I would never do again.

'It's not you who should be sorry, Mr Phinn,' said the Headteacher, turning in the direction of her colleague and glowering. 'I do wish you had consulted me, Marion, before telephoning the police. This is a very unfortunate start to the day. I cannot begin to imagine what Mr Phinn must be thinking.'

'Well, I'm sorry, Mrs Wilson, I'm sure,' the second woman replied, clearly stung by the rebuke, 'but I thought he might be a child molester. One has to be very vigilant these days.'

'This is Mrs Thickett,' said the Headteacher somewhat coldly. 'She's in charge of the infant class.'

'How do you do,' I said, attempting a smile.

'I mean, you can't be too careful,' said the infant teacher, twisting the ring on her finger nervously. 'Not where vulnerable little children are concerned. You read all the time in the papers about these abusers, sex offenders and child molesters. There was a terrible programme on the television last week about –'

'Mr Phinn hardly looks like a child molester, Marion,' interrupted the Headteacher sharply, still glaring at her.

'Oh, they don't all wear dirty raincoats, you know, Mrs Wilson. Some of them come in suits.'

'Well, there's no harm done.' I smiled reassuringly at Mrs Thickett. 'Mistakes do happen. Anyway, I was at fault not coming into school as soon as I arrived. Perhaps now that things have been cleared up . . .' I endeavoured to move the conversation on by beginning to explain what I wished to do during the morning visit but the little woman would not let it lie.

'You have to be so careful when it comes to the small ones. You hear all these dreadful stories of children being dragged into cars and driven off. It's a terrible world we live in, a terrible world.'

Oh dear, I thought, this does not bode well.

I eventually managed to have ten minutes alone with the Headteacher to explain the focus of my visit. I was there to monitor the teaching and learning of English and agreed to start the morning in the infant class.

Mrs Thickett's classroom was clean, orderly and decorated with bright posters and paintings. A few pieces of young children's first writing attempts were pinned alongside lists of key words, the alphabet and various arithmetical tables. Ranks of small melamine-topped tables were grouped together, each with a tray containing pencils, rulers, crayons and scissors. There was a small Reading Corner with a square of carpet, two large cushions and a bookcase full of assorted books, also a play area – the Home Corner – which had been set out as a café with a counter, plastic till, a table and a chair. The room smelt of bleach and lavender floor polish. I positioned myself at the rear of the classroom and watched as the children entered. They eyed me suspiciously as they filed past and took their seats.

When they were all settled and facing the teacher, Mrs Thickett began. 'Good morning, children,' she said jovially.

'Good morning, Mrs Thickett, good morning, everyone,' the children chorused.

'This morning, children, we have a special visitor.'

'It's the man in the car,' chirped up a cheeky-faced youngster swivelling round to get a better look at me. 'My mum phoned the bobbies about him.' Oh dear, oh dear! I thought, this little incident is not going to go away. All eyes were now trained on me. I smiled wearily.

'That was because your mother thought that Mr Phinn was a bad man, Shane,' said the teacher in a simpering voice. 'But Mr Phinn is not a bad man. He's a nice man.' I winced.

'Why did my mum phone the bobbies then, miss?' persisted the child, glancing again in my direction.

'Because she thought that Mr Phinn was somebody else.'

'A kidnapper, miss?'

'No, not a kidnapper.'

'A murderer?' The child's voice rose in excitement.

'Don't be silly, Shane. She thought Mr Phinn was a stranger and just to be on the safe side telephoned the police.

Remember that parents and teachers tell you not to talk to strangers so you all have to be very careful. But Mr Phinn is not a stranger because I know him.'

'But I don't know him, miss,' said the child.

'Well, you soon will,' replied the teacher, with a sharper ring to her voice. 'Now, let's hear no more about it. Mr Phinn's a school inspector, here this morning to see how well you are doing and to look at all the lovely work you do. So, don't be afraid to speak to him and answer his questions. He's very friendly.' I didn't feel at all friendly.

'My mummy says I haven't to speak to strangers,' announced a frightened-looking little girl at the front desk.

'Mr Phinn is not a stranger, Melanie,' Mrs Thickett said slowly and deliberately. 'I know him, Mrs Wilson knows him and I say it is all right to talk to him.'

Following the morning's unfortunate episode, I rather expected a quiet, nervous group of young children when I started my tour around the classroom but the contrary was true. During the course of the morning, I moved from desk to desk speaking to the children about their stories, examining their work and listening to them read. I found them lively and interested and full of questions. Things seemed to be taking a turn for the better.

In the Home Corner, set out as Fred's Café, I met a stocky, six-year-old boy dressed in a large blue apron. He was playing the part of Fred, the proprietor. All around him were notices and signs: NO DOGS ALLOWED, SPECIAL OF THE WEEK, COD 'N' CHIPS, NO SMOKING! WAITER SERVICE. I seated myself at the small table and looked at a blank piece of paper at the top of which was written in bold lettering: MENU. The little boy sidled up and stared at me intently. I looked up.

'What's it to be?' he asked.

'Oh,' I said, taking on the role of a customer, 'I think I'll just have something to drink.'

'Anything to eat?'

'No, I don't think so.'

'So you just want a drink?'

'Yes, please.'

'What about some fish 'n' chips?'

'No, I'm really not that hungry.'

'Just a drink?'

'That's right.'

The boy disappeared and returned a moment later with a small, empty plastic beaker which he placed before me. Then he watched intently as I drank the imaginary liquid, licked my lips and exclaimed, 'That was the nicest cup of tea I have had in a long while.'

'It's an 'arf o' bitter,' he told me bluntly and walked off.

On my tours of schools, I have visited many Home Corners: doctors' surgeries, opticians, banks, fish and chip shops, Victorian schoolrooms, dentists, florists, libraries, garages, corner shops, travel agents, clothes shops, strange planets and secret caves – a whole range of imaginary places where the small children enter make-believe worlds and where their language is often at its richest and most creative. I have seen infant children taking on a whole host of roles, imitating mothers and fathers, brothers and sisters, teachers and other adults with whom they come in contact.

On one occasion I visited a Home Corner set out as an estate agents. Rachel, the six-year-old receptionist, was sitting behind a desk on which had been arranged pens, pencils, a tape measure, a calculator, a plastic telephone and a toy cash dispenser. She had a name card bearing the name 'Miss R. Prentice' pinned to her dress and a pair of large spectacle frames on the tip of her nose. On a small table a range of brochures had been arranged, some made by the pupils themselves.

'Good morning,' she said cheerfully when I entered. 'May I help you?'

'I'm looking for a house,' I said, 'a big one.'

She pointed to the small table. 'There are lots to choose from,' she said confidently. 'Have a browse.'

'I like the look of this house,' I said, pointing to a photograph of the largest and the most expensive.

The girl shook her head. 'Sold,' she replied, 'subject to contract.'

'What about this one?' I said, picking up a photograph of another large residence. It had turrets and big bay windows, a great sweeping drive and tall iron gates.

She leaned forward and in a confidential voice informed me that 'Big houses cost a lot of money, you know. Why don't you buy a little one?' She thrust a picture of a small red-bricked terraced house into my hand. She clearly thought that big houses were way out of my league. 'This one should do you.'

I recall the time during my first year as an inspector when I had found a Home Corner set out as a baby clinic and a small girl clutching a large doll to her chest. She had been surrounded by scales, towels, feeding bottles, a plastic bath and a toy cot.

As I approached she had looked up alarmed. 'Go away!' she had cried. 'I'm breast feeding!'

The most memorable and dramatic incident in a Home Corner had taken place in a large infant school in the town of Crompton. It had been set out as a little post office and there were two small girls, clutching shopping bags, waiting to be served by a small pixie-like boy with enormous glasses that made his eyes look larger than ever. Suddenly a bruiser of a little boy had burst in brandishing a large plastic gun.

'This is a stick up!' he had shouted. 'Get them 'ands up in the air and let's be 'aving yer cash!'

The two little girls had looked unperturbed and had readily obliged and the child behind the counter had emptied various bits of paper, representing the takings, into the paper bag which had been held out to him. The little bank robber had snatched the papers that the two little girls had been holding and made a quick get-away.

'Isn't it terrible?' one little girl had complained, shaking her head. 'He's gone and nicked mi family allowance.'

'Ne'er mind, love,' the other child had consoled her, 'we'll call at t'Social on t'way 'ome and you can get a credit note.'

As I left Fred's Café that morning, I met another customer. It was Shane, the cheeky-faced youngster whose mum had telephoned the bobbies about me. There was a small plastic policeman's helmet on his head.

'Mornin',' he said. 'I wants a word wi' you.'

Oh dear, oh dear! I thought, and beat a coward's retreat to the staff room for coffee.

After morning break, I joined Mrs Wilson in the junior classroom and began by hearing the children read. The first child, Janine, was a strikingly pretty little black girl with long beaded hair and a bright, open smile.

'I love reading,' she announced in a matter-of-fact voice.

'Do you indeed?'

'I read all the time at home, you know.'

'Do you?'

'And Mummy reads to me and Daddy and Grampa and Grannie.'

'Really? You are a lucky girl.'

'And I get books for my birthday and at Christmas, and we go to the library every Saturday morning.'

'So you read a great deal?'

'My daddy calls me a bibliomaniac. He says it's because I'm mad about books. And I am. I love books.'

I smiled and looked into the shiny open face. 'And you probably have a lot of your own books, do you?'

'Enough to start a library. That's what my mummy says.'

'Will you read to me, then?'

'I'd love to.'

She was indeed a very good reader: clear and expressive and with all the self-assurance and high self-esteem of the achieving child who has experienced nothing but encouragement throughout her short life.

'Do you think I'm a good reader?' she asked when she had finished.

'No,' I replied, 'you're not a good reader.'

The child's sanguine expression disappeared in an instant, and she looked quite startled instead.

'You are a *brilliant* reader!' The smile returned, in triplicate. 'You are one of the very best readers I have ever heard.'

Later in the morning I came across Sam. He was a small rosy-cheeked boy with wiry blond hair, a round little biscuit barrel of a body and a doleful expression. He was not lively and interested and full of questions like Janine, and was unwilling to come with me into the Reading Corner with his book.

'I can't go on t'carpet,' he announced flatly.

'You can,' I replied.

'No, I can't. I can't go on that carpet.'

'Did Mrs Wilson say you couldn't go on the carpet?'

'No, but I'm not goin' on!'

'Why?'

'Because I'm not!'

'Is there some reason why you can't go on the carpet?' I persisted.

'Aye, there is.'

'Well, why can't you go on the carpet?'

'Because I've got shit on mi shoe.'

'Oh no!' I exclaimed dramatically. 'You must not say that word.'

278

The child maintained his carefully blank expression. 'What word?' he asked casually.

'That first word.'

'Why?'

'Because it's not a very nice word for a little boy to use.'

'Why?'

'Well, it's just not a nice word to use, that's all.'

'Well, what word should I use then?'

'Just say you've got dirt on your shoe.'

'But it's not dirt, is it? It's shit.'

Oh dear, I thought for the umpteenth time that day, another fine mess I have got myself into.

Mrs Wilson, who had obviously been privy to this exchange, suddenly appeared at my side and whispered in my ear, 'Perhaps he could say "excrement on his sole" or "faeces on his feet" or "poo on his shoe". I feel certain it will be somewhere in that inspectors' handbook of yours, Mr Phinn.' There was a hint of sarcasm in her voice.

I decided to persevere and turned back to Sam. 'What does your mum say if you have it on your shoe?'

'Have what on mi shoe?'

'You know what.' I pointed to his feet.

'She makes me tek mi shoes off.'

'Well, take them off, Sam, get your reading book and come into the Reading Corner with me.'

When I had finally prevailed upon him to come on the carpet, he stood close to me with an expressionless face. 'Yes?' he asked.

'Would you like to read to me?'

'Not particularly.'

'Well, I would really like you to.'

Sam took a blustering breath. 'No, I don't think so. I've bin heard reading already today by Mrs Wilson and I'm not in t'mood for another session at t'moment. Mebbe later on.'

With that he walked away, retrieved his shoes, examined the soles critically and returned to his desk.

Just before lunch Sam arrived with a rather dog-eared reading book with a grey cover. It was called *Dan and Nan have Fun*.

'I'll read to you now if you want,' he announced. 'But I'm not reight good. I'm a slow reader tha knaws and I'm still on the Reading Scheme books. Most others in t'class are free readers. I don't know why, but I just don't seem to tek to reading.'

'Don't worry about that, Sam,' I said, pleased to see him, 'just try your best.'

'I'll come on t'carpet an all, cos I've seen to mi shoes.'

'Right,' I said.

'Mrs Wilson let me scrape off all the sh –'

I jumped in as quick as a sudden crack of a whip. 'That's all right, then.'

His book was one in a series called the Funtime Reading Scheme. Judging by the cover, it did not appear to justify its title. There were other books in the series about pirates and princesses, gypsies and wizards, fairs and picnics, holidays and festivals. Perhaps the dreary cover of *Dan and Nan have Fun* belied a fast-moving story of adventure and excitement, but I strongly doubted it. When Sam, screwing up his eyes and furrowing his brow, started to bark out the words, I realised that the grey cover reflected the contents accurately. He read the text with steady determination, quickly flicking through the pages without pausing to look at the pictures in an effort to get it over with.

> Here is Dan.
> Dan is a boy.
> Here is Nan.
> Nan is a girl.
> Dan is a boy.

Nan is a girl.
Dan is Nan's brother.
Nan is Dan's sister.
They have fun.
Here is a house.
Dan and Nan live in the house.
They live near a river.
They have fun.
Dan has a canoe.
Dan and Nan go in the canoe.
They go on the river.
Dan paddles the canoe.
They have fun.
Nan sings a song.
Dan catches a fish.
Dan chops some wood.
Dan lights a fire.
Nan cooks the fish.
They eat the fish.
They have fun.

The pictures depicted a sparklingly clean little boy dressed in his school blazer and cap. He wore a spotless white shirt, neatly knotted tie, highly polished shoes and knee-length socks – rather inappropriate attire for a fishing trip in a canoe, one would have thought. He was beaming from the page. Nan, too, was gleaming, dressed in a colourful floral frock, bright blue shoes, dazzling white stockings and she was sporting great red ribbons in her long blonde plaits. She, like her brother, looked ecstatically happy.

'You read that very well, Sam,' I said when he had finished.

'Aye, I try,' he replied philosophically.

'Yes. You do try very hard,' I said, but thinking to myself what a pity that the material was so dry and dreary.

'What do you think of the story?' I asked.

'Bloody stupid!' I was just about to repeat the earlier exchange of 'Don't say *that* word' but thought better of it. The book *was* 'bloody stupid'. He could not have described it better. He shook his head before continuing. 'I mean going in a canoe on a fast-flowing river is asking for trouble. And you'd never catch a carp in them waters wi that rod. He wunt catch a cold wi' that. And as for chopping wood up with that gret axe. He could have taken his fingers off. I wouldn't let 'im loose wi penknife never mind a ruddy gret 'atchet. And another thing, tha should never light fires near a forest. They wants to get some work done them two instead of prattin' abaat all day havin' fun. I have to collect eggs on our farm, feed sows, fill troughs and coop up hens afore mi tea.' He paused and looked around him and sniffed the air. 'Can tha smell owt, Mester Phinn?' he asked.

'No,' I replied.

'I can. I reckons I didn't do such a good job on mi shoe.' With that he walked away.

As I drove back to the office in Fettlesham that balmy early summer afternoon, I thought of Janine returning to a warm, loving world of books and reading and I thought of Sam who would be about to start his many chores on the farm. What a different life those children led. I determined to find that little boy some books simple enough for him to read but with lively, realistic characters and an interesting storyline. He deserved better than *Dan and Nan*.

The view from the Headteacher's room in St Catherine's School was one of the most magnificent I had ever seen. Beneath a shining blue sky stretched a landscape of every conceivable colour: light purple mountains, brilliant green pastureland, swathes of yellow and red gorse which blazed like a bonfire, dark green hedgerows speckled in pinks and whites, twisted black stumps, striding silvered limestone walls and the grey snake of a road curling up the hill to the far distance. Light, the colour of melted butter, danced amongst the new leaves of early summer.

'It's quite a picture, isn't it?' said the Headteacher. Mrs Thomas was a small, ample, quietly spoken woman with a kindly presence and a gentle manner, the sort of teacher who sees good in every child.

'It is,' I agreed. It was at times like this that I realised how fortunate I was to have a job which enabled me to see such beauty day after day. Such sights never failed to fill me with awe.

It was Monday and the start of a two-day inspection of a school for physically disabled children. David, Gerry and I were undertaking what is colloquially known amongst inspectors as a 'dip stick' inspection. I was to look at the English and the arts in the school, David the mathematics and Gerry the sciences. We had formed a very favourable impression only five minutes after we had entered the building. We had arrived at the main entrance to be greeted by large lettering: WELCOME TO ST CATHERINE'S SCHOOL above the door. A welcoming party of four smart, smiling children signed us in and gave us badges. The building was immaculate: clean, bright walls, carpeted floors, displays of work well mounted. There was an atmosphere of calm about the school, a tranquillity which I had come across several times before in schools for the physically and mentally disabled.

'You know, I can smell a good school,' observed David as we headed for Mrs Thomas's office. 'The minute I walk through the door I can sense, in the very atmosphere and environment, whether it is a good or a bad school. I have a very positive feeling about this place.'

Not long after, with clipboard in hand, I made my way to the first lesson: drama. The teacher, Ms Pinkney, a strapping, jolly woman with long red hair gathered up in a tortoiseshell comb, and dressed in a bright pink and yellow Lycra outfit which clung to her as if she had been poured into it, greeted me cheerfully and confidently.

'Come along in, Mr Phinn. Shoes by the door, jacket on a peg. There's a spare leotard if you want to slip into it.' She beamed. 'Only joking about the leotard, but you do need to get rid of the coat and shoes. I hope you inspectors have a sense of humour. You'll need it in here.' Before I could respond she rattled on regardless. 'The children will arrive in a moment. This is my star group you are about to see, full of beans and keen as sharpened knives. You're in for a real treat this morning. Quite a number of children in this class are partially sighted or blind, and three have cerebral palsy. There's a couple with Down's syndrome, an autistic child – brilliant artist he is – and a dyspraxic boy. Wonderful athlete is Phillip. None of their disabilities holds them back one jot, as you'll see. They're an extremely talented group. In my opinion, what stops children like this achieving is not lack of ability but other people's low expectations of them. Don't you think?'

'It's usually me who asks the questions, Ms Pinkney,' I

replied, 'but now you come to mention it, I couldn't agree more. I think what you say, however, applies equally well to all children, whether disabled or not. High expectation and high self-esteem seem to me to be the keys to success in learning.'

'Spot on!' she cried. 'I can see we're going to get on, Mr Phinn. In the dim and distant past,' the teacher continued, 'many disabled people lived at home cosseted and protected, away from others, and dependent on well-meaning but indulgent parents. Scant demands were made upon them, you see. Some, of course, were packed off to institutions and given mindless tasks like making lampshades or weaving baskets. Few had proper jobs and were not expected to do much with their lives. "Well, of course, he's handicapped," they used to whisper. "I mean, what can you expect of her?" That's what they used to say about me, so I know how it feels. I had polio at five, wore callipers right the way through primary school, was called "a spastic" by the other children and was wrapped up in cotton wool by my parents – and then I met this fantastic teacher, Mrs Townsend, and this brilliant physiotherapist called Miss Pierpoint and they changed my life. They built up my self-confidence and believed in me. Anyhow, my drama group is due. I can't go on philosophising all morning, Mr Phinn, just get your kit off and find a chair.'

Smiling to myself, I divested myself of shoes and jacket and headed for the corner to sit unobtrusively to observe the lesson. The first child to arrive was a small fair-haired girl. Her eyelids were closed and she was, of course, unaware of my presence in the shadows. She was one of the pupils who had been in the welcoming party when we had arrived that morning.

'Hi, Ruth!' shouted the teacher. 'You're here nice and early.'

'Miss,' asked the girl, heading in the direction of the

voice, 'will we be having one of these school inspectors in with us this morning?'

'We will indeed,' answered the teacher, putting her arm round the girl's shoulder.

'Are you sure, miss?'

'Positive, Ruth.'

'Do you know who it will be, miss?'

'His name's Mr Phinn.'

'Oh, I met *him* this morning, miss,' cried the girl. 'He's from Yorkshire so he should be all right, shouldn't he, miss?'

'I'm sure he will be just fine.' Ms Pinkney cast a sideways glance in my direction.

'What does he look like, miss?'

'All these questions, Ruth Hardcastle. Now come along, shoes off, plimsolls on and cardigan on the peg.'

'I've never met a school inspector before,' continued the girl pulling off her shoes.

'Well, now's your chance.'

'Go on, miss, tell me what he looks like. I want to put a face to his voice.'

'Well,' said the teacher drawing out the word and glancing again in my direction with a mischievous smile on her lips, 'he's young, handsome, elegant, cultivated and very well dressed.'

Ruth thought for a moment before replying, 'And he's also in the room, isn't he, miss?'

'He is indeed, Ruth,' laughed Ms Pinkney. 'He's over by the sound deck in the corner. Perhaps you would like to take him your work and show him what we were doing last week.'

At this point the rest of the children began to arrive. They changed their shoes, hung up their coats and sat in a circle in the middle of the studio. I watched Ruth as she felt her way to a large cupboard and her fingers traced the names on the top of several large folders. A minute later she was by my side.

'Hello, Mr Phinn,' she said cheerfully.

'Hello, Ruth.'

'Would you like to see my work?'

'I'd love to.'

'Because that's what school inspectors do, isn't it, you look at children's work?'

'That's right.'

'To see how they are getting on.'

'And how do you think you're getting on, Ruth?' I asked.

'I think that's for you to say really,' she replied. 'I mean, you're the inspector.'

'Well, let me see then.'

'It's a monologue. Do you know about monologues, Mr Phinn?'

'I do, yes.'

'We all had to write about our inner thoughts, what we feel. Then we performed them in front of the rest of the group. Mine's a sort of poem.' She placed the large folder in my hands, stood back and waited. The pages were full of Braille: page after page of intricate dots. As part of a diploma course I had taken several years ago, I had learnt Braille. It is a simple, uncomplicated system of six dots in two vertical lines of three and while it is relatively easy to understand, Braille is immensely difficult to read. The problem is trying to distinguish the configurations of the small dots on the page. I took Ruth's folder, rested it on my lap and proceeded, at a snail's pace, to try and decipher the writing.

'My . . . thoughts . . . about . . . being . . . blind,' I read very slowly, trying to decode the dots on the page, 'by . . . Ruth . . . Hardcastle.'

'You're not too good a reader, Mr Phinn, are you?'

'No, Ruth, I'm not. I'm a bit rusty, I'm afraid. Perhaps you could help me out.'

She took the folder from my hands, sat at my feet and read to me in such a quiet, expressive voice that I became completely enthralled and totally oblivious of noise around me, of the teacher and the rest of the pupils.

I see with my ears.
I hear the leaves in the tall trees, whispering in the night.
I hear the sea, dark and deep, and the splash of the dolphin's
    leap.
I hear the flames crackling and the window frames rattling
    in the wind.
I see with my ears.

I see with my nose.
I smell the blossoms pearly-grey and hay new mown.
I smell the ploughed earth, cows in the byre, the smoky fire.
I smell Grandpa's pipe, Gran's lavender room and Mum's
    faint perfume.
I see with my nose.

I see with my mouth.
I taste the strong black coffee and the thick brown toffee
    between my teeth.
I taste the yellow of the lemon, the green of the melon and
    the red of the tomato.
I taste the orange of the carrot, the purple of the plum, the
    gold of the sun on my face.
I see with my mouth.

I see with my hands.
I feel the sharp edges, slippery floors, smooth ledges.
I feel lemonade in cold canisters, hard wooden banisters.
I feel hands to hold, arms on shoulders, faces to touch.
I see with my hands.

'Oh, that was excellent, Ruth,' I said gently when she closed the folder. 'I think it was one of the best monologues I have ever heard.'

'Really?'

'Yes, really. You are a very talented writer.'

'I like writing,' she said. 'Would you like a copy?'

'I'd love one.'

Ms Pinkney, like some large slice of Battenberg cake, was at my side. 'Come along now, Ruth, and join the rest of the group.' When she had gone she turned to me. 'She's a lovely little poet, isn't she?'

'She is,' I replied quietly and, I have to admit, there were tears in my eyes.

The next teacher I met that morning lacked Ms Pinkney's confidence. Miss Taylor's whole body seemed to tremble when I appeared at the classroom door and there was a distinct quavering in her voice.

'Oh . . . oh . . . the inspector . . . I never . . . oh dear . . . I thought . . . do come in.'

The art room she worked in was as colourful as the landscape outside. The tables were covered carefully in clean newsprint, and brushes and pencils, chalks and crayons were neatly arranged in trays. Walls were decorated with sketches and line drawings, bold outlines and pale watery scenes, collages and abstracts. There were clay models, sculptures and lino prints. In a breathless and hurried voice she attempted to explain what the eleven-year-olds in her care were doing.

'They're . . . er . . . painting . . . using poster paints . . . trying to mix the different colours to paint a scene . . . they are experimenting with different colours and shapes and textures. Some are using brushes, others palette knives or other objects to get an effect.' She wrung her hands nervously. 'I should say, Mr Phinn, that I'm not a specialist.'

I smiled reassuringly and whispered, 'Neither am I.'

Squatting before one little artist, I watched, fascinated by the child's dexterity and concentration. He was a small boy, with dark heavy eyes and long lashes, and a disarming smile. His small twisted body was hunched over the table and his thin legs were tucked beneath the sturdy chair on which he sat. He placed a small, soft rubber ball into a bowl of crimson paint and then, with delicate fingers, he rolled the ball across the sheet of dark blue paper creating the most striking effect.

'It's a sunset,' he explained. 'Sometimes when you look at the sky, it looks as if it's on fire. It's full of reds and yellows and oranges in long streaky flames.' He immersed the ball in a bowl of orange paint and repeated the process. 'I've used different things to get the different effects, you see,' he explained. I craned forward to get a better view. The boy suddenly sneezed. The ball he was holding, which was covered in thick sticky orange paint, shot out of his hand and, like a bullet from a gun, hit me smack between the legs. It fell to the floor, leaving behind a bright golden sunburst on my trousers. A deathly silence followed.

A faint voice said, 'I'm sorry, sir, it just sort of slipped.'

The teacher arrived, fluttering a large cloth like a flag and not having the first idea what to do with it. 'Oh dear, oh my goodness, oh how unfortunate.' She stared in disbelief at the stain for a moment and thrust the cloth into my hands. Out of the corner of my eye, I saw a care assistant take a handkerchief from her handbag and stuff it in her mouth in an attempt to stifle her laughter. By the door, another care assistant turned away, wiping her eyes. Then the children, who had been remarkably quiet, began to giggle, then chuckle and finally everyone was laughing: children, teacher, assistants and me. I stood there, the centre of attention – a grey-suited figure with a great splash of gold like some magnificent codpiece.

My attempts, later in the privacy of the gents, to remove paint proved fruitless. If anything I made it worse. The bright orange had been transformed into a much larger sickly brown blotch. With the aid of my clipboard, I covered the mark and headed for the next lesson, a lower junior English class, confident that I could hide the blemish. If I remained seated at the back of the classroom with the clipboard positioned strategically on my lap there was little chance of anyone seeing the stain. At lunch-time I planned to nip into the nearby town and buy a pair of grey flannels.

I had not banked, however, on meeting Little Miss Eagle Eyes. As I entered the classroom, a small girl of about seven or eight, with Down's syndrome, must have spotted the mark on my trousers and no sooner had I positioned myself at the rear of the room out of everyone's way than she approached me. I smiled warmly at the serious face. She continued to observe me as if I were some rather strange specimen in a museum case. Then she gently lifted the clipboard and peered underneath. She looked up. Then back at the stain and then back at me. Recognition suddenly dawned and she shouted the full length of the classroom.

'Miss! Miss! This man's done a runny poo!'

Every head in the classroom turned in my direction. 'I . . . er . . . had a accident with some paint in the previous class,' I explained, making my hasty apologies to an astonished teacher and an open-mouthed class, before scurrying from the room. With clipboard clasped to my stomach, I headed quickly for the school office, intending to explain the situation to the school secretary and say I would be out of school for a short while. But Lady Luck was not with me. Halfway down the corridor I met Mrs Thomas herself, beaming madly.

'Oh, Mr Phinn, I heard what happened from Miss Taylor.' She stared at the stain. 'Oh dear, it does look rather conspicuous, doesn't it? Not to worry, it's only poster paint and will not be hard to remove. It's not uncommon for some of our children to have a little accident now and again and we have a laundry on the premises. I'm sure we can soon find you a change of clothes if you would like to follow me.'

The change of clothes consisted of a pair of white cotton trousers. They looked ridiculous worn with my grey jacket, white shirt and college tie so I put on the matching white cotton jacket, and was soon dressed in the sort of outfit worn by physiotherapists, care assistants, support staff and ancillaries. The suit was rather small and tight-fitting but I felt a great deal more at ease and, picking up my clipboard, headed for lunch in the dining-room.

The first lesson of the afternoon was a music class with the older juniors. On my way there I passed several people, all dressed in the same white attire as me. I found the music teacher hovering outside the music room, looking furtively in each direction. She had a long, pale, worried face and was twitching nervously as I approached.

'Good afternoon –' I began.

'Quick!' she snapped, pulling the sleeve of my jacket. 'Quick! Come in!' She glanced over my shoulder and then down the corridor before pushing me into an empty classroom on the other side of the corridor. She pushed the door to, and whispered in a confidential tone of voice, 'Did you see any?'

'See any?' I repeated.

'Inspectors. Did you see any school inspectors? We've got inspectors in.'

'Yes, I know, I'm –' I tried to explain but with little success.

'I'm terrified, I don't mind telling you. I've seen the old one prowling about in the mathematics block this morning. He looks as if he's been dug up.'

'Well, you see –'

'I've got the piano tuner in the music room mending two broken keys on the baby grand, a whistling window cleaner up a ladder outside, the classroom assistant off ill, a really lively group of children arriving any moment and you can bet your bottom dollar I'll have a school inspector watching points and ticking his little boxes.'

'If I might –'

'They descend on you like hungry vultures, you know. They look into everything – folders, files, desks, drawers, books, bags, storeroom, cupboards. I wouldn't put it past them to rootle through my handbag.'

'Oh no, they –'

'It's a nightmare. Then they interrogate you, ask you all sorts of questions before sitting at the back of the room scribbling away, and you never know what they write. It's all very upsetting. I've not had a wink of sleep for a month.'

'It's not that bad,' I reassured her.

'Well, how would you know?' she said sharply, but did not wait for a reply. 'You should have it done to you and you'll find out how stressful it is. Have you ever been observed?' She did not wait for an answer to that either, but rattled on regardless. 'I mean, my job is on the line here. I just know I'll get one in with me at some point today. I have a sort of premonition. I can feel it in my bones. Are you sure you didn't see anybody heading this way?'

'Well, no, I didn't, but if I might explain why I am –'

'Thank God for that! I might just be lucky.' She peered out of the door. 'Anyway, the children are arriving now.'

I followed her as she darted across the corridor into the music room where she spoke to a group of very ebullient children who were finding their places. 'Listen a moment, everyone, and that includes you, Michael Thompson.' The children stopped their chatter and faced the teacher. 'Did any of you see a stranger heading this way?'

'No, miss,' the class chorused.

'Because we might be having a school inspector with us this afternoon and I want everyone on their best behaviour.' The teacher flourished a hand in my direction. 'Here's your physio, Peter, so you can get straight off.'

A young man in a wheelchair approached me. 'Is it hydrotherapy today, sir?' he asked.

'I've no idea,' I replied.

'It's usually hydrotherapy on a Monday, sir, if the pool's available.'

'This is a new physiotherapist, Peter, and he's probably not aware of all the –'

'Actually, I'm not,' I interrupted quite forcefully. I could not let this deception continue.

'You're not? Well, who are you then?' asked the teacher. 'You need to wear your badge so if you do meet an inspector, he'll know who you are.'

I reached into my pocket for my badge and pinned it on my lapel. In bold black lettering it read: **G. R. Phinn, Inspector of Schools**.

At first the teacher did not register and then her face drained of colour. She stared at the badge as if mesmerised, before whispering, 'You never are. Oh Lord, you never are.'

'I'm afraid so.' I smiled weakly. 'I have been attempting to tell you.'

'I feel faint,' she murmured, and then added, 'I never knew inspectors came incognito.' Then, turning to the window, she gestured at the whistling window cleaner, polishing away outside. 'Is he one as well?' she asked faintly.

Once we had got over that little trauma, the lesson was fine. The children were keen and interested and demonstrated their not inconsiderable skills on various instruments. When the teacher saw the smiles and heard the easy, pleasant conversations between us, she visibly relaxed. It was towards the end of the lesson that a pale, gentle-eyed boy with long delicate hands and an ashen complexion wheeled himself towards me. Matthew, I later found out, had Muscular Dystrophy, a cruel and debilitating disease which wastes away the muscles in the body.

'Would you like me to sing?' he asked simply.

I had never been asked such a question in a classroom before. Children often offered to read to me or show me their writing or tell me about the work they were undertaking but never sing.

'I should like that very much,' I replied.

The boy sang a haunting melody in a high, clear and perfectly pitched voice. The classroom fell utterly silent. Not a child moved. The window cleaner stopped his whistling and froze on his ladder, the piano tuner – who had stayed behind to hear the lesson – had an expression of utter astonishment and I felt tears beginning to well up in my eyes for the second time that day.

When he had finished, the teacher sighed loudly. 'Oh Matthew,' she said, putting an arm around his shoulder, 'that song always makes me cry.'

A shy smile came to the boy's lips, the smile of one who has unexpectedly scored the winning goal, who has finally reached a summit. It was a smile of pure success.

I spent the remainder of the afternoon observing the English lessons. In one class I came upon an earnest-looking young man of about sixteen drafting an essay which was placed on a tray fixed across the front of his wheelchair. His tongue stuck out of the corner of his mouth, his face was fierce with concentration.

'Good afternoon,' I said, sitting down next to him and looking over his shoulder.

'Oh, hi!' he replied, staring up and smiling.

'Would you like to tell me what you are doing?'

'Excuse me?'

'Tell me what you're doing?' I repeated.

'Well, as you can see, I'm writing.' There was a mischievous glint in the bright, intelligent eyes.

'Writing what?'

He placed his pen down carefully in front of him. 'Who are you?'

'I'm Gervase Phinn, a school inspector,' I told him.

'Really? I thought you were a care assistant or one of the medical staff. Do all school inspectors usually dress like dentists?'

'No, they don't. It's a long story.'

'I like stories,' he said, placing his elbows on the desk and propping his chin in his cupped hands. 'I want to be a professional writer. I've got a place at Oxford to read English next year.'

'Well done,' I said.

'If I get the grades. So, what's the story with the white outfit, then?'

'I spilt something on my suit and hence the change of clothes,' I explained.

'And here I was thinking there was something sinister about it – that you were creeping round classrooms incognito, disguised as a care assistant to spy on the teachers. It would make a good story that, don't you think?'

'You'll have to write it and send me a copy,' I told him, smiling. 'Now, would you tell me what you are doing?'

He explained to me that the texts he was studying for his exams were *The Cherry Orchard* by Anton Chekhov and *Othello* by William Shakespeare.

'And which do you prefer?' I asked.

He looked down at his desk for a moment in thoughtful silence. 'The Chekhov, I think,' he eventually replied.

'That's an interesting choice,' I remarked.

'Why do you say that?' he asked.

'I would have thought that a boy of sixteen would have preferred *Othello*.'

'Really?'

'Perhaps you would tell me why you prefer Chekhov to Shakespeare?' I asked.

'Perhaps before I do that, Mr Phinn,' he replied, 'you would explain why you think it is surprising that a boy of sixteen might prefer the Shakespeare?' There was a slight smile playing on his lips.

'Well, I suppose it's because there's more excitement and action in the Shakespeare. It's more of a boy's play, I would have thought.'

'I guess most people, like you, would assume that a boy would prefer a play with more action, intrigue and violence rather than the more contemplative and thoughtful Russian drama but I'm rather perverse in that I like the Chekhov. Boys can be sensitive as well, you know.'

'Yes, of course,' I replied, feeling firmly put in my place.

At the end of the day David, Gerry and I sat in the Head-teacher's room giving some feedback. My colleagues, like the pupil to whom I had been speaking, were greatly intrigued as to why I was dressed 'like a trainee doctor' but I explained to them that all would be revealed later.

'Well, as for mathematics, Mrs Thomas . . .' David began.

His voice became fainter and fainter as I stared through the window at the great sweep of the fells, the tumbling woods and distant moorland. I could feel the warmth of the mellow afternoon sun on my face and caught a waft of roses from the garden. I was in another world.

'Would you like to say a few things about English and the arts, Mr Phinn?' David's voice broke into my reverie.

Before I could respond, there was a knock on the door and what appeared like a delegation entered the room. The little artist presented me with his painting of the sunset, Ruth gave me a copy of her poem and Miss Taylor held out a pair of clean, neatly pressed trousers. The Headteacher smiled broadly, Gerry frowned in obvious puzzlement and David's eyes popped out, as we say in Yorkshire, like chapel hat pegs.

'Here are your trousers, Mr Phinn,' said Miss Taylor, suppressing a smile. 'We wouldn't want you to leave without them.'

It was a glorious early summer day when I visited Scarthorpe Primary School. I sat uncomfortably in an already hot car, parked in a gateway, becoming increasingly frustrated. It was as well that I had set off early that morning because I had been over hill and dale in a futile search for the elusive little school. I had checked the route to the village of Scarthorpe on the Ordnance Survey map before setting out and it had seemed simple enough. Indeed, the route via quiet, snaking lanes was quite straightforward until I had arrived at some crossroads where none of the old, pointed wooden signs made any mention of Scarthorpe. It was as if the village had been suddenly swallowed up. I tossed a mental coin, turned right and drove for a couple of miles until I came to a sign for Scarthorpe pointing in the opposite direction. I retraced my route, crossed over the original crossroads and came to more crossroads with another set of signs but, again, none with the name of the village I wanted. I turned left and arrived at a sign which indicated that Scarthorpe was, yet again, in the direction from which I had just come. So, back I went and after a couple more miles, with no signs in sight, I pulled off the road. I was now sitting, fuming, in the car, deciding which way to go next. I pushed the totally unhelpful road atlas aside – its scale was far too small – and stared through the windscreen at the magnificent view which stretched before me.

Beneath a vast, blank curve of blue there stretched the brilliant greens of the pastureland, rolling and billowing up to the richer, darker hues of the far-off fells. Fat, creamy sheep grazed lazily behind the white-silvered limestone walls in fields, while their lambs frisked and raced. In the still, windless sky a wedge of birds moved slowly south, high above a trembling kestrel. There was the heady scent of may blossom and buttercups blending with the smells of earth and grass. I returned to the map and followed with my finger the route which I had taken from Fettlesham earlier that morning: the straight road to Hawksrill, over Butterwick Fell, through Whisterton, by Castle Crags, past the United States Airforce Base at Ribbon Bank, into Wargrave village, on to the Thresherton road, to arrive at the first enigmatic crossroads. I leaned back in the hot seat, the sun on my face, wiped my brow and sighed aloud. 'Where, in heaven's name, am I?'

I realised that it would have been far more sensible if I had stopped to ask directions at the pub a couple of miles back or at a house close to the road. Now, with time ticking on, I was in the middle of nowhere. I sighed and wondered what to do next. Across the road an ancient millstone announced the entrance to Providence Farm and a long, narrow, pot-holed track led to a distant cluster of buildings. If only I had brought the Ordnance Survey map with me; it would have surely shown the farm and pinpointed my whereabouts. The road atlas was useless. There's nothing for it, I thought, I will have to ask. The track looked good only for tractors and jeeps so I decided to walk.

The muddy track seemed endless, and it was a long, hot trek to the farm. In a field beside the track, a herd of black and white cows stared with elaborate indifference as I passed, and continued to swish their tails slowly and chew methodically. In the field on the other side, standing alone, was a huge, square-bodied bull with a brass ring through its nose. It looked like a box on legs. The creature regarded me with utmost suspicion as I came closer and when I was level it bellowed loudly and lengthily. On closer examination it looked abnormally large. Its back was as wide as a trestle table and its neck as thick as the sentinel chestnut tree which cast a shadow over the farmhouse. As I approached the cattle grid and the buildings, I became aware I was being observed. Two men were standing at the entrance to a barn watching me as bright-eyed cats might watch a mouse. The older of the two had a stern, weathered face the colour of bruised parchment, grizzled, smoky-grey hair and a sharp beak of a nose. He was dressed in a clean, long-sleeved, collarless shirt, open waistcoat and ancient wellington boots. His companion was a fair, thick-set young man with an equally weathered face and tight, wiry hair. He was dressed in a T-shirt and shorts but, incongruously, he wore large heavy military-style boots. His arms and legs were wind-burned to the colour of copper.

'Can't tha read?' demanded the older of the men.

'Pardon?'

'Sign on t'gate. Can't tha read? Feed reps only by appointment.'

'I'm not a rep,' I panted. 'I'm a school inspector.'

'Well, tha'll not find any scoil up 'ere and that's for sure.'

'I gather that,' I said, getting my breath, 'but I'm well and truly lost.'

The younger man screwed up his face, surveyed the sky, empty apart from skimming swallows, and sucked in his breath.

'What scoil are tha looking fer?'

'Scarthorpe Primary School. Do you know where it is?'

''appen I do.'

'Well, would you be so kind as to tell me?'

The young man pointed across the fields. 'See yonder spire. That's t'church. Scoil's next door.'

'Tha'r a bit on t'early side to go a-visitin',' said the older man. 'It's just past eight. There'll be nob'dy theer at this time.'

'Well, I always set off early to make certain I get there.' There was no reply, just a couple of slow nods of the head. 'As you might have guessed, I'm not too good at directions and, I have to say, the road signs around here are very confusing.'

'Been t'same since time o' t'Vikings. They had difficulty finding their way around this part o' t'dale, I'll be bound. We don't go advertisin' ourselves up here, tha knaws.'

'Nay,' agreed his young companion. 'We don't want rooad full o' caravans!'

'And coaches.'

'And ramblers climbin' ovver t'walls and knockin' 'em down.'

I felt it politic to make a hasty retreat. 'Well, thank you for your help. I'll be on my way. Just head in the direction of the church, you say?'

'Nay, it's not quite as easy as that,' explained the older man. 'Rooad comes back on itsen at t'bottom o' yonder 'ill. When tha gets to t'crossroads, tek sign for Whisterton, and you pass Thresherton Hall on yer right. Turn left at Holloway Farm, stay on t'rooad and you'll get to t'scoil.'

'Thank you,' I said, trying to memorise the instructions and turning to go.

''old on,' said the older man, 'we'll walk to t'gate wi' thee and see thee off t'premises.' I was thus accompanied by the two farmers, in silence, down the long muddy track which seemed to stretch endlessly to the road. Our pace was leisurely to say the least and they kept their eyes suspiciously on me from the start.

The farmer stopped when we came level with the fearsome bull. The beast eyed us malevolently, scraped and stamped the ground with a cudgel of a hoof, snorted contemptuously and filled the air with loud and mournful bellowing.

'Telling us who's t'boss,' announced the older man, his

face screwing up with pleasure. 'Showing off for t'benefit o' t'cows.' All the cows I could see in the fields surrounding us ceased their swishing and chewing and stared in the direction of the bull. 'Leads a life of owd Riley, does Samson. Spends all t'winter inside in t'warm, eatin' and drinkin' and sleepin', and all summer in t' field, in t'sun, eatin' and drinkin' and sleepin' and mekkin love. Not a bad old life, is it?'

'I could imagine worse,' I agreed.

'Mind you,' commented the younger man, 'many a bull nivver gets t'chance of any o' that, eh, Dad?'

'They don't,' agreed his father seriously. 'Most of 'em get castrated and end up as beefburgers.'

'Really,' I said.

'Tha'd be 'ard pushed to imagine owt worse than that, wun't tha?'

'You would,' I agreed, with feeling.

'Gerrin castrated and endin' up beefburgered. But that's the way o' things. Aye, that's the way o' things.'

'How many cows do you have?' I asked, attempting to get on to less delicate ground.

'Near on three 'undred,' replied the older man as we set off down the track again.

'And do you have sheep?'

'We do. Up on t'fells.'

'And pigs?'

'No, we don't keep pigs. Not a lot o'money in pigs these days. Not a lot o'money in owt, if truth be told. Poor relations are yer farmers. Hardly worth keeping livestock what wi price o'feed.'

'And how many acres have you?'

'I can see tha'r an inspector,' said the farmer stopping in his tracks. 'Tha'r full o' bloody questions, aren't tha?'

We walked on without another word. However, after a minute or two, I found the silence rather embarrassing so

I commented cheerfully, 'The farm's a fair old distance from the road.'

'Aye, it is that,' agreed the older man.

'Yes, quite a distance,' I said, not expecting a reply.

'That's what t'local MP said when he comes up 'ere a-canvassin' last year. "Aye," I said to 'im, "it is a fair distance, but if it were any shorter it wun't reach, would it?"'

At getting on for a quarter to nine, I finally arrived at Scarthorpe Primary School. The small stone building was tucked away behind the ancient Norman church and half-hidden by a huge, stunted oak tree, its twisted roots grasping the thin soil like arthritic fingers. The school was further obscured by the overhanging branches of laurel and syca-more. Mrs Fox, the Headteacher, was a vast and jolly woman with a shock of streaky curls and large friendly eyes behind enormous coloured frames. She wore a bright tartan smock, a rope of large, blue glass beads and yellow dangly earrings. Mrs Fox had the sort of voice which would penetrate bricks and mortar.

'My goodness, Mr Phinn, you are the early bird,' she chortled. I explained that I would have arrived even earlier had I not taken so many wrong turnings at the mysterious crossroads. I was also foolish enough to mention that I had broken my journey at Providence Farm and related the conversation with the two farmers about the bull.

'Oh, you met Mr Purvis and his son, Jack, did you? I was at school with the one and taught the other. Both are real characters, aren't they?'

'They are indeed,' I agreed. 'Well, Mrs Fox, what I intend to do this morning –'

'He dotes on that bull of his. Soft as a brush when it comes to Samson. We often take the children up to Providence Farm as part of our environmental studies work.'

At this point I attempted for a second time to explain what form my day's inspection would take, but Mrs Fox continued blithely. 'My great-uncle Beecham had the land adjoining Providence Farm and knew his grandfather really well. Old Mr Purvis – lived right up to his ninety-eighth birthday he did, without a day's illness – didn't have the patience of his grandson when it came to bulls. My great-uncle Beecham always used to tell the tale which never fails to bring a smile to my lips.'

'What I hope to be doing today, Mrs Fox –' I tried again.

'His bull was called Caesar. He was a great, fat, pompous creature, no good at all except for breeding purposes. He looked like the emperor himself the way he strutted round the field and proceeded to . . . er . . . do his duty to the cows, as one might say. But he had a really vicious streak had Caesar, and many's the time Old Mr Purvis stamped back to the farmhouse, cursing and swearing, and black and blue with bruises. The bull broke his arm a couple of times when he was trying to get hold of him. Anyway, when Young Mr Purvis was about eleven, as the story goes, he rushed into the farmhouse kitchen one morning shouting blue murder. "Grandfather! Grandfather!" he cries. "Caesar's gone! He's not in his field! Somebody's stolen Caesar!" His grandfather didn't bat an eyelid but carried on drinking his tea. Then he nodded in the direction of the window. In the field beyond was poor old Caesar yoked to a plough pulling away down the furrows, with two of the farmhands flicking his haunches with sharp switches. Caesar snorted and bellowed and puffed and heaved and looked very hard done by. "I'll show him that there's more to life than love-making!" said Old Mr Purvis.' Mrs Fox chuckled loudly, her body heaving and her eyes filling with tears of pleasure.

'What I hope to be doing today, Mrs Fox –' I attempted a third time.

'Did Mr Purvis tell you about the incident when that poor young vet was called out to see to Samson?'

I took the bull firmly by the horns. 'Mrs Fox, I really would like to make a start, if I may.'

'Why, of course you do, Mr Phinn,' she replied smiling broadly. 'That's why you're here. Come along and I'll let you look through our planning documents while the children arrive. I'll tell you about Samson, the vet and the bottle of liquid paraffin later, if you like.'

I thought it would be the last time that day that I would hear about bulls but sadly I was mistaken. In the junior classroom later that morning, I joined two boys of about ten or eleven. Both were miniature versions of the farmers I had met at Providence Farm: plain, stocky individuals with sturdy legs, brown faces, tightly curled hair, short, sandy eyelashes and bright eyes. Neither was a very good reader but each tried hard and barked out the words with grim determination. The reading book depicted an idyllic town with sparkling shops, gleaming hotels, brightly painted houses with well-tended gardens and white gates, and a manicured park with a friendly, waving park-keeper standing at the entrance. There were no traces of litter or graffiti and not a sign of a public house, betting office, job centre or charity shop. Everyone in this Utopia looked happy and well dressed, from the jolly policeman to the beaming vicar to the smiling shoppers. The most exciting things that happened in the story were a walk round the lake to look at the ducks and a ride on the bus. It came as no surprise therefore to discover that it was called Merrytown.

'Do you enjoy reading?' I asked one of the boys when he finished and had snapped the book shut with a vengeance.

He lifted a sandy eyebrow. 'No.'

'Do you read at home?'

'No.'

'Why is that?'

'Don't 'ave t'time.'

'Do you have any books at home?'

'A few.'

'And what are they about?'

'Tractors.'

'Do you like reading about tractors?'

'Not particularly.'

It was like extracting blood from a stone but I persisted and tried, by changing tack, to get him to open up a little.

'You live on a farm, do you?'

'I do.'

'I visited a farm on my way here this morning.'

'Oh, aye.' He appeared a little more interested.

'Providence Farm. Do you know it?'

''appen I do.'

The other boy looked up from his work at the mention of the farm. 'Did tha see Samson?'

'I did indeed,' I replied.

''e's a champion beast is Samson, 'e is that.'

'Do you live on a farm as well?'

'Aye.'

'Do you have a bull?'

'Nay, only bull we 'ave on our farm is t'bull wi t'bowler 'at.'

'Pardon?'

'A I man.'

'I'm sorry?'

The boy sighed and gave me such a world-weary look. Then, as a teacher might explain to a particularly slow child, he articulated, 'Artificial Inseminator. 'e comes round and sees to t'cows.'

'I see,' I said somewhat uncertainly.

'So, there's no need for t'bull.'

The first boy decided to contribute to the discussion. 'French sperm's best, tha knaws.'

'Really?' I sighed. 'And do you have a bull on your farm?'

'Nay, we 'ave all our cows done, like on Roger's farm. We did 'ave two bulls but they're both deead now. One were called Eric, he were an 'olstein and t'other were called Oscar and he were a Belgian Blue. Samson's a Limosan and not near as big.'

'You mean there are bulls which are bigger than Samson?' I gasped.

'Oh aye, Belgian Blues can weigh owt up to a ton and an 'arf. Double-muscled, tha sees. Bred for their meat.' He was now quite animated. 'Yer Belgian Blue 'as muscles on muscles and is so big tha can only deliver a calf through a Caesarean. Tha knaws what a Caesarean is, dust tha?'

'I do.'

'Can't gerrem out natural way, Belgian Blues. Vets just zip 'em oppen down t'belly.'

His companion added, 'If tha was to cross 'em wi' a Fresian you'd 'ave a fair chance of a natural birth, Jacob.' He turned to me. 'Tha sees most Belgian Blue cows bred wi' another breed, so it meks it easier for 'em to calve.'

'Still large, though,' said the other seriously. 'Anyroad, we dun't bother wi' bulls any more. Best bull is t'bull out of a test tube.'

'What a pity,' I said. 'To think that those wonderful creatures, those great, snorting, bellowing beasts with their massive bodies and sharp horns might not be seen again.'

'They don't 'ave 'orns,' Jacob told me bluntly.

'They don't? But I thought all bulls have horns?'

'They 'ave 'em tekken off after three month. You de-bud 'em. Burn off their 'orns. Bulls are bad enough wi'out 'orns on. Tha dun't go lookin' fer trouble. It's 'ard enough gerrin' 'em in from t'fields as it is. Old Samson's a devil. Belgian Blues are placid usually, but your Limosan, they can be reight frisky. Toss you up in t'air or butt thee as soon as look at thee.'

'And tha's talkin' money,' interrupted Roger. 'Best o' breed at Fettlesham Show this year, Pride o' Brussels 'e were called, fetched fotty thousand quid. Serious money is that, tha knaws. And o' course, if owt 'appens to 'em like if they 'ad an accident or come down wi summat and tek badly, then they're no good to man nor beast.'

'That's what 'appened wi' Oscar and Eric, weren't it, Jacob?'

'Aye,' replied the boy sagely.

'What sort of accident did they have?' I enquired innocently.

'Well, Eric were feeling a bit lively like and made a move for cows in t'next field. 'e went through a thick 'awthorn 'edge, a drystone wall and two gates afore mi dad blocked him wi' tractor. Anyroad, Eric charged tractor and bust a few bones. Got an infection and had to be put down.'

'I thought the idea was for the bull to get to the cows?' I commented.

Both boys looked at me with disdainful expressions. 'We're talkin' big bulls 'ere. A ton and an 'arf – 'ed have brok every cow's back.'

'I see,' I said feebly. 'Well, shall we look at your books?'

'In olden days, when Mr Purvis's granddad up at Providence Farm had Caesar, he used to dig a pit, put t'cow in it and lower t'bull on with two reight big, thick leather straps.'

'I see,' I said weakly. 'Could you get your English books out, please?'

'Nowadays it's all mechanised,' the boy continued regardless. 'They put t'bull in a serving cage and lower him on and lift him off, lower him on and lift him off.'

'My granddad says it's not a bad old life,' remarked Roger, echoing the comments I had heard earlier that morning at Providence Farm.

I tried again to move the conversation away from what

was becoming an increasingly embarrassing conversation. 'So what have you been doing in English this week?'

'Now, t'other bull, Oscar, 'e went and 'ad t'accident.'

'What accident was that?' I asked somewhat stupidly.

'Accident what Belgian Blues 'ave.'

'And what is that?'

'Tha knaws,' said the boy, eyeing me seriously.

'I don't.'

'Tha' does.'

'Really I don't. What accident did he have?'

The boy gave his companion another knowing look, the tired, long-suffering look of the expert attempting to explain a simple concept to an ignoramus. 'Well, Mester Phinn, sometimes when a bull gets to t'fust cow, he's very keen . . .' At this point I wished I had stayed with the fantasy world of Merrytown and its cardboard inhabitants, for I anticipated that what was to follow would be as blunt as a sump hammer. 'And 'e gets a bit carried away like and sometimes 'e overdoes it and 'is willy snaps.' I could hear my great in-drawing of breath and feel a red flush creeping up my neck.

I retreated to the classroom window and stared at the view outside, attempting to regain my composure. I felt decidedly weak at the knees and was entirely at a loss for words. A flood of sunlight poured into the room, slanting in long bars across the dusty air. All was still. Through the window the vast, green rolling fells shimmered in the bright light, the narrow road curled endlessly between the fields, and far off an invisible bird called plaintively from the sun-warmed grass. I was brought back to reality by Jacob, who tapped me gently on the arm and looked up with a twinkle in his bright eyes.

'It's all reight, Mester Phinn,' he said winking, 'it only 'appens wi' bulls!'

I was in love. Since the first moment I had set eyes on Christine, appearing round the side of Winnery Nook Nursery and Infant School like some vision, with those deep blue eyes and the soft mass of golden hair, I had been smitten. Over the twenty-one months I had known her, that love had become so powerful that it felt like a wearying sickness. She was always in my thoughts. I was like a love-lorn schoolboy, day-dreaming at the back of the class-room during a rather tedious lesson and staring vacantly out of the window whilst thinking of Christine. In the middle of meetings at the Education Office, my thoughts would inevitably drift to a picture of her smiling or laughing or humming to herself as she frequently did. On a course, the words of the speaker would flow over me as my mind would be fixed on Christine, visualising her sitting in the middle of a group of happy infants, sharing a book with them or reading a poem or singing a nursery rhyme in that soft, hypnotic voice. And people were beginning to notice.

Late one afternoon towards the end of the Summer term I stopped focusing on the report I was supposed to be reading and began to dream of the woman I loved.

'Gervase!' snapped Sidney. 'Are you entirely with us this afternoon? You look as if you are wired up to a brick!'

'Pardon?'

'I have just asked you an important question and, rather than do me the courtesy of responding, you completely ignored me and continued to peer into the middle distance like Macbeth upon seeing the ghost of Banquo.'

'I'm sorry, Sidney, I was miles away.'

'Indeed you were. Now, what do you think?'

'What do I think about what?'

Sidney gave a great heaving sigh. 'I was asking about the arrangements for the Creative Arts Course in Oxford next weekend.'

'Well, what about them?'

'Give me strength!'

Following her visit to the Staff Development Centre last December, Miss de la Mare had written to say how impressed she had been with the training and had invited Sidney and me to be tutors on a Ministry of Education course the weekend before the end of the Summer term. We had both been very flattered to have been asked and readily agreed. It had seemed so far ahead then that I had put it to the back of my mind. Now the course was about to happen, I realised that I had not given a single thought to it. Help! My mind was completely occupied with higher thoughts.

'I said that it would be a sensible idea if we both travelled down to Oxford together.'

'Pardon?'

'What *is* the matter with you? Are you sickening for something? I asked if we should travel down to Oxford together?'

'Yes, that's fine, Sidney.'

'It would be better, I think, if we went in your old Volvo estate. I will have to take all my materials, easels and equipment, display boards and, of course, the stuffed animals.'

David, who had been working quietly until this point, raised his head slowly like a weary tortoise, peered over the top of his spectacles and said, 'You are not taking those wretched stuffed animals with you, are you, Sidney?'

'Of course! They are the next best thing to first-hand experience. I always take my stuffed animals with me when I run a course. I would be lost without them.'

David shook his head. 'Well, I'm glad I'm not travelling down to Oxford with you and a car full of flea-ridden, dead creatures glaring and snarling out of the window.'

'I never glare and snarl out of windows,' said Sidney calmly. 'Anyway, I don't hear Gervase complaining.' He turned to me. 'You have no problem with my stuffed animals, do you, Gervase? *Gervase!*' Once again, I was only half-listening to the office chatter. 'I said you don't have a problem, do you?'

'Who said I had a problem?'

'I give up,' sighed Sidney. 'We will talk about this when you emerge from the catatonic trance.'

'You *are* unusually unforthcoming this afternoon, Gervase,' remarked David. 'Not your old self at all. Is there something on your mind?'

'No, no, there's nothing on my mind.'

'Is it that dreadful dragon of a headteacher from Henderson Road School?' asked Sidney grimacing. 'She complains about all the inspectors so I shouldn't worry.'

'No, nothing like that.'

'The Ugglemattersby inspection?'

'No, no, that's all been done and dusted and the governors accepted the report and Mr Sharples is taking early retirement.'

'It'll be Mrs Savage, then,' announced David almost gleefully. 'That Ice Maiden would put the wind up a banshee. She's been after me about those ridiculous coloured forms of hers. Has she been chasing you?'

'No, it's not Mrs Savage.'

'Well, what is it?' both my colleagues asked in unison.

'I can't say. It's . . . it's . . . I need to sort it out myself.'

'Now come along, Gervase!' exclaimed Sidney, turning his full attention on me. 'We are your friends as well as your colleagues. You can tell us whatever it is. I've been on the county's counselling course and was singled out for

313

my ability to listen sympathetically, so if you want to confide in me, get things off your chest, I'm all ears. I've also done art therapy and a stress management weekend so I am well equipped to help.'

'Help!' snorted David. 'Well equipped to help! You forget, Sidney, that I was also on that disastrous counselling course and you were singled out, as I remember, for your complete inability to listen to other people and the total insensitivity of your advice. After contact with you, the people in your group were suicidal at the end. As I recall, your solution to whatever problem that arose was to look the person in the eye and tell them to pull themselves together, stop whinging and snap out of it. I well remember that poor tutor's words: "With you, Mr Clamp, a trouble shared is a trouble doubled." And on the stress management weekend I heard that the tutor went down with severe depression herself, remarking that you did not so much suffer from stress, you were more of a carrier. She headed for her car a gibbering wreck.'

'I shall choose to ignore those slanderous comments, David, because my dear friend here is in need of some help and support. Now, Gervase, what is the matter? Tell, tell.'

'I'm in love!' I blurted out.

There was a stunned silence.

'In love?' repeated Sidney, after what seemed a long, long pause. 'Oh, that is serious. Is it someone we know?'

'Yes, of course it is!' I snapped, already regretting my confession.

'Is it a certain desirable doctor of philosophy, with alluring Irish eyes and a smile like a rainbow?'

'No, it's not Gerry. I hardly know her.'

'Is it a certain well-preserved, power-dressed widow with a predatory look and a smile like a shark?'

'Mrs Savage? Do me a favour!'

'The *femme fatale* with the feather duster in the crackling nylon overall who inhabits the SDC?'

'Sidney, will you be serious!'

'Then it must be the Nordic beauty, the blonde bombshell, the delectable Miss Bentley of Winnery Nook.'

'You know full well it is.'

'I don't see a problem, myself.'

'What did I say?' announced David shaking his head. 'All the sensitivity of a sledge hammer.'

'Well, I don't,' continued Sidney. 'He's been taking her out for the best part of two years.' He turned his attention back to me. 'I mean, it's hardly a whirlwind romance.'

'I've not been taking her out for the best part of two years,' I said. 'I only started seeing Christine last summer.'

'Well, you want to look sharpish. She's an extremely attractive young woman. Very marriageable. If you don't start pulling your finger out, being a bit more dynamic, proactive and determined, you'll be getting a "Dear John" letter. She'll go back to that dreadful soldier and give you the old heave-ho!'

'Now, does that make you feel a lot better, Gervase?' asked David sarcastically. 'Has that wonderfully sympathetic advice helped you with your little problem? You know, Sidney, with such obvious sensitivity and understanding, you ought to work for the Samaritans.'

'I am only telling him to gird up his loins and go for it. I mean, look at him. He's like a sick calf, mooning about the office. I certainly do not relish a weekend in Oxford with him in this powerless state.'

'Well, that's what love does for you,' said David. 'I recall someone saying that love was like the measles – that it is something we all have to go through. I know I did.'

'More like the mumps with me!' exclaimed Sidney. 'Incredibly painful and all the more so when you're older. You see, David, the problem with Gervase is –'

'Excuse me, Sidney, would you mind not talking about me as if I'm not here?' I said.

'You see, your problem, Gervase, is what I was saying about the mumps. It's happening to you late in life so it's affecting you far worse.'

'Late in life!' I cried. 'I'm just over thirty, not in my dotage!'

'But as you get older, you get more picky, more difficult to please. My advice, if you really love Christine, is to face up to things, take the bull by the horns, grasp the nettle and be decisive. Stop shilly-shallying, ask her straight out to marry you.'

My stomach gave a great lurch at the very word 'marry'.

'And pull yourself together, stop whinging and snap out of it,' added David mimicking Sidney's voice. 'You see what I mean about Sidney's sensitive approach to a problem? As tactful as a charging elephant.'

'It's not as easy as that, Sidney,' I said sighing. 'She might not be ready for . . . er . . . marriage. She's so involved with her work in school. We've never discussed any future together and she might not feel the same way about me. She might not be the marrying sort. She's a very independent woman is Christine. I know she likes my company and we enjoy the same things but –'

'Have you told her how lovely she is and that you can't stop thinking about her?' asked Sidney.

'No.'

'Have you told her that when she smiles the birds begin to sing and the sun begins to shine?'

'No.'

'Have you told her that you can't live without her?'

'No.'

'Have you told her that you love her?'

'No.'

Sidney snorted. 'Then how, in heaven's name, is she to

know how you feel? She might think that *you* are the one who isn't ready for marriage. She might think that *you* are too involved with your work to think about anything else. She might think that *you* don't feel the same way about her as she might think about you. She might think that *you* are not the marrying sort.'

'Much as I am loath to admit it,' ventured David, who had been listening intently, 'Sidney, despite his bluntness, is perfectly right. You have to let her know how you really feel about her.'

'You, of all people, Gervase,' continued Sidney, 'are supposed to possess the higher order language skills, the ability to use words at their richest and most persuasive. Can't you pen her a poem and write it in chalk down the path to Winnery Nook School? – something along the lines of "Oh dearest heart, come kiss me gently, Be my love, my Christine Bentley."'

'I'd stick to painting and stuffed animals if I were you, Sidney,' said David. 'He doesn't want to frighten her off with that sort of doggerel, or get arrested for defacing school property.'

'I'll have you know it worked with my wife,' retorted Sidney. 'When I painted my Lila a poem on the wall of her flat she was putty in my hands.'

'Probably drunk,' said David, before turning his attention back to the topic under discussion. 'I think Gervase ought to take Christine out for a really romantic dinner in a remote country inn,' he said. 'Champagne, roses, soft music. That's the way it's done. And I know the very place. A delightful French restaurant with superb food and magnificent views, not too far from here.'

'Is that the way you proposed?' I asked.

'Well, no, actually,' replied David. 'I asked Gwynneth in a bus shelter on a rainy Sunday afternoon in Pontypool. We were having a little *cwtch* and –'

'A little what?' exclaimed Sidney. 'What in the world is a cutch?'

'A *cwtch* – Welsh for a cuddle,' explained David. 'And I said, "What about it, *Cariad*?" She said it was quite unexpected and she would have to think about it as her mother had not taken to me at all. Thirty years later and her mother's still not too sure about me. It took her three months – Gwynneth, that is, not her mother – to make up her mind and then she said she would have to iron out my irritating habits.'

'She was singularly unsuccessful on that count,' murmured Sidney.

'You see, that's just what I mean,' I said. 'Suppose Christine says she likes me but couldn't marry me. It would be the end of everything. I couldn't go on seeing her. If I delay it a bit, carry on as we are, she might grow to love me in time – like your wife, David. I just think it might be better to do nothing for the time being.'

'Faint heart, dear boy, faint heart!' exclaimed Sidney. 'She might think you are trifling with her affections and get tired of waiting about. Have you ever thought of that? I mean, it's been getting on for two years, well, over a year anyway, that you have been taking her out. She won't go on waiting for ever. And you're no spring chicken. The summer holidays are nearly upon us. She'll be gadding off to some exotic location full of rich, eligible, unattached men who will buzz around her like bees around a honey pot. You've got to go for it. Be decisive. You could start by giving her a quick clutch in a bus shelter.'

'A *cwtch*!' snapped David. 'And it worked for me!'

'Look, Gervase, do you love her?' asked Sidney, suddenly turning very serious.

'Yes, I do,' I replied.

'Well, why don't you ask her to marry you?'

'I'm frightened she'll say no. I haven't got much money

saved, I drive an old car and I live in a rented flat. It wouldn't be an offer she couldn't refuse.'

Sidney got up from his desk and came and perched on the corner of my desk. 'That's not the real reason though, is it?' he continued.

'What?' I replied.

'The fact that you've not much money and live in a rented flat.'

'No,' I replied. 'I'm just frightened that she doesn't love me.'

Sidney sighed and put his hand on my shoulder. 'Well, old boy, there's only one way to find out, isn't there?'

Sidney was right, of course. I could not delay any longer. I decided that when I returned from the course in Oxford I would take Christine out for that romantic dinner suggested by David and ask her to marry me.

I arrived at Sidney's house early on the Saturday morning as arranged, to find my colleague dressed like an ageing pop star in wildly bright T-shirt and jeans. He was in the garage, collecting together an assortment of stuffed animals and equipment. He stopped what he was doing when he caught sight of me heading down the path towards him. I was about to ask him the question he put to me.

'Gervase, what *are* you wearing?'

'A suit. Why?'

'Do you always have to wear that dreadful grey outfit? We are contributing to a creative arts course, not attending a Foreign Office funeral. Relax, get casual. It's a residential course for lively teachers, not an undertakers' convention. You want to look colourful, expressive, exciting, artistic. You're not inspecting this weekend, you know!'

'I didn't stop to think about what to put on, to be honest. My mind was on other things.'

'Oh dear, I do hope this is not a taster of things to come.

I sincerely hope that you are not going to mope around Oxford like some medieval mystic contemplating the meaning of life. You really will have to ask her, you know.'

'I know.'

'This weekend will give you a perfect opportunity to get your thoughts together and rehearse what you will say to her when you get back and pop the question. I'll give you the benefit of my extensive experience with the opposite sex. We will have some rehearsals. Now, come and help me load up.'

We packed the car with Sidney's boxes of paints and brushes, great plastic bags of clay, folders and files, easels and display boards, drapes and canvasses, dried flowers and gnarled lumps of driftwood and, on the very top, we wedged a ferocious-looking stuffed stoat savaging a rabbit, a snarling fox, a pair of fat hedgehogs and assorted sharp-beaked birds.

'I shall carry the badger on my knee,' announced Sidney. 'He is very precious is Barry.'

We said goodbye to his long-suffering wife, Lila, who smiled and shook her head as I pulled away and headed for the main road.

Sidney spent the first part of the journey chattering inconsequentially and the second part in deep sleep with his arms wrapped lovingly round the stuffed badger. The sight of him in an amorous embrace with the black and white creature drew many a stare from other motorists.

When we arrived in Oxford, Sidney rubbed his eyes, stretched, yawned and peered through the window. 'Drop me off at the college, will you, Gervase,' he directed. 'I shall unpack and find Miss de la Mare and tell her we've arrived. You park the car somewhere and then would you book us in while I sort out the workshop rooms? I'll see you in an hour for lunch.'

During the summer months, after the undergraduates have gone down for the Long Vac, the university becomes available for a huge variety of outside courses and conferences. Miss de la Mare's art course was to take place at one of the oldest, most beautiful and prestigious of the colleges.

Having dropped off Sidney and parked the car as instructed, I made my way to the entrance of Wentworth College, a large, square, imposing building of honey-coloured stone. Moving round various tourists who were peeking through the small opening set in a vast ancient door stretching across an entrance archway, I arrived at the Porter's Lodge. I peered through a leaded window for a sign of life, and found myself staring into the face of a gaunt, lugubrious-looking porter with a hatchet of a nose. The nose could have cut a rock in two. A few seconds later the funereal figure emerged through the portal like some black beetle creeping out from a hole.

'Good morning, sir,' he intoned. 'May I be of assistance?'

'Good morning,' I replied cheerily. 'I'm here for the meeting.'

'You will find your colleagues in the Stafford Chamber.' He gestured with a long stick of a finger across the quadrangle. 'I'll enter your name, sir, if I may.'

'Gervase Phinn,' I replied.

'Thank you, Dr Phinn. Pre-prandial drinks are at present being served.'

'And I am expecting my colleague, so if you could direct him to where the meeting is taking place?'

'Of course, Dr Phinn,' replied the porter, smiling like a frog.

I walked out from under the archway and into the quadrangle, in the middle of which was set a large beautifully mown square of lawn. The hum of the traffic outside hardly permeated this peaceful sanctum.

I made my way across the quadrangle to the Stafford Chamber. It was a magnificently ornate room with dark oak wainscoting, a great domed ceiling, and an uneven but highly polished floor. Portraits of former Earls of Wentworth lined the walls, and a great imposing portrait of Charles I on horseback, resplendent in silver armour and flowing blue cloak, hung at the head of the room. There was a pleasant smell of old wood and beeswax. A small gathering of formally dressed people was chatting away amiably and sipping sherry, but I could see no sign of Miss de la Mare. Everyone seemed to be remarkably relaxed. I was relieved to be in a suit. I would have been entirely out of place in one of Sidney's suggested outfits and wondered if he would be allowed in when he arrived.

A distinguished, elderly gentleman, with the face of a Roman senator, approached me. 'Have we met?' he asked amiably.

'I don't think so,' I replied, holding out my hand. 'I'm Gervase Phinn.'

'John Morton, Emeritus Professor of Medieval History. I am very pleased to meet you. I once knew a bishop called Gervase. A very saintly man. You are a new face at our gathering, are you not?'

'Yes, and very honoured to have been invited.'

'Whereabouts are you from?'

'Yorkshire.'

'Ah yes, I did detect a certain northern burr in the voice. You'll know Professor de Longue, of course. He's a Halifax man. And David Willett-Smith is from your part of the country, Sheffield I think.' As I cast my eyes around the throng, I had an uneasy feeling that this august gathering was not a group of primary school teachers on a weekend creative arts course. My suspicions were strengthened as my friendly companion took me round and introduced me to one distinguished person after another. They were confirmed when a large begowned individual appeared and announced: 'Fellows of the College, luncheon is served.' I had gate-crashed a meeting of the Fellows of Wentworth College.

'So you are Dr Finn, are you?' I turned to face a rather portly, elderly man with grey nibbled eyebrows and skin as white and shiny as a waxwork figure. 'I'm Herbert Rawnsley and have been so looking forward to meeting you.'

I shook a cold hand. 'You have?' I replied nervously.

'Yes, indeed. I was so delighted to hear that you had been elected one of our Honorary Fellows. You are a Cambridge man, are you not? Trinity, was it?'

'Er . . . well . . . I . . .'

'Your book on Multi-Dimensional Scaling and Log-Linear Contingency Analysis was refreshingly readable. We must get together after lunch.'

'Yes, we must,' I replied, thinking how, in heaven's name, was I to get out of this place.

'I must say, you have lost your Canadian accent,' continued the wax-faced individual.

'Gervase is from Yorkshire, Herbert,' said Professor Morton who had just joined us.

'I thought you were Canadian? It is Maurice Finn, isn't it, author of *Statistical Measurements in Social Science*?'

'I'll just wash my hands, if I may,' I replied, turning in the direction of the exit.

'There's a lavatory through here,' my companion said helpfully and, grasping my arm, he added, 'I'll come with you. We'll sit together at lunch and compare notes. I'm working on some economic models in which you may very well be interested.'

I hid in a toilet cubicle for a few minutes, then crept away unobserved. Once outside in the quadrangle, I breathed great gulps of air in relief. I found Sidney pacing up and down near the main entrance.

'There you are!' he cried. 'I thought you'd thrown yourself in the river or something. Where have you been?' Before I could answer, he rattled on. 'Never mind, it's all sorted. I've seen Miss de la Mare, found where we are to work and have copies of the programme. I've taken the larger room because I need the space. You'll be all right in the little annexe, won't you? Yes, of course, you will, you don't need equipment for poetry, do you? Now, let's go and have some lunch.'

Miss de la Mare was waiting for me in the entrance to the seminar room where I was to lead the poetry workshop later that afternoon. She was wearing a beige cotton safari concoction, with pockets and zips everywhere. Her summer ensemble ended with a pair of pink plimsolls. There was a broad grin on her plump face.

'Mr Phinn, Gervase!' she cried, grasping my hand and shaking it vigorously. 'How very nice to see you. Always a great relief to know that the speakers and tutors have arrived. I saw Mr Clamp earlier and he said you'd found the college without too much difficulty. Now, come along in and see if you've got everything you need. There's a flip chart, screen, overhead projector, plenty of paper and materials.' Miss de la Mare seemed more nervous than I.

'It's fine, Miss de la Mare,' I reassured her, glancing around the small room.

'But is the room big enough, do you think?'

'It's fine,' I repeated.

'Because I could see if there is something a little larger if not.'

'It really is fine,' I said laughing.

'Good show!' she cried, rubbing her hands together. 'I'm sure your session will go really well.'

My afternoon workshop did, in fact, go well. The teachers were good-humoured and interested and produced some splendid poems. Sidney's session, however, did not turn out quite as planned. I was sitting in a small rose garden, enclosed by handsome wrought-iron railings, to the rear of the college, when I caught sight of him striding across the quadrangle with the stuffed badger tucked under his arm and a thunderous look on his face. I called to him and a few moments later he banged noisily through the gate, flopped on to the seat next to me and rather unceremoniously, I thought, dumped the badger at his feet.

'I was harangued by a mad woman!' he exclaimed, eyes blazing and beard bristling. 'A mad woman in crimson dungarees with bright red hair and clanking metal jewellery. Compared to her, Mrs Savage is a veritable Mother Teresa.'

'Who was she?' I asked, trying to suppress a smile.

'Some animal rights activist, by the way she behaved. She took against my stuffed creatures from the start and refused to put brush to canvas. "How would you like to be murdered, gutted, stuffed and mounted and then painted by all and sundry?" she screeched at me, as I was arranging the heron. The whole session went from bad to worse and deteriorated into a debate on the rights and wrongs of stuffed animals.' Sidney's eyes were now fairly crackling with anger. 'I endeavoured to explain to her that the animals were not deliberately killed, but had been found dead, but would she have it?' My colleague caught sight of the slight smile on my lips. 'You may find this amusing, Gervase, but that smile will rapidly disappear when I tell you that, at my suggestion, Boadicea in the red dungarees and battle jewellery is moving to the poetry workshop with you tomorrow morning. I suggested that she might find poetry more to her liking.'

'Well, thanks a bundle, Sidney!'

'We are doing pottery tomorrow and I certainly don't intend having that red she-devil savaging me for digging up the environment, stripping clay from river beds, disturbing the natural habitat of snails and generally ruining the planet. I'll tell you this, Gervase –'

'Excuse me, sir.' It was the gaunt, lugubrious-looking porter.

'Yes?' snapped Sidney. 'What is it?'

'Your voice is carrying across the quadrangle – sir.'

'Really?'

'It's echoing.'

'You don't say.'

'This garden is reserved for the Fellows of the college.' He scrutinized Sidney as if looking for dirt and then his eyes rested on the stuffed badger. 'And pets are not allowed.'

'Pets!' exclaimed Sidney. 'It's not a pet, it's a stuffed badger.'

'I can see what it is, sir.'

Sidney patted the creature on the head. 'And it's dead.'

'I take it you are not a Fellow of the college, sir?' continued the man unperturbed.

'Do I look like a Fellow of the college?' exclaimed Sidney wearily. He was dressed in a coloured T-shirt and bandanna, paint-spattered jeans and multi-coloured plimsolls.

'No, sir, you do not.'

'You are correct! I am not a Fellow of the college.'

'Well, would you mind vacating the garden then, please, sir, taking the animal with you?'

'Am I doing any harm? Am I doing anything heinously wrong in merely sitting on a bench in the sunshine, minding my own business? Is my stuffed companion ripping up the lawn or savaging the flowers?'

'The garden is for the exclusive use of Fellows of Wentworth College,' the porter persisted. 'I must ask you to leave.' With a great exhalation of breath, Sidney got to his feet angrily, snatched up the badger and strode away. I got up to follow him.

'I am sorry that you were disturbed, Dr Finn,' said the porter. 'We do get all sorts of unsavoury itinerants over the summer who slide in when my back is turned. I trust you were not too inconvenienced?' Without waiting for an answer he walked away but turned as if he had suddenly forgotten something. 'Oh, by the way, Dr Finn, Professor Rawnsley has been looking for you.'

'Bringing the stuffed animals was a complete and utter disaster,' growled Sidney as I helped him load the car the following afternoon. 'I feel like throwing the blasted badger in the river. It's brought me nothing but grief. I should have got them to paint insipid watercolours of the college and the gardens, do pretty little sketches of flowers. Mind you, we would have been banned no doubt by that gate-keeper from Hell from drawing anything in his wretched Fellows' garden.'

Before I could answer, a stately, crimson-gowned figure entered the quadrangle. It was the elderly don with the face of the Roman senator whom I had met the previous day. He smiled benignly at me.

'You missed a very good lunch yesterday, Gervase,' he said, approaching me. 'We all wondered where you had got to. Herbert is very keen to speak to you.'

'I was feeling a little unwell,' I replied sheepishly.

'Oh, I am sorry. I trust you are now recovered?'

'Yes, I feel fine today.'

'That's good. Are you coming?'

'Coming?' I repeated.

'To Evensong in the chapel. It's the special service for the Fellows.'

'I'll be along in a moment,' I replied, smiling weakly.

'I look forward to seeing you there.' There was a swish of red gown and Professor Morton was gone.

'Who the devil was that?' asked Sidney.

'Oh, just someone I met yesterday.'

'Well, what was all that about lunch and a meeting of the Fellows? You are a dark horse, you know. There are one or two questions I want answering, Gervase, starting with why you were not asked to vacate the Fellows' garden when I was evicted, who are these important people that you seem to know and, more importantly, how you coped with the wild woman in the red dungarees.'

'Come along, Sidney, let's go. All will be revealed on the journey home. I need to get back to Fettlesham. There's a very important question *I* need to ask and it really can't be put off any longer.'

I had booked a table at Le Bon Appetit restaurant in the little market town of Ribsdyke for the Saturday after my return from Oxford. Christine would be in a good mood because term would have ended and she would be looking forward to the long summer break. There would be soft music, subdued lights and, from our secluded table, we would look out along the dale and watch the sun go down behind the noble fells. I would reach out and take Christine's hand in mine. Our eyes would lock. I would gaze into those deep blue eyes and whisper, 'Christine, I think you know how I feel about you. Over the year, I've grown closer and closer to you. You're always in my thoughts, you're forever in my dreams. I love you.' I would pause for effect. 'Darling, will you marry me?' Her eyes would fill with tears. 'Of course,' she would sigh.

That is what I had carefully rehearsed in Oxford but it did not quite work out like that.

The taxi arrived late. I thought it would set the scene much better if I arrived at Christine's house in a sleek black taxi rather than in my old, distinctly grubby, Volvo estate. It would also mean that I could have more than one glass of wine. I might need some Dutch courage, I thought, imagining the ordeal ahead of me. My heart sank when I saw the vehicle which spluttered to a halt outside The Rumbling Tum café. It was without a doubt the oldest and smelliest in the fleet, reeking of diesel and stale cigarettes.

'I didn't know I were pickin' up t'Prince of Wales,' said the driver facetiously, when I complained about the state of the interior. 'You should have asked for t'limousine.'

When we finally arrived at Christine's parents' house, I could see my future bride staring anxiously through the window.

'I'm really sorry,' I said as I hurried her down the path, 'the taxi was late.'

'I thought you'd stood me up,' she said smiling. Then she caught sight of the vehicle. 'And we're going by taxi. How nice.'

Le Bon Appetit was heaving. We squeezed through a crowd of loud young men in smart suits holding pints of lager who were blocking the door, to be greeted by the head waiter. He was a small, dark-eyed, Gallic-looking individual, who eyed me superciliously as I pushed my way forward, clearing a path for Christine. He asked, in a strong French accent, if I had a reservation and, hearing that I had, ran a fat finger down a list in his hand.

'Ah, oui, Meester and Meesis Pinn.'

'Phinn!' I corrected.

'Meester Phinn. Eef you would like to come zees way, I will show you to your table.' We followed him through a noisy, crowded restaurant to a small table positioned between two larger tables full of loud, laughing people and directly opposite the doors to the kitchens.

'Is there somewhere which is a little more private?' I asked, immediately regretting that I had not asked for a quiet table when I had booked.

'Private?' he repeated, arching a thick, black eyebrow. 'Private?'

'More secluded, quieter.'

'Oh, no, no, no! I am afraid not. Le Bon Appetit ees always ver' busy at zer weekend. You 'ave to book early for zer best tables.' He gave me a look which clearly said, 'It is this table or nothing.'

'It's fine,' said Christine squeezing into a chair.

'Aperitif?' demanded the waiter, before I could sit down.

'In a minute!' I snapped, attempting to get into the chair.

After we had ordered them, the drinks took an age to arrive and, try as I might to have a conversation with Christine, my voice was drowned by the noise of the other diners, the banging of the double swing doors to the kitchen, the shouts of the chef and over-loud background music. To make matters worse, the waiter, another small, dark-eyed, Gallic-looking individual, insisted on taking us through the menu in maximum, dreary detail.

'You can 'ave for starters zer warmed asparagus with a lightly poached egg, fresh spinach salad, garden 'erbs and parmesan shavings or you can 'ave tempura of deep-fried queenie scallops with red pepper sauce on a bed of rocket leaves and crispy prosciutto, or you can 'ave confit of plump pigeon, served with an 'onest red wine reduction, ragout of Schitake, oyster and Piedmont wild mushrooms, or you can 'ave casserole of numerous mussels in a garlic shellfish broth, or you can 'ave oven-roasted 'alibut tandoori tikka marsala with pickled lime chutney and naan bread, or you can 'ave fresh Scottish smoked salmon served on a platter of chicory leaves, caper, gherkins and roasted crusty bread, fresh from zer oven, or you can 'ave hot feta cheese with sweet plum tomatoes, black olives and diced oregano, or you can 'ave fruit terrine featuring strawberries, blackberries, redcurrants, blueberries, all set in apple jelly and served with citrus crème fraîche, or you can 'ave zer fresh tomato soup with zer croutons.'

'I'll 'ave the mussels!' I snapped, when finally the drone came to a halt.

'And soup for me,' said Christine, attempting to suppress a smile.

'Bon,' scowled the waiter, bristling like an angry cat and

then proceeded to scribble down the order. 'And now for zer main courses. We 'ave . . .' And the whole thing was repeated. He took my order for the food and strode away with a flourish.

'Sounds delicious,' shouted Christine across the table.

'David recommended it,' I shouted back. 'I didn't think it would be quite as crowded.' At this point there were shrieks of cackling laughter from the large, rowdy office party at the next table.

'Would you care to see the wine list, sir?' The wine waiter, with hair slicked back in rippling boot-black waves, offered an enormous leather-bound volume in his long white fingers.

'Just a bottle of dry house white, please,' I replied. I could not contemplate listening to him working through the catalogue of wines. He inclined his head, nodded and departed through the mêlée.

The restaurant grew noisier and noisier and hotter and hotter and every time a waiter swept out of the kitchen, a great gust of humid air hit us in the face. It was quite impossible to have any sort of intimate conversation in such an atmosphere. The food finally arrived. The numerous mussels numbered five, the soup looked about as appetising as grey dishwater, the main courses were barely warm and the white wine too sweet.

'I'm really sorry about this, Christine!' I shouted across the table. 'David said this place was really good. He came here for his twenty-fifth wedding anniversary. I certainly wasn't expecting it to be like this. I wanted this evening to be so special.'

'Could you take a photo of us, please, young man?' asked a man with a clarety complexion and heavy jowls who was sitting at the next table. 'Office outing,' he explained. 'Do you mind?'

'Of course not,' I replied, smiling maniacally. The

evening was developing into a farce. I took three or four photographs, thrust the camera into his hands and wiped my brow.

'To be what?' asked Christine when I turned back to face her.

'Sorry, what did you say?'

'You said something about wanting the evening to be . . .'

'Special! I wanted it to be special. But this place has all the ambience of an abattoir!' Christine laughed and nearly spilt her wine. 'And there was something very particular I wanted to ask you. Something I've been wanting to say for weeks now and . . .' She looked at me expectantly, as did a couple of the office revellers on the next table to whom my raised voice had obviously carried. 'Would you . . . would you . . . would you like another glass of wine?'

'No thanks, it's a little too sweet for me,' she replied.

I tried again. 'Christine . . . would you . . .'

'Would you care to 'ear what we 'ave for dessert?' It was the waiter again.

No, I felt like saying, let me guess. 'Would you like a pudding, Chris?' I asked.

'No, thanks, just coffee, please.'

'Could we just have coffee, please,' I said to the waiter. He stuck his tongue in the corner of his mouth, shrugged and nodded as if deliberating on a difficult arithmetical problem. 'And is there anywhere less crowded and noisy for us to have it?' I continued.

'Oh, no, no, no! I am afraid not. Le Bon Appetit ees always ver' busy at zer weekend.'

This was just impossible. There should have been soft music, subdued lighting, the outstanding view down the dale, a wonderful calm. I could not possibly ask her here in this place. I wanted this evening to be memorable.

'Shall we skip the coffee?' suggested Christine helpfully. 'We could go back to my house. I make an excellent cup and I know Mum and Dad would love to see you again. They hoped you might have time to pop in.'

'No coffee, then, thank you,' I told the waiter. 'Just the bill, please.'

'*Certainement*,' murmured the waiter and strode off.

Turning back to Christine, I said in a resigned voice, 'Yes, let's go back to your house for coffee.' I had not planned for the evening to end like this. How could I propose with Christine's parents making polite conversation and smiling at me over the rims of their coffee cups? 'I'll just go and rustle up the taxi. I ordered it for eleven, but we don't want to be hanging about here for the next hour. Would you excuse me? I won't be long.'

Having finally persuaded the head waiter to ring for the taxi, I headed for the only cool and quiet place in the building: the gents. I had to get my thoughts straight and think through another plan of attack. In the deserted cloak-room, I splashed cold water over my face and stared into the mirror. Perhaps Christine's parents would leave us to ourselves and then I could pop the question. I had rehearsed what I would say so many times I knew it backwards. Or perhaps we could sit outside in the warm air, I could take her in my arms and propose beneath the moon. I looked in the mirror, smiled and said out loud: 'I think you know how I feel about you. Over the year I've grown closer and closer to you. You're always in my thoughts, you're forever in my dreams. I love you, I've always loved you, I've loved you since I first saw you.' I paused for effect. 'I just cannot live without you. I want to spend the rest of my life with you. Darling, will you marry me?'

There was a loud flushing noise, a cubicle door opened and the man with a clarety complexion and heavy jowls from the next table emerged with a bemused expression. He joined me at the washbasin where he proceeded to wash his hands vigorously.

'I'm afraid I can't,' he said bluntly.

'I'm sorry?'

'Marry you. I'm married already. I've been married for fotty-five years. But thank you for asking – I shall always treasure the memory.' Then, chuckling to himself, he left me to my thoughts.

The evening had been a total disaster. What else could possibly happen next? I had not long to wait. At the bar, having settled the bill, I became aware of a familiar voice.

'Could you order me a taxi, please, to collect us in about thirty minutes?' It was Dr Gore.

'Dr Gore!' I exclaimed.

The Chief Education Officer smiled his hungry vampire smile and came down the bar to join me. 'Hello, Gervase, I didn't see you there. I take it you too have been celebrating the end of term? Are you here with your colleagues?'

'No, no, just with a friend,' I replied.

'Well, you must come and join us for a coffee.'

'That's very kind, but I'm expecting a taxi –'

'What time?' he interrupted.

'Well, it was for eleven actually, but I've just asked the waiter to telephone and see if it could collect us earlier.'

'I'm sure that you have time for a cup of coffee. In any case, if your taxi does arrive it can wait for ten minutes or so.' He smiled a thin-lipped, self-satisfied smile, reminding me of Count Dracula before he sinks his fangs into a helpless victim. 'Now, I won't take no for an answer. You run along and fetch your friend. We're through the archway, near the window, in a little alcove.'

'And where have you been?' Christine demanded in a mock angry voice when I arrived back at the table. 'I've been sitting here for ages.'

'I'm really sorry. I met Dr Gore and just couldn't get away. He's asked us to join him for coffee and I couldn't get out of it. He insisted. Do you mind awfully?'

'Of course not.'

I led Christine through the crowd still thronging the bar area, under the archway and headed in the direction of the window where Dr Gore had said he was sitting. This was where Christine and I should have been, I thought crossly. There was soft background music, subdued lights, tables for two in secluded alcoves. I could have proposed here, I thought to myself.

'He's over there,' said Christine taking my arm.

I stopped in my tracks as if turned to stone when I saw who was in animated conversation with the CEO. At a pretty table, bathed in pink light from a nearby lamp, sat a streamlined figure in exquisite acid-green silk and bedecked in an assortment of heavy gold jewellery. It was Mrs Savage.

'I do not believe it,' I heard myself whisper. 'I do not believe it.'

'What is it?' asked Christine. 'You look as if you've seen a ghost.'

'Something worse,' I murmured.

Dr Gore stood as we reached the table. 'Ah, there you are,' he said. 'Good, good. Miss Bentley, how very nice to see you. Gervase never mentioned who his friend was. Bit of a dark horse is our English inspector. Come, come, do take a seat. I've ordered some more coffee.'

Mrs Savage placed the china cup she was holding carefully between finger and thumb on the saucer and our eyes met. She arched an eyebrow and gave me a twisted little smile. We sat down on chairs pulled up by Dr Gore. 'You know Brenda, of course, Gervase,' continued Dr Gore jovially. He turned to Christine and gave her the thin-lipped grin. 'This is my personal assistant, Brenda Savage,' he explained. 'You keep me in order, don't you, Brenda?' She gave a self-satisfied little smirk before extending a green-nailed hand like some member of royalty. 'Delighted to meet you,' she said softly.

'And this is Christine Bentley,' Dr Gore told her. 'One of our most distinguished and hard-working headteachers.'

'Hello,' said Christine warmly. 'I think I saw you with Dr Gore when he came to talk at the Headteachers' Conference.'

'That's right,' said Mrs Savage. 'I spend a lot of time with Dr Gore.' She gave me what could only be termed a challenging look.

Dr Gore and Mrs Savage, I thought to myself. Well, well. The evening was collapsing into a complete shambles – but what a story I would have to tell David and Sidney.

'Well, isn't this nice,' chortled the CEO leaning back in his chair.

The next ten minutes of trivial conversation seemed an eternity. Mrs Savage never missed an opportunity to remind me how hard Dr Gore worked and how much he relied on her. I could have yelped for joy when I saw the little French waiter heading in our direction.

'Meester and Meesis Pinn, your taxi is 'ere.'

I thanked Dr Gore for the coffee, shook his hand, wished him a pleasant summer holiday, smiled weakly at Mrs Savage and turned to Christine, 'Shall we go then?'

Christine slid her hand into mine and smiled. 'If you're ready,' she replied.

I was lost for words, just as I had been the very first time I had seen her. She had the deepest blue eyes and the fairest complexion I had ever seen, the softest mass of golden hair, the sweetest mouth. She was strikingly beautiful. It had been a *coup de foudre* – an instantaneous falling in love and I had to tell her. 'Gervase,' she repeated, 'are you ready?'

'Yes,' I murmured. 'I'm ready.'

'That was an unexpected meeting, wasn't it?' Christine said as we headed for the door. 'Fancy coming across Dr Gore and Mrs Savage, together. Do you think there's something going on between them? He's a widower, isn't he?'

'Christine –'

'Of course, it might be quite innocent – just be a sort of thank-you meal, you know –'

'Christine! I am really totally uninterested in Dr Gore and Mrs Savage at the moment. There really is something I have to ask you. It won't wait. Could we just sit down for a moment?' We found an empty table in a smoky part of the room near the bar. I took a deep breath and tried to remember the words I had endlessly rehearsed. My mind went blank and my throat dry. 'I know this is not the best place to say this, but I really have to say it now. You don't have to answer me right away. You might want to think about it. It's just that I think you are the most beautiful, wonderful, amazing person I've ever met and, well, I love you. Yes, I do, I love you. I can't stop thinking about you. It's making me ill. I want you to be my wife.'

'Oh.'

'Will you marry me, Christine? You may want to think about it –'

'The answer is "No",' Christine replied immediately.

'No? Oh, no!' Her answer was like a bullet to the heart.

'No, I don't need to think about it, Gervase. Of course I'll marry you.'

'*You will?*' I shouted loud enough to turn the entire noisy restaurant silent. 'You'll marry me?'

'Of course, I will.'

Making his way to the bar was the claret-faced man who had heard the final rehearsal of my speech in the gents.

'Well done, lad,' he chuckled, thumping me on the back. 'I knew thy'd fettle it.'

This was followed by a clatter of clinking glasses and noisy applause from the rest of the diners. I caught sight of Dr Gore raising a very large brandy glass in our direction. He was smiling his vampire smile while Mrs Savage, with her beringed hand on his arm, had an enigmatic smirk playing about her lips.

'Ees everything all right?' It was the head waiter who had materialised at my arm.

'*Oui! Oui!*' I exclaimed jumping up, grasping him by the shoulders and kissing him on both cheeks.

''Ere, steady on, squire,' he replied in a distinctly Yorkshire accent, looking acutely embarrassed. 'You've no need to carry on like that.'

'*Le repas était excellent*,' exclaimed Christine suddenly, '*en dépit du fait que la soupe était froide, la viande pas assez cuite, le vin tiède, et l'ambiance celle d'un abattoir. A part ça, tout était superbe.*'

'Thanks very much, madam,' said the waiter with a wan smile. 'Very kind of you, I'm sure.' He looked distinctly uncomfortable. 'I'm not all that good with French,' he whispered, retaining the weak smile. 'The boss just likes us to put on the accent. Gives the place a bit of class, you know.' He added in a feeble voice, 'Actually, I was born in Barnsley.' Then he continued as an afterthought, 'They don't speak much French in Barnsley.'

We let the taxi wait and stood with our arms around each other on the little hump-backed bridge in front of the restaurant. In the clear moonlight, the swirling waters beneath were speckled in myriad colours: rose-pink and silver, slate-grey and russet red, shimmering yellow and tenderest blue. A few leaves eddied in the pools, while old dead oaks, garlanded in ivy, stood upright with roots agape to the sky and willows wept and shivered in the breeze. From its banks, shadowy pastures climbed up the fellside and the great buffs of limestone towered above us like tall castle walls. The smell of wet wood and honeysuckle mingled in the still air. A distant farm dog yapped, and high above an owl gave a hunting shriek.

Christine's blue eyes were bright with pleasure and her

blonde hair shone golden in the moonlight. I stooped to kiss her.

'I'd like six,' I said, wrapping my arms around her waist.

'Six what?' Christine asked.

'Children. I'd like six children.'

'Let's think about that later, shall we?' she replied, reaching up to kiss me.

'You *do* want children?' I asked.

'Yes, of course, but not right at this moment and I might want eight.'

'Ey up! Are tha ready or what?' said a loud voice in my ear.

I very nearly tumbled off the bridge, and turned to face the taxi driver standing with hands on hips. 'I've got a lot o' calls toneet, tha knaws. Can't be messin' abaat whilst tha looks at t'river. It's been theer since Battle o' Ribsdyke 'undreds o' years back. It'll still be theer in t' mornin'. So let's be 'avin' thee.'

Christine and I hooted with laughter so loudly that it was the taxi driver's turn to jump with surprise.

'Are you two all reight?'

'We're champion, aren't we, Chris?' I exclaimed robustly, in true Yorkshire fashion. 'Just champion!'

Remember Me?

'Do you remember me?' asked the young man.
The old man at the bus stop,
Shabby, standing in the sun, alone,
Looked round.
He stared for a moment screwing up his eyes,
Then shook his head.
'No, I don't remember you.'
'You used to teach me,' said the young man.
'I've taught so many,' said the old man, sighing.
'I forget.'
'I was the boy you said was useless,
Good for nothing, a waste of space.
Who always left your classroom crying,
And dreaded every lesson that you taught.'
The old man shook his head and turned away.
'No, I don't remember you,' he murmured.
'Well, I remember you,' the young man said.

refresh yourself at penguin.co.uk

Visit penguin.co.uk for exclusive information and interviews with
bestselling authors, fantastic give-aways and the
inside track on all our books, from the Penguin Classics
to the latest bestsellers.

BE FIRST

first chapters, first editions, first novels

EXCLUSIVES

author chats, video interviews, biographies, special
features

EVERYONE'S A WINNER

give-aways, competitions, quizzes, ecards

READERS GROUPS

exciting features to support existing groups and
create new ones

NEWS

author events, bestsellers, awards, what's new

EBOOKS

books that click – download an ePenguin today

BROWSE AND BUY

thousands of books to investigate – search, try
and buy the perfect gift online – or treat yourself!

ABOUT US

job vacancies, advice for writers and company
history

Get Closer To Penguin ... www.penguin.co.uk

TOUS LES MATINS DU MONDE

PASCAL QUIGNARD

TOUS LES MATINS
DU MONDE

roman

nrf

GALLIMARD

Il a été tiré de l'édition originale de cet ouvrage cinquante exemplaires sur vergé blanc de Hollande numérotés de 1 à 50.

Colombe allait s'asseoir le soir quand le temps était agréable. Il n'était pas riche sans qu'il pût se plaindre de pauvreté. Il possédait une terre dans le Berry qui lui laissait un petit revenu et du vin qu'il échangeait contre du drap et parfois du gibier. Il était maladroit à la chasse et répugnait à parcourir les forêts qui surplombaient la vallée. L'argent que ses élèves lui remettaient complétait ses ressources. Il enseignait la viole qui connaissait alors un engouement à Londres et à Paris. C'était un maître réputé. Il avait à son service deux valets et une cuisinière qui s'occupait des petites. Un homme qui appartenait à la société qui fréquentait Port-Royal, Monsieur de Bures, apprit aux enfants les lettres, les chiffres, l'histoire sainte et les rudiments du latin qui permettent de la comprendre. Monsieur de Bures logeait dans le cul-de-sac de la rue Saint-Dominique-d'Enfer. C'est Madame de Pont-Carré qui avait recommandé Monsieur de Bures à Sainte Colombe. Celui-ci avait inculqué à ses filles, dès l'âge le plus tendre, les notes et les clés. Elles chantaient bien et avaient de réelles dispositions pour la musique. Tous les trois, quand Toinette eut cinq ans et Madeleine neuf, firent des petits trios à voix qui présentaient un certain nombre de difficultés et il était content de l'élégance avec laquelle ses filles les résolvaient. Alors, les petites ressemblaient plus à Sainte Colombe qu'elles n'évoquaient les traits de leur mère ; cependant le souvenir de cette dernière était intact en lui. Au bout de trois ans, son apparence était toujours dans ses yeux. Au bout de cinq ans, sa voix chuchotait toujours dans ses oreilles. Il était le plus souvent taciturne, n'allait ni à Paris ni à Jouy. Deux années après la mort de Madame de Sainte Colombe, il vendit son cheval. Il ne pouvait contenir le regret de ne pas avoir été présent quand sa femme avait rendu l'âme. Il était alors au chevet d'un étaient à leurs leçons ou à leurs jeux; ou encore après que Guignotte, la cuisinière, les avait couchées. Il estimait que la musique aurait mis de l'encombrement à la conversation des deux petites filles qui papotaient dans le noir avant de s'endormir. Il trouva une façon différente de tenir la viole entre les genoux et sans la faire reposer sur le mollet. Il ajouta une corde basse à l'instrument pour le doter d'une possibilité plus grave et afin de lui procurer un tour plus mélancolique. Il perfectionna la technique de l'archet en allégeant le poids de la main et en ne faisant porter la pression que sur les crins, à l'aide de l'index et du médius, ce qu'il faisait avec une virtuosité étonnante. Un de ses élèves, Côme Le Blanc le père, disait qu'il arrivait à imiter toutes les inflexions de la voix humaine : du soupir d'une jeune femme au sanglot d'un homme qui est âgé, du cri de guerre de Henri de Navarre à la

CHAPITRE II

La route qui menait chez Sainte Colombe était boueuse dès que les froids venaient. Sainte Colombe avait de la détestation pour Paris, pour le claquement des sabots et le cliquetis des éperons sur les pavés, pour les cris que faisaient les essieux des carrosses et le fer des charrettes. Il était maniaque. Il écrasait les cerfs-volants et les hannetons avec le fond des bougeoirs : cela produisait un bruit singulier, les mandibules ou les élytres craquant lentement sous la pression

15

régulière du métal. Les petites aimaient le voir faire et y prendre plaisir. Elles lui apportaient même des coccinelles.

L'homme n'était pas si froid qu'on l'a décrit; il était gauche dans l'expression de ses émotions; il ne savait pas faire les gestes caressants dont les enfants sont gloutons; il n'était pas capable d'un entretien suivi avec personne, sauf Messieurs Baugin et Lancelot. Sainte Colombe avait fait ses études en compagnie de Claude Lancelot et il le retrouvait quelquefois les jours où Madame de Pont-Carré recevait. Au physique, c'était un homme haut, épineux, très maigre, jaune comme un coing, brusque. Il se tenait le dos très droit, de façon étonnante, le regard fixe, les lèvres serrées l'une sur l'autre. Il était plein d'embarras mais il était capable de gaieté.

Il aimait jouer aux cartes avec ses filles, en buvant du vin. Il fumait alors, chaque soir, une longue pipe en terre d'Ardennes. Il n'était guère assidu à suivre la mode. Il portait les cheveux noirs ramassés comme au temps des guerres et, autour du cou, la fraise quand il sortait. Il avait été présenté au feu roi dans sa jeunesse et de ce jour, sans qu'on sût pourquoi, n'avait plus mis les pieds au Louvre ni au château-vieux de Saint-Germain. Il ne quitta plus le noir pour les habits.

Il était aussi violent et courrouçable qu'il pouvait être tendre. Quand il entendait pleurer durant la nuit, il lui arrivait de monter la chandelle à la main à l'étage et, agenouillé entre ses deux filles, de chanter :

Sola vivebat in antris Magdalena
Lugens et suspirans die ac nocte...

ou bien :

Il est mort pauvre et moi je vis comme il est mort
Et l'or
Dort
Dans le palais de marbre où le roi joue encore.

Parfois les petites demandaient, surtout Toinette :

« Qui était maman ? »

Alors il se rembrunissait et on ne pouvait plus tirer de lui un mot. Un jour, il leur dit :

« Il faut que vous soyez bonnes. Il faut que vous soyez travailleuses. Je suis content de vous deux, surtout de Madeleine, qui est plus sage. J'ai le regret de votre mère. Chacun des souvenirs que j'ai gardés de mon épouse est un morceau de joie que je ne retrouverai jamais. »

Il s'excusa une autre fois auprès d'elles de ce qu'il ne s'entendait guère à parler ; que leur mère, quant à elle, savait parler et rire ; que pour ce qui le concernait il n'avait guère d'attachement pour le langage et qu'il ne prenait pas de plaisir dans la compagnie des gens, ni dans celle des livres et des discours. Même les poésies de Vauquelin des Yveteaux et de ses anciens amis ne lui conve-

naient jamais entièrement. Il avait été lié à
Monsieur de La Petitière, qui avait été
garde du corps du Cardinal et s'était fait
depuis solitaire et cordonnier de ces messieurs en substitution à Monsieur Marais le
père. Même chose pour la peinture, outre
Monsieur Baugin. Monsieur de Sainte
Colombe ne louait pas la peinture que faisait
alors Monsieur de Champaigne. Il la jugeait
moins grave que triste, et moins sobre que
pauvre. Même chose pour l'architecture, ou
la sculpture, ou les arts mécaniques, ou la
religion, n'était Madame de Pont-Carré. Il
est vrai que Madame de Pont-Carré jouait
très bien du luth et du théorbe et qu'elle
n'avait pas sacrifié complètement ce don à
Dieu. Elle lui envoyait son carrosse de temps
à autre, n'en pouvant plus de tant de
privation de musique, le faisait venir dans
son hôtel et l'accompagnait au théorbe jusqu'à avoir la vue brouillée. Elle possédait
une viole noire qui datait du roi François Ier

et que Sainte Colombe maniait comme s'il s'était agi d'une idole d'Egypte.

Il était sujet à des colères sans raison qui jetaient l'épouvante dans l'âme des enfants parce que, au cours de ces accès, il brisait les meubles en criant : « Ah ! Ah ! » comme s'il étouffait. Il était très exigeant avec elles, ayant peur qu'elles ne fussent pas bien instruites par un homme seul. Il était sévère et ne manquait pas à les punir. Il ne savait pas les réprimander ni porter la main sur elles ni brandir le fouet ; aussi les enfermait-il dans le cellier ou dans la cave, où il les oubliait. Guignotte, la cuisinière, venait les délivrer.

Madeleine ne se plaignait jamais. A chaque colère de son père, elle était comme un vaisseau qui chavire et qui coule inopinément : elle ne mangeait plus et se retirait dans son silence. Toinette se rebellait, réclamait contre son père, criait après lui. Elle ressemblait par le caractère, au fur et à mesure qu'elle grandissait, à Madame de Sainte Colombe. Sa sœur, le nez baissé dans la peur, ne soufflait mot et refusait jusqu'à une cuillerée de soupe. Au reste, elles le voyaient peu. Elles vivaient dans la compagnie de Guignotte, de Monsieur Pardoux et de Monsieur de Bures. Ou elles allaient à la chapelle nettoyer les statues, ôter les toiles d'araignée et disposer les fleurs. Guignotte, qui était originaire du Languedoc et qui avait pour coutume de laisser ses cheveux toujours dénoués dans le dos, leur avait confectionné des gaules en rompant des branches dans les arbres. Toutes trois, avec un fil, un hameçon et une papillote nouée pour voir la touche, dès que les beaux jours étaient là, troussaient leur jupe et glissaient les pieds nus dans la vase. Elles sortaient de la Bièvre la friture du soir, qu'elles mêlaient ensuite dans la poêle avec un peu de farine de blé et de vinaigre tiré du vin de la vigne de Monsieur de Sainte Colombe, qui était

CHAPITRE III

Quand sa fille aînée eut atteint la taille nécessaire à l'apprentissage de la viole, il lui enseigna les dispositions, les accords, les arpèges, les ornements. L'enfant la plus petite fit de vives colères et presque des tempêtes que lui fût refusé l'honneur que son père consentait à sa sœur. Ni les privations de nourritures ni la cave ne purent réduire Toinette et calmer l'ébullition où elle se trouvait.

Un matin, avant que l'aube parût, Monsieur de Sainte Colombe se leva, suivit la Bièvre jusqu'au fleuve, suivit la Seine jusqu'au pont de la Dauphine, et s'entretint tout le jour avec Monsieur Pardoux, qui était son luthier. Il dessina avec lui. Il calcula avec lui, et il revint le jour tombant. Pour les pâques, alors que la cloche de la chapelle sonnait, Toinette trouva dans le jardin une étrange cloche enveloppée comme un fantôme dans une toile de serge grise. Elle souleva le tissu et découvrit une viole réduite à un demi-pied pour un pied. C'était, avec une exactitude digne d'admiration, une viole comme celle de son père ou celle de sa sœur, mais plus petite, comme les ânons sont aux chevaux. Toinette ne se tint pas de joie.

Elle était pâle, pareille à du lait, et elle pleura dans les genoux de son père tant elle était heureuse. Le caractère de Monsieur de Sainte Colombe et son peu de disposition au langage le rendaient d'une extrême pudeur et son visage demeurait inexpressif et sévère quoi qu'il sentît. Il n'y avait que dans ses compositions qu'on découvrait la complexité et la délicatesse du monde qui était caché sous ce visage et derrière les gestes rares et rigides. Il buvait du vin en caressant les cheveux de sa fille qui avait la tête enfouie dans son pourpoint et dont le dos était secoué.

Très vite les concerts à trois violes des Sainte Colombe furent renommés. Les jeunes seigneurs ou les fils de la bourgeoisie auxquels Monsieur de Sainte Colombe enseignait la manière de jouer de la viole prétendirent y assister. Les musiciens qui appartenaient à la corporation ou qui avaient de l'estime pour Monsieur de Sainte Colombe s'y rendirent aussi. Celui-ci alla jusqu'à organiser une fois tous les quinze jours un concert qui commençait à vêpres et qui durait quatre heures. Sainte Colombe s'efforçait, à chaque assemblée, de donner à

CHAPITRE IV

Monsieur Caignet et Monsieur Chambon-
nières étaient de ces assemblées de musique
et les louaient fort. Les seigneurs en avaient
fait leur caprice et on vit jusqu'à quinze
carrosses arrêtés sur la route boueuse, outre
les chevaux, et obstruer le passage pour les
voyageurs et les marchands qui se rendaient à Jouy ou à Trappes. A force qu'on
lui en eut rebattu les oreilles, le roi voulut
entendre ce musicien et ses filles. Il dépêcha
Monsieur Caignet — qui était le joueur de

viole attitré de Louis XIV et qui appartenait à sa chambre. Ce fut Toinette qui se précipita pour ouvrir la porte cochère de la cour et qui mena Monsieur Caignet au jardin. Monsieur de Sainte Colombe, blême et furieux qu'on l'eût dérangé dans sa retraite, descendit les quatre marches de sa cabane et salua.

Monsieur Caignet remit son chapeau et déclara :

« Monsieur, vous vivez dans la ruine et le silence. On vous envie cette sauvagerie. On vous envie ces forêts vertes qui vous surplombent. »

Monsieur de Sainte Colombe ne desserra pas les lèvres. Il le regardait fixement.

« Monsieur, reprit Monsieur Caignet, parce que vous êtes un maître dans l'art de la viole, j'ai reçu l'ordre de vous inviter à vous produire à la cour. Sa majesté a marqué le désir de vous entendre et, dans le cas où elle serait satisfaite, elle vous accueillerait parmi les musiciens de la chambre.

Dans cette circonstance j'aurais l'honneur de me trouver à vos côtés. »

Monsieur de Sainte Colombe répondit qu'il était un homme âgé et veuf; qu'il avait la charge de deux filles, ce qui l'obligeait à demeurer dans une façon de vivre plus privée qu'un autre homme; qu'il ressentait du dégoût pour le monde.

« Monsieur, dit-il, j'ai confié ma vie à des planches de bois grises qui sont dans un mûrier; aux sons des sept cordes d'une viole; à mes deux filles. Mes amis sont les souvenirs. Ma cour, ce sont les saules qui sont là, l'eau qui court, les chevesnes, les goujons et les fleurs du sureau. Vous direz à sa majesté que son palais n'a rien à faire d'un sauvage qui fut présenté au feu roi son père il y a trente-cinq ans de cela.

— Monsieur, répondit Monsieur Caignet, vous n'entendez pas ma requête. J'appartiens à la chambre du roi. Le souhait que marque sa majesté est un ordre. »

Le visage de Monsieur de Sainte Colombe s'empourpra. Ses yeux luisirent de colère. Il s'avança à le toucher.

« Je suis si sauvage, Monsieur, que je pense que je n'appartiens qu'à moi-même. Vous direz à sa majesté qu'elle s'est montrée trop généreuse quand elle a posé son regard sur moi. »

Monsieur de Sainte Colombe poussait Monsieur Caignet vers la maison tout en parlant. Ils se saluèrent. Monsieur de Sainte Colombe regagna la vorde tandis que Toinette allait au poulailler, qui se trouvait à l'angle du mur clos et de la Bièvre.

Pendant ce temps-là, Monsieur Caignet revint avec son chapeau et son épée, s'approcha de la cabane, écarta avec sa botte un dindon et des petits poussins jaunes qui picoraient, se glissa sous le plancher de la cabane, s'assit dans l'herbe, dans l'ombre et les racines et écouta. Puis il repartit sans qu'on le vît et regagna le Louvre. Il parla au roi, rapporta les raisons que le musicien avait avancées et lui fit part de l'impression merveilleuse et difficile que lui avait faite la musique qu'il avait entendue à la dérobée.

CHAPITRE V

Le roi était mécontent de ne pas posséder Monsieur de Sainte Colombe. Les courtisans continuaient de vanter ses improvisations virtuoses. Le déplaisir de ne pas être obéi ajoutait à l'impatience où se trouvait le roi de voir le musicien jouer devant lui. Il renvoya Monsieur Caignet accompagné de l'abbé Mathieu.

Le carrosse qui les menait était accompagné par deux officiers à cheval. L'abbé Mathieu portait un habit noir en satin, un petit collet à ruché de dentelles, une grande croix de diamants sur la poitrine.

Madeleine les fit entrer dans la salle. L'abbé Mathieu, devant la cheminée, posa ses mains garnies de bagues sur sa canne en bois rouge à pommeau d'argent. Monsieur de Sainte Colombe, devant la porte-fenêtre qui donnait sur le jardin, posa ses mains nues sur le dossier d'une chaise étroite et haute. L'abbé Mathieu commença par prononcer ces mots :

« Les musiciens et les poètes de l'Antiquité aimaient la gloire et ils pleuraient quand les empereurs ou les princes les tenaient éloignés de leur présence. Vous enfouissez votre nom parmi les dindons, les poules et les petits poissons. Vous cachez un talent qui vous vient de Notre-Seigneur dans la poussière et dans la détresse orgueilleuse. Votre réputation est connue du roi et de sa cour, il est donc temps pour vous de brûler vos vêtements de drap, d'accepter ses bienfaits, de vous faire faire une perruque à grappes. Votre fraise est passée de mode et...

— ... c'est moi qui suis passé de mode, Messieurs, s'écria Sainte Colombe, soudain vexé qu'on s'en prît à sa façon de s'habiller. Vous remercierez sa majesté, cria-t-il. Je préfère la lumière du couchant sur mes mains à l'or qu'elle me propose. Je préfère mes vêtements de drap à vos perruques in-folio. Je préfère mes poules aux violons du roi et mes porcs à vous-mêmes.

— Monsieur ! »

Mais Monsieur de Sainte Colombe avait brandi la chaise et la soulevait au-dessus de leurs têtes. Il cria encore :

« Quittez-moi et ne m'en parlez plus ! Ou je casse cette chaise sur votre tête. »

Toinette et Madeleine étaient effrayées par l'aspect de leur père tenant à bout de bras la chaise au-dessus de sa tête et craignaient qu'il ne se possédât plus. L'abbé

Mathieu ne parut pas effrayé et tapota avec sa canne le carreau en disant :

« Vous mourrez desséché comme une petite souris au fond de votre cabinet de planches, sans être connu de personne. »

Monsieur de Sainte Colombe fit tourner la chaise et la brisa sur le manteau de la cheminée, en hurlant de nouveau :

« Votre palais est plus petit qu'une cabane et votre public est moins qu'une personne. »

L'abbé Mathieu s'avança en caressant des doigts sa croix de diamants et dit :

« Vous allez pourrir dans votre boue, dans l'horreur des banlieues, noyé dans votre ruisseau. »

Monsieur de Sainte Colombe était blanc comme du papier, tremblait et voulut saisir une seconde chaise. Monsieur Caignet s'était approché ainsi que Toinette. Monsieur de Sainte Colombe poussait des « Ah ! » sourds pour reprendre souffle, les mains sur le dossier de la chaise. Toinette dénoua ses doigts et ils l'assirent. Tandis que Monsieur Caignet enfilait ses gants et remettait son chapeau et que l'abbé le traitait d'opiniâtre, il dit tout bas, avec un calme effrayant :

« Vous êtes des noyés. Aussi tendez-vous la main. Non contents d'avoir perdu pied, vous voudriez encore attirer les autres pour les engloutir. »

Le débit de sa voix était lent et saccadé. Le roi aima cette réponse quand l'abbé et le violiste de sa chambre la lui rapportèrent. Il dit qu'on laissât en paix le musicien tout en enjoignant à ses courtisans de ne plus se rendre à ses assemblées de musique parce qu'il était une espèce de récalcitrant et qu'il avait eu partie liée avec ces Messieurs de Port-Royal, avant qu'il les eût dispersés.

CHAPITRE VI

Pendant plusieurs années ils vécurent dans la paix et pour la musique. Toinette quitta sa petite viole et vint le jour où, une fois par mois, elle mit du linge entre ses jambes. Ils ne donnaient plus qu'un concert toutes les saisons où Monsieur de Sainte Colombe conviait les musiciens ses confrères, quand il les estimait, et auquel il n'invitait pas les seigneurs de Versailles ni même les bourgeois, qui gagnaient en ascendant sur l'esprit du roi. Il notait de moins en moins de compositions nouvelles sur son cahier couvert de cuir rouge et il ne voulut pas les faire imprimer et les soumettre au jugement du public. Il disait qu'il s'agissait là d'improvisations notées dans l'instant et auxquelles l'instant seul servait d'excuse, et non pas des œuvres achevées. Madeleine devenait belle, d'une beauté mince, et pleine d'une curiosité dont elle ne percevait pas le motif et qui lui procurait des sentiments d'angoisse. Toinette progressait en joie, en invention et en virtuosité.

Les jours où l'humeur et le temps qu'il faisait lui en laissaient le loisir, il allait à sa barque et, accroché à la rive, dans son ruisseau, il rêvait. Sa barque était vieille et prenait l'eau : elle avait été faite quand le surintendant réorganisait les canaux et était peinte en blanc, encore que les années eussent écaillé la peinture qui la recouvrait. La barque avait l'apparence d'une grande viole que Monsieur Pardoux aurait ouverte.

Il aimait le balancement que donnait l'eau, le feuillage des branches des saules qui tombait sur son visage et le silence et l'attention des pêcheurs plus loin. Il songeait à sa femme, à l'entrain qu'elle mettait en toutes choses, aux conseils avisés qu'elle lui donnait quand il les lui demandait, à ses hanches et à son grand ventre qui lui avaient donné deux filles qui étaient devenues des femmes. Il écoutait les chevesnes et les goujons s'ébattre et rompre le silence d'un coup de queue ou bien au moyen de leurs petites bouches blanches qui s'ouvraient à la surface de l'eau pour manger l'air. L'été, quand il faisait très chaud, il faisait glisser ses chausses et ôtait sa chemise et pénétrait doucement dans l'eau fraîche jusqu'au col puis, en se bouchant avec les doigts les oreilles, y ensevelissait son visage.

Un jour qu'il concentrait son regard sur les vagues de l'onde, s'assoupissant, il rêva qu'il pénétrait dans l'eau obscure et qu'il y séjournait. Il avait renoncé à toutes les choses qu'il aimait sur cette terre, les instruments, les fleurs, les pâtisseries, les partitions roulées, les cerfs-volants, les visages, les plats d'étain, les vins. Sorti de son songe, il se souvint du Tombeau des Regrets qu'il avait composé quand son épouse l'avait quitté une nuit pour rejoindre la mort, il eut très soif aussi. Il se leva, monta sur la rive en s'accrochant aux branches, partit chercher sous les voûtes de la cave une carafe de vin cuit entourée de paille tressée. Il versa sur la terre battue la couche d'huile qui préservait le vin du contact de l'air. Dans la nuit de la cave, il prit un verre et il le goûta. Il gagna la cabane du jardin où il s'exerçait à la viole, moins, pour dire toute la vérité, dans l'inquiétude de donner de la gêne à ses filles que dans le souci où il était de n'être à portée d'aucune oreille et de pouvoir essayer les positions de la main et tous les mouvements possibles de son archet sans que personne au monde pût porter quelque jugement que ce fût sur ce qu'il lui prenait envie de faire. Il posa sur le tapis bleu clair qui recouvrait la table où il dépliait son pupitre la carafe de vin garnie de paille, le verre à vin à pied qu'il remplit, un plat d'étain contenant quelques gaufrettes enroulées et il joua le Tombeau des Regrets.

Il n'eut pas besoin de se reporter à son livre. Sa main se dirigeait d'elle-même sur la touche de son instrument et il se prit à pleurer. Tandis que le chant montait, près de la porte une femme très pâle apparut qui lui souriait tout en posant le doigt sur son sourire en signe qu'elle ne parlerait pas et qu'il ne se dérangeât pas de ce qu'il était en train de faire. Elle contourna en silence le pupitre de Monsieur de Sainte Colombe. Elle s'assit sur le coffre à musique qui était dans le coin auprès de la table et du flacon de vin et elle l'écouta.

C'était sa femme et ses larmes coulaient.

CHAPITRE VII

Cette visite ne fut pas seule. Monsieur de
Sainte Colombe, après avoir craint qu'il
pût être fou, considéra que si c'était folie,
elle lui donnait du bonheur, si c'était vérité,
c'était un miracle. L'amour que lui portait
sa femme était plus grand encore que le
sien puisqu'elle venait jusqu'à lui et qu'il
était impuissant à lui rendre la pareille. Il
prit un crayon et il demanda à un ami
appartenant à la corporation des peintres,
Monsieur Baugin, qu'il fît un sujet qui

représentât la table à écrire près de laquelle sa femme était apparue. Mais il ne parla de cette visitation à personne. Même Madeleine, même Toinette ne surent rien. Il se confiait simplement à sa viole et parfois recopiait sur son cahier en maroquin, sur lequel Toinette avait tiré à la règle des portées, les thèmes que ses entretiens ou que ses rêveries lui avaient inspirés. Dans sa chambre, dont il fermait la porte à clef parce que le désir et le souvenir de sa femme le poussaient parfois à descendre ses braies et à se donner du plaisir avec la main, il posait côte à côte, sur la table près de la fenêtre, sur le mur qui faisait face au grand lit à baldaquin qu'il avait partagé douze années durant avec sa femme, le livre de musique en maroquin rouge et la petite toile qu'il avait commandée à son ami, entourée d'un cadre noir. Il éprouvait en la voyant du bonheur. Il était moins souvent courroucé et ses deux filles le remarquèrent mais n'osèrent pas le lui dire. Au fond de lui, il avait le sentiment que quelque chose s'était achevé. Il avait l'air plus quiet.

CHAPITRE VIII

Un jour, un grand enfant de dix-sept ans, rouge comme la crête d'un vieux coq, vint frapper à leur porte et demanda à Madeleine s'il pouvait solliciter de Monsieur de Sainte Colombe qu'il devînt son maître pour la viole et la composition. Madeleine le trouva très beau et le fit entrer dans la salle. Le jeune homme, la perruque à la main, posa une lettre pliée en deux et cachetée à la cire verte sur la table. Toinette revint avec Sainte Colombe qui s'assit à l'autre extrémité de la table en silence, ne décacheta pas la lettre et fit signe qu'il écoutait. Madeleine, tandis que le garçon parlait, disposait sur la grande table, qui était couverte d'une pièce d'étoffe bleue, une fiasque de vin enveloppée de paille et une assiette en faïence qui contenait des gâteaux.

Il s'appelait Monsieur Marin Marais. Il était joufflu. Il était né le 31 mai 1656 et, à l'âge de six ans, avait été recruté à cause de sa voix pour appartenir à la maîtrise du roi dans la chantrerie de l'église qui est à la porte du château du Louvre. Pendant neuf ans, il avait porté le surplis, la robe rouge, le bonnet carré noir, couché dans le dortoir du cloître et appris ses lettres, appris à noter, à lire et à jouer de la viole autant qu'il restait de temps disponible, les enfants ne cessant de courir à l'office des matines, aux services chez le roi, aux grand-messes, aux vêpres.

Puis, quand sa voix s'était brisée, il avait été rejeté à la rue ainsi que le contrat de chantrerie le stipulait. Il avait honte encore. Il ne savait où se mettre ; les poils lui étaient poussés aux jambes et aux joues ; il barrissait. Il évoqua ce jour d'humiliation dont la date était demeurée inscrite dans son esprit : 22 septembre 1672. Pour la dernière fois, sous le porche de l'église, il s'était arc-bouté, il avait pesé avec son épaule sur la grande porte de bois doré. Il avait traversé le jardin qui bornait le cloître de Saint-Germain-l'Auxerrois. Il y avait vu des quetsches dans l'herbe.

Il se mit à courir dans la rue, passa le For-L'Evêque, descendit la pente brusque qui menait à la grève et s'immobilisa. La Seine était couverte par une lumière immense et épaisse de fin d'été, mêlée à une brume rouge. Il sanglotait et il suivit la rive pour retourner chez son père. Il donnait des coups de pied ou tamponnait les cochons, les oies, les enfants qui jouaient dans l'herbe et la boue craquelée de la grève. Les hommes nus et les femmes en chemise se lavaient dans la rivière, l'eau au mollet.

Cette eau qui coulait entre ces rives était une blessure qui saignait. La blessure qu'il avait reçue à la gorge lui paraissait aussi irrémédiable que la beauté du fleuve. Ce pont, ces tours, la vieille cité, son enfance et le Louvre, les plaisirs de la voix à la chapelle, les jeux dans le petit jardin du cloître, son surplis blanc, son passé, les quetsches violettes reculaient à jamais emportés par l'eau rouge. Son compagnon de dortoir, Delalande, avait encore sa voix et il était resté. Il avait le cœur plein de nostalgie. Il se sentait seul, comme une bête bêlante, le sexe épais et poilu pendant entre les cuisses.

Perruque à la main, il ressentit tout à coup de la honte de ce qu'il venait de dire. Monsieur de Sainte Colombe demeurait le dos tout droit, les traits impénétrables. Madeleine tendit vers l'adolescent une des pâtisseries avec un sourire qui l'encourageait à parler. Toinette s'était assise sur le coffre, derrière son père, les genoux au menton. L'enfant poursuivit.

Quand il était arrivé à la cordonnerie, après qu'il eut salué son père, il n'avait pu retenir plus longtemps ses sanglots et était monté avec précipitation s'enfermer dans la pièce où on disposait le soir les paillasses, au-dessus de l'atelier où son père travaillait. Son père, l'enclume ou bien la forme en fer sur la cuisse, ne cessait de taper ou de râper le cuir d'un soulier ou d'une botte. Ces coups de marteau lui faisaient sauter le cœur et l'emplissaient de répugnance. Il haïssait l'odeur d'urine où les peaux macéraient et l'odeur fade du seau d'eau sous l'établi où son père laissait à tremper les contreforts. La cage aux serins et leurs piaillements, le tabouret à lanières qui grinçait, les cris de son père — tout lui était insupportable. Il détestait les chants oiseux ou grivois que son

comme il la tripotait, expliqua qu'au sortir
de Saint-Germain-l'Auxerrois il était allé
chez Monsieur Caignet qui l'avait gardé
durant presque un an puis qui l'avait
adressé à Monsieur Maugars : c'était le fils
du violiste qui avait appartenu à Monsieur
de Richelieu. Quand il le reçut, Monsieur
Maugars lui demanda s'il avait entendu
parler de la renommée de Monsieur de
Sainte Colombe et de sa septième corde : il
avait conçu un instrument en bois qui
couvrait toutes les possibilités de la voix
humaine : celle de l'enfant, celle de la
femme, celle de l'homme brisée, et aggravée.
Durant six mois Monsieur Maugars l'avait
fait travailler puis lui avait enjoint d'aller
trouver Monsieur de Sainte Colombe, qui
habitait au-delà du fleuve, en lui présentant
cette lettre et en se recommandant de lui. Le
jeune garçon poussa alors la lettre en direction de Monsieur de Sainte Colombe. Ce
dernier rompit le cachet, la déplia mais, sans

l'avoir lue, désira parler, se leva. C'est ainsi qu'un adolescent qui n'osait plus ouvrir la bouche rencontra un homme taciturne. Monsieur de Sainte Colombe ne parvint pas à s'exprimer, reposa la lettre sur la table et s'approcha de Madeleine et lui murmura que c'était jouer qu'il fallait. Elle quitta la salle. Vêtu de drap noir, la fraise blanche à son cou, Monsieur de Sainte Colombe se dirigea vers la cheminée, près de laquelle il s'assit dans un grand fauteuil à bras.

Pour la première leçon, Madeleine prêta sa viole. Marin Marais était encore plus confus et rouge que lorsqu'il était entré dans la maison. Les filles s'assirent plus près, curieuses de voir comment l'ancien enfant de chœur de Saint-Germain-l'Auxerrois jouait. Il s'accoutuma rapidement à la taille de l'instrument, l'accorda, joua une suite de Monsieur Maugars avec beaucoup d'aisance et de virtuosité.

Il regarda ses auditeurs. Les filles baissaient le nez. Monsieur de Sainte Colombe dit :

« Je ne pense pas que je vais vous admettre parmi mes élèves. »

Un long silence suivit qui fit trembler le visage de l'adolescent. Il cria soudain avec sa voix rauque :

« Au moins dites-moi pourquoi !

— Vous faites de la musique, Monsieur. Vous n'êtes pas musicien. »

Le visage de l'adolescent se figea, les larmes montèrent à ses yeux. Il bégaya de détresse :

« Au moins laissez-moi... »

Sainte Colombe se leva, retourna le grand fauteuil en bois face à l'âtre. Toinette dit :

« Attendez, mon père. Monsieur Marais a peut-être en mémoire un air de sa composition. »

Monsieur Marais inclina la tête. Il s'empressa. Il se pencha aussitôt sur la viole pour l'accorder plus soigneusement qu'il n'avait fait et joua le Badinage en si.

« C'est bien, père. C'est très bien ! » dit Toinette quand il eut fini de jouer et elle applaudit.

« Qu'en dites-vous ? » demanda Madeleine en se tournant vers son père avec appréhension.

Sainte Colombe était resté debout. Il les quitta brusquement et alla pour sortir. Au moment de franchir la porte de la salle, il tourna son visage, dévisagea l'enfant qui était demeuré assis, la face rouge, épouvantée, et dit :

« Revenez dans un mois. Je vous dirai alors si vous avez assez de valeur pour que je vous compte au nombre de mes élèves. »

CHAPITRE IX

Le petit air de badinage que lui avait joué l'enfant lui revenait parfois à l'esprit et il en était ému. C'était un air mondain et facile mais qui avait de la tendresse. Il oublia enfin l'air. Il travailla davantage dans la cabane.

La quatrième fois où il sentit le corps de son épouse à ses côtés, détournant les yeux de son visage, il lui demanda :

« Parlez-vous, Madame, malgré la mort ?

— Oui. »

Il frémit parce qu'il avait reconnu sa voix. Une voix basse, du moins contralto. Il avait le désir de pleurer mais n'y parvint pas tant il était surpris, dans le même temps, que ce songe parlât. Le dos tremblant, au bout d'un moment, il trouva le courage pour demander encore :

« Pourquoi venez-vous de temps à autre ? Pourquoi ne venez-vous pas toujours ?

— Je ne sais pas, dit l'ombre en rougissant. Je suis venue parce que ce que vous jouiez m'a émue. Je suis venue parce que vous avez eu la bonté de m'offrir à boire et quelques gâteaux à grignoter.

— Madame ! » s'écria-t-il.

Il se leva aussitôt, plein de violence, au point qu'il fit tomber son tabouret. Il éloigna la viole de son corps parce qu'elle le gênait et la posa contre la paroi de planches, sur sa gauche. Il ouvrit les bras comme s'il entendait déjà l'étreindre. Elle cria :

« Non ! »

Elle se reculait. Il baissa la tête. Elle lui dit :

« Mes membres, mes seins sont devenus froids. »

Elle avait du mal à retrouver son souffle. Elle donnait l'impression de quelqu'un qui a fait un effort trop grand. Elle touchait ses cuisses et ses seins tandis qu'elle disait ces mots. Il baissa la tête de nouveau et elle revint s'asseoir alors sur le tabouret. Quand elle eut recouvré un souffle plus égal, elle lui dit doucement :

« Donnez-moi plutôt un verre de votre vin de couleur rouge pour que j'y trempe mes lèvres. »

Il sortit en hâte, alla au cellier, descendit à la cave. Quand il revint, Madame de Sainte Colombe n'était plus là.

CHAPITRE X

Quand il arriva pour son deuxième cours, ce fut Madeleine, très mince, les joues roses, qui ouvrit la grande porte cochère.

« Parce que je vais me baigner, dit-elle, je vais relever mes cheveux. »

Sa nuque était rose, avec des petits poils noirs ébouriffés dans la clarté. Comme elle levait ses bras, ses seins se serraient et gonflaient. Ils se dirigèrent vers la cabane de Monsieur de Sainte Colombe. C'était une belle journée de printemps. Il y avait des primevères et il y avait des papillons. Marin Marais portait sa viole à l'épaule. Monsieur de Sainte Colombe le fit entrer dans la cabane sur le mûrier et il l'accepta pour élève en disant :

« Vous connaissez la position du corps. Votre jeu ne manque pas de sentiment. Votre archet est léger et bondit. Votre main gauche saute comme un écureuil et se faufile comme une souris sur les cordes. Vos ornements sont ingénieux et parfois charmants. Mais je n'ai pas entendu de musique. »

Le jeune Marin Marais éprouvait des sentiments mêlés en entendant les conclusions de son maître : il était heureux d'être accepté et il bouillait de colère devant les réserves que Monsieur de Sainte Colombe mettait en avant les unes après les autres sans marquer plus d'émotion que s'il s'était agi d'indiquer au jardinier les boutures et les semences. Ce dernier continuait :

« Vous pourrez aider à danser les gens qui

dansent. Vous pourrez accompagner les acteurs qui chantent sur la scène. Vous gagnerez votre vie. Vous vivrez entouré de musique mais vous ne serez pas musicien.

« Avez-vous un cœur pour sentir ? Avez-vous un cerveau pour penser ? Avez-vous idée de ce à quoi peuvent servir les sons quand il ne s'agit plus de danser ni de réjouir les oreilles du roi ?

« Cependant votre voix brisée m'a ému. Je vous garde pour votre douleur, non pour votre art. »

Quand le jeune Marais descendit les marches de la cabane, il vit, dans l'ombre que faisaient les feuillages, une jeune fille longue et nue qui se cachait derrière un arbre et il détourna en hâte la tête pour ne pas sembler l'avoir vue.

CHAPITRE XI

Les mois passèrent. Un jour où il faisait très froid et où la campagne était recouverte de neige, ils ne purent travailler longtemps qu'ils ne fussent transis. Leurs doigts étaient gourds et ils quittèrent la cabane, regagnèrent la maison et, près de l'âtre, firent chauffer du vin, y ajoutèrent des épices et de la cannelle, et le burent.

« Ce vin réchauffe mes poumons et mon ventre, dit Marin Marais.

« — Connaissez-vous le peintre Baugin? lui demanda Sainte Colombe.

— Non, Monsieur, ni aucun autre peintre.

— Je lui ai naguère passé commande d'une toile. C'est le coin de ma table à écrire qui est dans mon cabinet de musique. Allons-y.

— Sur-le-champ?

— Oui. »

Marin Marais regardait Madeleine de Sainte Colombe : elle se tenait de profil près de la fenêtre, devant le carreau pris de givre, qui déformait les images du mûrier et des saules. Elle écoutait avec attention. Elle lui lança un regard singulier.

« Allons voir mon ami, disait Sainte Colombe.

— Oui », disait Marin Marais.

Ce dernier, comme il regardait Madeleine, ouvrait son pourpoint, ajustait et relaçait son collet de buffle.

« C'est à Paris, disait Monsieur de Sainte Colombe.

— Oui », lui répondait Marin Marais.

Ils s'emmitouflèrent. Monsieur de Sainte Colombe entoura son visage dans un carré de laine ; Madeleine tendait chapeaux, capes, gants. Monsieur de Sainte Colombe décrocha près de l'âtre le baudrier et l'épée. Ce fut la seule fois où Monsieur Marais vit Monsieur de Sainte Colombe porter l'épée. Le jeune homme tenait les yeux fixés sur l'estocade signée : on y voyait, bosselée, en relief, la figure du nocher infernal, une gaffe à la main.

« Allons, Monsieur », dit Sainte Colombe.

Marin Marais releva la tête et ils sortirent. Marin Marais rêvait au forgeron à l'instant où il avait frappé l'épée sur l'enclume. Il revit la petite enclume de cordonnier que son père posait sur sa cuisse et sur laquelle il frappait avec son marteau.

Il rêva à la main de son père et à la callosité qu'y avait empreinte le marteau quand il la passait sur sa joue, le soir, quand il était âgé de quatre ou cinq ans, avant qu'il quittât l'échoppe pour la chantrerie. Il songea que chaque métier avait ses mains : les cals aux gras des doigts de la main gauche des gambistes, les durillons aux pouces droits des savetiers-bottiers. Il neigeait quand ils sortirent de la maison de Monsieur de Sainte Colombe. Ce dernier était enveloppé dans une grande cape brune et on ne voyait que ses yeux sous son carré de laine. Ce fut l'unique fois où Monsieur Marais vit son maître au-dehors de son jardin ou de sa maison. Il passait pour ne jamais les quitter. Ils rejoignirent la Bièvre en aval. Le vent sifflait ; leurs pas faisaient craquer la terre prise de gel. Sainte Colombe avait saisi son élève par le bras et il posait son doigt sur ses lèvres en signe de se taire. Ils marchaient bruyam-

CHAPITRE XII

« C'est Saint-Germain-l'Auxerrois, dit Monsieur de Sainte Colombe.

— Je le sais plus qu'un autre. J'y ai chanté dix ans, Monsieur.

— Voici », dit Monsieur de Sainte Colombe.

Il frappait le marmot. C'était une porte étroite de bois ouvragé. On entendit sonner le carillon de Saint-Germain-l'Auxerrois. Une vieille femme passa la tête. Elle portait une ancienne coiffe en pointe sur le front. Ils se retrouvèrent près du poêle dans l'atelier de Monsieur Baugin. Le peintre était occupé à peindre une table : un verre à moitié plein de vin rouge, un luth couché, un cahier de musique, une bourse de velours noir, des cartes à jouer dont la première était un valet de trèfle, un échiquier sur lequel étaient disposés un vase avec trois œillets et un miroir octogonal appuyé contre le mur de l'atelier.

« Tout ce que la mort ôtera est dans sa nuit », souffla Sainte Colombe dans l'oreille de son élève. « Ce sont tous les plaisirs du monde qui se retirent en nous disant adieu. »

Monsieur de Sainte Colombe demanda au peintre s'il pouvait recouvrer la toile qu'il lui avait empruntée : le peintre avait voulu la montrer à un marchand des Flandres qui en avait tiré une copie. Monsieur Baugin fit un signe à la vieille femme qui portait la coiffe en pointe sur le front ; elle s'inclina et alla chercher les gaufrettes entourées d'ébène. Il la montra à Monsieur Marais, pointant le doigt sur le verre à pied et sur l'enroulement des petites pâtisseries jaunes. Puis la vieille femme impassible s'occupa à l'envelopper de chiffons et de cordes. Ils regardèrent le peintre peindre. Monsieur de Sainte Colombe souffla de nouveau dans l'oreille de Monsieur Marais :

« Ecoutez le son que rend le pinceau de Monsieur Baugin. »

Ils fermèrent les yeux et ils l'écoutèrent peindre. Puis Monsieur de Sainte Colombe dit :

« Vous avez appris la technique de l'archet. »

Comme Monsieur Baugin se retournait et les interrogeait sur ce qu'ils murmuraient entre eux :

« Je parlais de l'archet et je le comparais à votre pinceau, dit Monsieur de Sainte Colombe.

— Je crois que vous vous égarez, dit le peintre en riant. J'aime l'or. Personnellement je cherche la route qui mène jusqu'aux feux mystérieux. »

Ils saluèrent Monsieur Baugin. La coiffe blanche en pointe s'inclina sèchement devant eux tandis que la porte se refermait dans leur dos. Dans la rue la neige avait redoublé de violence et d'épaisseur. Ils n'y voyaient rien et trébuchaient dans la couche de la neige. Ils entrèrent dans un jeu de paume qui se trouvait là. Ils prirent un bol de soupe et le burent, soufflant sur la vapeur qui l'enveloppait, en marchant dans les salles. Ils virent des seigneurs qui jouaient entourés de leurs gens. Les jeunes dames qui les accompagnaient applaudissaient aux meilleurs coups. Ils virent dans une autre salle, montées sur des tréteaux, deux femmes qui récitaient. L'une disait d'une voix soutenue :

« Ils brillaient au travers des flambeaux et

des armes. Belle, sans ornements, dans le simple appareil d'une beauté qu'on vient d'arracher au sommeil. Que veux-tu ? Je ne sais si cette négligence, les ombres, les flambeaux, les cris et le silence... »

L'autre répondait lentement, à l'octave plus basse :

« J'ai voulu lui parler et ma voix s'est perdue. Immobile, saisi d'un long étonnement, de son image en vain j'ai voulu me distraire. Trop présente à mes yeux, je croyais lui parler, j'aimais jusqu'à ses pleurs que je faisais couler... »

Tandis que les actrices déclamaient avec de grands gestes étranges, Sainte Colombe chuchotait à l'oreille de Marais :

« Voilà comment s'articule l'emphase d'une phrase. La musique aussi est une langue humaine. »

Ils sortirent du jeu de paume. La neige avait cessé de tomber mais arrivait à la hauteur de leurs bottes. La nuit était là sans qu'il y eût de lune ni d'étoiles. Un homme passa avec une torche qu'il protégeait avec la main et ils le suivirent. Quelques flocons tombaient encore.

Monsieur de Sainte Colombe arrêta son disciple en lui prenant le bras : devant eux un petit garçon avait descendu ses chausses et pissait en faisant un trou dans la neige. Le bruit de l'urine chaude crevant la neige se mêlait au bruit des cristaux de la neige qui fondaient à mesure. Sainte Colombe tenait une fois encore le doigt sur ses lèvres.

« Vous avez appris le détaché des ornements, dit-il.

— C'est aussi une descente chromatique », rétorqua Monsieur Marin Marais.

Monsieur de Sainte Colombe haussa les épaules.

« Je mettrai une descente chromatique dans votre tombeau, Monsieur. »

C'est ce qu'il fit en effet, des années plus tard. Monsieur Marais ajouta :

« Peut-être la véritable musique est-elle liée au silence ?

— Non », dit Monsieur de Sainte Colombe. Il était en train de remettre le carré de laine sur sa tête et enfonça son chapeau pour le retenir. Déplaçant le baudrier de son épée qui entravait ses jambes, tenant toujours serrées les gaufrettes sous son bras, il se retourna et pissa lui-même contre le mur. Il pivota de nouveau vers Monsieur Marais en disant :

« La nuit est avancée. J'ai froid aux pieds. Je vous donne mon salut. »

Il le quitta tout à trac.

CHAPITRE XIII

C'était le commencement du printemps. Il le poussait hors de la cabane. Chacun la viole à la main, sans un mot, sous la pluie fine, ils traversèrent le jardin en direction de la maison où ils entrèrent en faisant du vacarme. Il appela en criant ses filles. Il avait l'air courroucé. Il dit :

« Allez, Monsieur. Allez. Il s'agit de faire naître une émotion dans nos oreilles. »

Toinette descendit l'escalier en courant. Elle s'assit près de la porte-fenêtre. Madeleine vint embrasser Marin Marais qui lui dit, tout en disposant sa viole entre ses jambes et en cherchant l'accord, qu'il avait joué devant le roi à la chapelle. Les yeux de Madeleine se firent plus graves. L'atmosphère était tendue, pareille à une corde sur le point de rompre. Tandis que Madeleine essuyait les gouttes de pluie sur la viole avec son tablier, Marin Marais répétait en chuchotant à son oreille :

« Il est furieux parce que j'ai joué hier devant le roi à la chapelle. »

Le visage de Monsieur de Sainte Colombe se rembrunit encore. Toinette fit un signe. Sans s'en soucier, Marin Marais expliquait à Madeleine qu'on avait glissé sous les pieds de la reine une chaufferette à charbon. La chaufferette...

« Jouez ! dit Monsieur de Sainte Colombe.

— Regarde, Madeleine. J'ai brûlé le bas de ma viole. C'est un des gardes qui a remarqué que ma viole brûlait et qui m'a fait signe avec sa pique. Elle n'est pas brûlée. Elle n'est pas vraiment brûlée. Elle est noircie et... »

Deux mains claquèrent avec une grande violence sur le bois de la table. Tous sursautèrent. Monsieur de Sainte Colombe hurla entre ses dents :

« Jouez !

— Madeleine, regarde ! continuait Marin.

— Joue ! » dit Toinette.

Sainte Colombe courut à travers la salle, lui arracha l'instrument des mains.

« Non ! » cria Marin qui se leva pour récupérer sa viole. Monsieur de Sainte Colombe ne se possédait plus. Il brandissait la viole en l'air. Marin Marais le poursuivait dans la salle tendant les bras pour reprendre son instrument et l'empêcher de faire une chose monstrueuse. Il criait : « Non ! Non ! » Madeleine, figée de terreur, tordait son tablier entre ses mains. Toinette s'était levée et courait après eux.

Sainte Colombe s'approcha de l'âtre, dressa la viole en l'air, la fracassa sur le manteau de pierre de la cheminée. Le miroir qui le surplombait se rompit sous le choc. Marin Marais s'était accroupi soudain et hurlait. Monsieur de Sainte Colombe jeta ce qui restait de la viole à terre, sautait dessus avec ses bottes à entonnoir. Toinette tirait par le pourpoint son père en prononçant son nom. Au bout d'un moment, tous les quatre se turent. Ils se tenaient immobiles et hébétés. Ils regardaient sans comprendre le saccage. Monsieur de Sainte Colombe, la tête baissée, pâle, ne regardait que ses mains. Il cherchait à soupirer des « Ah ! Ah ! » de douleur. Il ne le pouvait pas.

« Mon père, mon père ! » disait Toinette en étreignant les épaules et le dos de son père en sanglotant.

Il mouvait ses doigts et poussait peu à peu des petits cris « Ah! Ah!» comme un homme qui se noie sans retrouver le souffle. Enfin il quitta la pièce. Monsieur Marais pleurait dans les bras de Madeleine qui s'était agenouillée auprès de lui et qui tremblait. Monsieur de Sainte Colombe revint avec une bourse dont il dénouait le lacet. Il compta les louis qu'elle contenait, s'approcha, jeta la bourse aux pieds de Marin Marais et se retira. Marin Marais cria dans son dos en se remettant debout :

« Monsieur, vous pourriez rendre raison de ce que vous avez fait! »

Monsieur de Sainte Colombe se retourna et dit avec calme :

« Monsieur, qu'est-ce qu'un instrument? Un instrument n'est pas la musique. Vous avez là de quoi vous racheter un cheval de cirque pour pirouetter devant le roi. »

Madeleine pleurait dans sa manche en

cherchant elle-même à se relever. Les sanglots faisaient frissonner son dos. Elle demeurait à genoux entre eux.

« Ecoutez, Monsieur, les sanglots que la douleur arrache à ma fille : ils sont plus près de la musique que vos gammes. Quittez à jamais la place, Monsieur, vous êtes un très grand bateleur. Les assiettes volent au-dessus de votre tête et jamais vous ne perdez l'équilibre mais vous êtes un petit musicien. Vous êtes un musicien de la taille d'une prune ou bien d'un hanneton. Vous devriez jouer à Versailles, c'est-à-dire sur le Pont-Neuf, et on vous jetterait des pièces pour boire. »

Monsieur de Sainte Colombe quitta la salle en lançant la porte derrière lui. Monsieur Marais courut lui-même vers la cour pour partir. Les portes claquaient.

Madeleine courut derrière lui sur la route, le rejoignit. La pluie avait cessé. Elle le prit par les épaules. Il pleurait.

« Je vous enseignerai tout ce que mon père m'a appris, lui dit-elle.

— Votre père est un homme méchant et fou, dit Marin Marais.

— Non. »

En silence, elle faisait « Non » avec la tête. Elle dit encore une fois :

« Non. »

Elle vit ses larmes qui coulaient et essuya l'une d'entre elles. Elle aperçut les mains de Marin qui s'approchaient des siennes, toutes nues sous la pluie. Elle avança ses doigts. Ils se touchèrent et ils sursautèrent. Puis ils étreignirent leurs mains, avancèrent leurs ventres, avancèrent leurs lèvres. Ils s'embrassèrent.

CHAPITRE XIV

Marin Marais venait en cachette de Monsieur de Sainte Colombe. Madeleine lui montrait sur sa viole tous les tours que son père lui avait enseignés. Debout devant lui, elle les lui faisait répéter, disposant sa main sur la touche, disposant le mollet pour repousser l'instrument en avant et le faire résonner, disposant le coude et le haut du bras droit pour l'archet. Ainsi ils se touchaient. Puis ils se baisèrent dans les coins d'ombre. Ils s'aimèrent. Ils se mussaient

81

parfois sous la cabane de Sainte Colombe
pour entendre à quels ornements il en était
venu, comment progressait son jeu, à quels
accords ses préférences allaient désormais.

Quand il eut vingt ans, durant l'été 1676,
Monsieur Marais annonça à Mademoiselle
de Sainte Colombe qu'il était engagé à la
cour comme « musicqueur du roy ». Ils
étaient au jardin ; elle le poussait pour qu'il
s'installe sous le cabinet de planche édifié
dans les branches basses du vieux mûrier.
Elle lui avait tout donné de sa pratique.

Il arriva un jour que l'orage éclata alors
que Marin Marais s'était embusqué sous la
cabane et qu'ayant pris froid il éternua
violemment à plusieurs reprises. Monsieur
de Sainte Colombe sortit sous la pluie, le
surprit le menton dans les genoux sur la
terre humide et lui donna des coups de pied
en appelant ses gens. Il parvint à le blesser
aux pieds et aux genoux et à le faire sortir, le
prit au collet, demanda au valet le plus

proche qu'il allât quérir le fouet. Madeleine de Sainte Colombe s'interposa. Elle dit à son père qu'elle aimait Marin, le calma enfin. Les nuages de l'orage étaient passés aussi vite qu'ils avaient été violents et ils tirèrent au jardin des fauteuils de toile dans lesquels ils s'assirent.

« Je ne veux plus vous voir, Monsieur. C'est la dernière fois, dit Sainte Colombe.

— Vous ne me verrez plus.

— Désirez-vous épouser ma fille aînée ?

— Je ne puis encore donner ma parole.

— Toinette est chez le luthier et rentrera tard », dit Madeleine en détournant son visage.

Elle vint s'asseoir dans l'herbe auprès de Marin Marais, adossée à la grande chaise de toile de son père. L'herbe était déjà presque séchée et sentait fort le foin. Son père regardait, au-delà du saule, les forêts vertes. Elle regarda la main de Marin qui l'approchait lentement. Il posa ses doigts sur le sein de Madeleine et glissa lentement jusqu'au ventre. Elle serra les jambes et frissonna. Monsieur de Sainte Colombe ne pouvait les voir. Il était occupé à parler :

« Je ne sais pas si je vous donnerai ma fille. Sans doute avez-vous trouvé une place qui est d'un bon rapport. Vous vivez dans un palais et le roi aime les mélodies dont vous entourez ses plaisirs. A mon avis, peu importe qu'on exerce son art dans un grand palais de pierre à cent chambres ou dans une cabane qui branle dans un mûrier. Pour moi il y a quelque chose de plus que l'art, de plus que les doigts, de plus que l'oreille, de plus que l'invention : c'est la vie passionnée que je mène.

— Vous vivez une vie passionnée? dit Marin Marais.

— Père, vous menez une vie passionnée? »

Madeleine et Marin avaient parlé en

même temps et en même temps avaient dévisagé le vieux musicien.

« Monsieur, vous plaisez à un roi visible. Plaire ne m'a pas convenu. Je hèle, je vous le jure, je hèle avec ma main une chose invisible.

— Vous parlez par énigmes. Je n'aurai jamais bien compris ce que vous vouliez dire.

— Et c'est pourquoi je n'escomptais pas que vous cheminiez à mes côtés, sur mon pauvre chemin d'herbes et de pierrailles. J'appartiens à des tombes. Vous publiez des compositions habiles et vous y ajoutez ingénieusement des doigtés et des ornements que vous me volez. Mais ce ne sont que des noires et des blanches sur du papier ! »

Avec son mouchoir, Marin Marais effaçait les traces de sang sur ses lèvres. Il se pencha soudain vers son maître.

« Monsieur, il y a longtemps que je souhaite vous poser une question.

— Oui.

— Pourquoi ne publiez-vous pas les airs que vous jouez?

— Oh! mes enfants, je ne compose pas! Je n'ai jamais rien écrit. Ce sont des offrandes d'eau, des lentilles d'eau, de l'armoise, des petites chenilles vivantes que j'invente parfois en me souvenant d'un nom et des plaisirs.

— Mais où est la musique dans vos lentilles et vos chenilles?

— Quand je tire mon archet, c'est un petit morceau de mon cœur vivant que je déchire. Ce que je fais, ce n'est que la discipline d'une vie où aucun jour n'est férié. J'accomplis mon destin. »

Dominique-d'Enfer, les enfants aussi se disaient entre eux « Monsieur » et ils ne se tutoyaient pas. Parfois un de ces Messieurs lui faisait envoyer un carrosse pour qu'il vînt jouer pour la mort d'un des leurs ou pour les Ténèbres. Monsieur de Sainte Colombe ne pouvait s'empêcher alors de songer à son épouse et aux circonstances qui avaient précédé sa mort. Il vivait un amour que rien ne diminuait. Il lui semblait que c'était le même amour, le même abandon, la même nuit, le même froid. Un mercredi saint, alors qu'il avait joué lors de l'office des Ténèbres dans la chapelle de l'hôtel de Madame de Pont-Carré, il avait rangé sa partie et s'apprêtait à s'en retourner. Il était assis dans la petite allée latérale, sur une chaise en paille. Sa viole était posée à ses côtés, recouverte de sa housse. L'organiste et deux sœurs interprétaient un morceau nouveau qu'il ne connaissait pas et qui était beau. Il tourna sa tête sur sa droite : elle était assise à ses côtés. Il inclina la tête. Elle lui sourit, leva un peu la main ; elle portait des mitaines noires et des bagues.

« Maintenant il faut rentrer », dit-elle.

Il se leva, prit sa viole et la suivit dans l'obscurité de l'allée, longeant les statues des saints couverts de linges violets.

Dans la ruelle il ouvrit la porte du carrosse, déplia le marchepied et monta après elle en mettant sa viole devant lui. Il dit au cocher qu'il rentrait. Il sentit la douceur de la robe de son épouse près de lui. Il lui demanda s'il lui avait bien témoigné autrefois à quel point il l'aimait.

« J'ai en effet le souvenir que vous me témoigniez votre amour, lui dit-elle, encore que je n'eusse pas été blessée si vous me l'aviez exprimé de façon un peu plus bavarde.

— Etait-ce si pauvre et si rare ?

— C'était aussi pauvre que fréquent, mon ami, et le plus souvent muet. Je vous aimais. Comme j'aimerais encore vous proposer des pêches écrasées ! »

Le carrosse s'arrêta. Ils étaient déjà devant la maison. Il était sorti du carrosse et lui tendit la main pour qu'elle descendît à son tour.

« Je ne puis pas », dit-elle.

Il eut un air de douleur qui donna à Madame de Sainte Colombe le désir de porter la main vers lui.

« Vous n'avez pas l'air bien », dit-elle.

Il sortit la viole habillée de sa housse et la posa sur le chemin. Il s'assit sur le marchepied et il pleura.

Elle était descendue. Il se releva en hâte et ouvrit la porte cochère. Ils traversèrent la cour pavée, grimpèrent le perron, pénétrèrent dans la salle où il laissa sa viole contre la pierre de cheminée. Il lui disait :

« Ma tristesse est indéfinissable. Vous avez raison de m'adresser ce reproche. La parole ne peut jamais dire ce dont je veux parler et je ne sais comment le dire... »

Il poussa la porte qui donnait sur la balustrade et le jardin de derrière. Ils marchèrent sur la pelouse. Il montra du doigt la cabane en disant :

« Voilà la cabane où je parle ! »

Il s'était mis de nouveau à pleurer doucement. Ils allèrent jusqu'à la barque. Madame de Sainte Colombe monta dans la barque blanche tandis qu'il en retenait le bord et la maintenait près de la rive. Elle avait retroussé sa robe pour poser le pied sur le plancher humide de la barque. Il se redressa. Il tenait les paupières baissées. Il ne vit pas que la barque avait disparu. Il reprit au bout d'un certain temps, les larmes glissant sur ses joues :

« Je ne sais comment dire, Madame. Douze ans ont passé mais les draps de notre lit ne sont pas encore froids. »

CHAPITRE XVI

Les visites de Monsieur Marais devinrent plus exceptionnelles. Madeleine le rejoignait à Versailles ou à Vauboyen où ils s'aimaient dans une chambre d'auberge. Madeleine lui confiait tout. C'est ainsi qu'elle lui avoua que son père avait composé les airs les plus beaux qui fussent au monde et qu'il ne les faisait entendre à personne. Il y avait les Pleurs. Il y avait la Barque de Charon.

Une fois ils eurent peur. Ils étaient à la maison parce que Marin Marais cherchait à

surprendre, en se glissant sous les branches
du mûrier, les airs dont Madeleine lui avait
parlé. Elle était debout devant lui, dans la
salle. Marin était assis. Elle s'était appro-
chée. Elle tendait ses seins en avant, près de
son visage. Elle dégrafa le haut de sa robe,
écarta sa chemise de dessous. Sa gorge
jaillit. Marin Marais ne put qu'y jeter son
visage.

« Manon ! » criait Monsieur de Sainte
Colombe.

Marin Marais se cacha dans l'encoignure
de la fenêtre la plus proche. Madeleine était
pâle et remettait en hâte sa chemise de
dessous.

« Oui, mon père.

— Il faut que nous fassions nos gammes
par tierce et quinte.

— Oui, mon père. »

Il entra. Monsieur de Sainte Colombe ne
vit pas Marin Marais. Ils partirent aussitôt.
Quand, au loin, il les entendit s'accorder,

Marin Marais sortit de son encoignure et voulut quitter de façon furtive la demeure en passant par le jardin. Il tomba sur Toinette, accoudée à la balustrade, qui contemplait le jardin. Elle l'arrêta par le bras.

« Et moi, comment me trouves-tu ? »

Elle tendit ses seins comme avait fait sa sœur. Marin Marais rit, l'embrassa et s'esquiva en se précipitant.

CHAPITRE XVII

Une autre fois, à quelque temps de là, un jour d'été, alors que Guignotte, Madeleine et Toinette étaient convenues d'aller à la chapelle nettoyer les statues des saints, enlever les toiles d'araignée, laver le pavé, épousseter les chaises et les bancs, fleurir l'autel, Marin Marais les accompagna. Il monta à la tribune et joua une pièce d'orgue. En bas, il voyait Toinette qui frottait avec une serpillière le pavé et les marches qui entouraient l'autel. Elle lui fit signe. Il descendit. Il faisait très chaud. Ils se prirent la main, passèrent par la porte de la sacristie, traversèrent en courant le cimetière, sautèrent le muret et se retrouvèrent dans les buissons à la limite du bois.

Toinette était tout essoufflée. Sa robe laissait voir le haut des seins qui luisaient de sueur. Elle avait les yeux qui brillaient. Elle tendit les seins en avant.

« La sueur mouille le bord de ma robe, dit-elle.

— Vous avez des seins plus gros que ceux de votre sœur. »

Il regardait ses seins. Il voulut approcher ses lèvres, lui prit les bras, voulut se séparer d'elle et repartir. Il avait l'air égaré.

« J'ai le ventre tout chaud », lui dit-elle en prenant sa main et en la mettant entre les siennes. Elle le tira à elle.

« Votre sœur... », murmurait-il et il l'enferma dans ses bras. Ils s'étreignaient. Il baisait ses yeux. Il désordonna sa chemise.

« Mettez-vous nu et prenez-moi », lui dit-elle.

C'était encore une enfant. Elle répétait : « Mettez-moi nue ! Puis mettez-vous nu ! »

Son corps était celui d'une femme ronde et épaisse. Après qu'ils se furent pris, à l'instant de passer sa chemise, nue, illuminée de côté par la lumière du jour finissant, les seins lourds, les cuisses se détachant sur le fond des feuillages du bois, elle lui parut la plus belle femme du monde.

« Je n'ai pas honte, dit-elle.

— J'ai honte.

— J'ai eu du désir. »

Il l'aida à lacer sa robe. Elle levait les bras et les tenait ployés en l'air. Il serrait la taille. Elle ne portait pas de pantalon sous sa chemise. Elle dit :

« En plus, maintenant, Madeleine va devenir maigre. »

CHAPITRE XVIII

Ils étaient à demi nus dans la chambre de
Madeleine. Marin Marais s'adossa au mon-
tant du lit. Il lui disait :

« Je vous quitte. Vous avez vu que je
n'avais plus rien au bout de mon ventre
pour vous. »

Elle prit ses mains et lentement, mettant
son visage dans les deux mains de Marin
Marais, elle se mit à pleurer. Il poussa un
soupir. L'embrasse qui retenait le rideau du
lit tomba tandis qu'il tirait sur ses chausses

pour les lacer. Elle lui prit des mains les cordons des chausses et y porta ses lèvres.

« Vos larmes sont douces et me touchent. Je vous abandonne parce que je ne songe plus à vos seins dans mes rêves. J'ai vu d'autres visages. Nos cœurs sont des affamés. Notre esprit ne connaît pas le repos. La vie est belle à proportion qu'elle est féroce, comme nos proies. »

Elle se taisait, jouait avec les cordons, caressait son ventre et ne le regardait pas. Elle releva la tête, lui fit face soudain, toute rouge, lui murmurant :

« Arrête de parler et va-t'en ! »

CHAPITRE XIX

Mademoiselle de Sainte Colombe tomba malade et devint si maigre et si faible qu'elle s'alita. Elle était grosse. Marin Marais n'osait prendre de ses nouvelles mais il avait convenu avec Toinette d'un jour où il venait, au-delà du lavoir sur la Bièvre. Là, il donnait du foin à son cheval et il s'enquérait des nouvelles sur la grossesse de Madeleine. Elle accoucha d'un petit garçon qui était mort-né. Il confia à Toinette un paquet qu'elle remit à sa sœur : il contenait des

chaussures montantes jaunes en veau à
lacets, que son père avait confectionnées à
sa demande. Madeleine voulut les mettre à
cuire dans l'âtre mais Toinette l'en empê-
cha. Elle se rétablit. Elle lut les Pères
du désert. Le temps passant, il cessa de
venir.

En 1675, il travaillait la composition avec
Monsieur Lully. En 1679, Caignet mourut.
Marin Marais, à vingt-trois ans, fut nommé
Ordinaire de la Chambre du roi, prenant la
place de son premier maître. Il assuma aussi
la direction d'orchestre auprès de Monsieur
Lully. Il composa des opéras. Il se maria
avec Catherine d'Amicourt et il en eut dix-
neuf enfants. L'année où on ouvrit les char-
niers de Port-Royal (l'année où le roi exigea
par écrit qu'on rasât les murs, qu'on exhu-
mât les corps de Messieurs Hamon et
Racine et qu'on les donnât aux chiens), il
reprit le thème de la Rêveuse.

En 1686, il habitait rue du Jour, près de

CHAPITRE XX

La neuvième fois où il sentit près de lui que son épouse était venue le rejoindre, c'était au printemps. C'était lors de la grande persécution de juin 1679. Il avait sorti le vin et le plat de gaufrettes sur la table à musique. Il jouait dans la cabane. Il s'interrompit et lui dit :

« Comment est-il possible que vous veniez ici, après la mort ? Où est ma barque ? Où sont mes larmes quand je vous vois ? N'êtes-vous pas plutôt un songe ? Suis-je un fou ?

« — Ne soyez pas dans l'inquiétude.
Votre barque est pourrie depuis longtemps
dans la rivière. L'autre monde n'est pas
plus étanche que ne l'était votre embarcation.

— Je souffre, Madame, de ne pas vous
toucher.

— Il n'y a rien, Monsieur, à toucher
que du vent. »

Elle parlait lentement comme font les
morts. Elle ajouta :

« Croyez-vous qu'il n'y ait pas de souf-
france à être du vent ? Quelquefois ce vent
porte jusqu'à nous des bribes de musique.
Quelquefois la lumière porte jusqu'à vos
regards des morceaux de nos apparences. »

Elle se tut encore. Elle regardait les
mains de son mari, qu'il avait posées sur
le bois rouge de la viole.

« Comme vous ne savez pas parler ! dit-
elle. Que voulez-vous, mon ami ? Jouez.

— Que regardiez-vous en vous taisant ?

— Jouez donc ! Je regardais votre main vieillie sur le bois de la viole. »

Il s'immobilisa. Il regarda son épouse puis, pour la première fois de sa vie, ou du moins comme s'il ne l'avait jamais vue jusque-là, il regarda sa main émaciée, jaune, à la peau desséchée en effet. Il mit devant lui ses deux mains. Elles étaient tachées par la mort et il en fut heureux. Ces marques de vieillesse le rapprochaient d'elle ou de son état. Son cœur battait à rompre par la joie qu'il éprouvait et ses doigts tremblaient.

« Mes mains, disait-il. Vous parlez de mes mains ! »

CHAPITRE XXI

A cette heure, le soleil avait déjà disparu. Le ciel était rempli de nuages de pluie et il faisait sombre. L'air était plein d'humidité et laissait pressentir une averse prochaine. Il suivit la Bièvre. Il revit la maison et sa tourelle et se heurta aux hauts murs qui la protégeaient. Au loin, par instants, il percevait le son de la viole de son maître. Il en fut ému. Il suivit le mur jusqu'à la rive et, empoignant les racines d'un arbre qu'une crue du ruisseau avait mises à nu, il parvint à contourner le mur et à rejoindre le talus de la rive qui appartenait aux Sainte Colombe. Du grand saule, il ne restait plus que le tronc. La barque n'était plus là non plus. Il se dit : « Le saule est rompu. La barque a coulé. J'ai aimé des filles qui sont sans doute des mères. J'ai connu leur beauté. » Il ne vit pas les poules ni les oies s'empresser autour de ses mollets : Madeleine ne devait plus habiter ici. Autrefois elle les rentrait le soir dans leur cabane et on les entendait piailler et s'ébrouer dans la nuit.

Il se glissa dans l'ombre du mur et, se guidant au son de la viole, s'approcha de la cabane de son maître et, s'enveloppant dans son manteau de pluie, il approcha l'oreille de la cloison. C'étaient de longues plaintes arpégées. Elles ressemblaient aux airs qu'improvisait Couperin le jeune, dans ce temps-là, sur les orgues de Saint-Gervais. Par le petit créneau de la fenêtre filtrait la lueur d'une bougie. Puis, comme la viole de ces visites, elle demanda à son père qu'il jouât la Rêveuse qu'avait composée pour elle jadis Monsieur Marais, du temps où il l'aimait. Il refusa et quitta la chambre fort courroucé. Pourtant Monsieur de Sainte Colombe, à peu de temps de là, alla trouver Toinette dans l'île, dans l'atelier de Monsieur Pardoux, et lui demanda d'avertir Monsieur Marais. Il s'ensuivit la tristesse qu'on sait. Non seulement il ne parla plus durant dix mois mais Monsieur de Sainte Colombe ne toucha plus sa viole : c'était la première fois que ce dégoût lui naissait. Guignotte était morte. Il n'avait jamais usé d'elle, ni touché ses cheveux qu'elle portait dénoués dans le dos, quoiqu'il l'eût convoitée. Plus personne ne lui préparait sa pipe de terre et son pichet de vin. Il disait aux valets qu'ils pouvaient aller dans leur soupente se coucher ou jouer aux cartes. Il préférait rester seul, avec un chandelier, assis près de la table, ou avec un bougeoir, dans sa cabane. Il ne lisait pas. Il n'ouvrait pas son livre de maroquin rouge. Il recevait ses élèves sans un regard et en se tenant immobile, si bien qu'il fallut leur dire de ne plus se déranger pour venir faire de la musique.

Dans ces temps-là, Monsieur Marais venait tard dans la soirée et écoutait, l'oreille collée à la paroi de planches, le silence.

CHAPITRE XXIII

Une après-midi, Toinette et Luc Pardoux
étaient venus trouver Monsieur Marais
alors que celui-ci était de service à Versailles : Madeleine de Sainte Colombe avait
une grande fièvre soudaine, due à la petite
vérole. On craignait qu'elle ne mourût. Un
garde prévint l'Ordinaire de la Chambre
qu'une Toinette l'attendait sur le pavé.

Il arriva embarrassé, avec ses dentelles,
ses talons à torsades d'or et de rouge. Marin
Marais fut maussade. Montrant le billet

cloître, Madeleine de Sainte Colombe rétorqua que la sainteté, c'était le service de son père, le cloître, c'était cette « vorne » sur la Bièvre et que cette connaissance étant faite il lui paraissait inutile de la renouveler. Quant à être défigurée, elle dit qu'elle ne demandait pas à en être plainte ; elle était déjà maigre comme les chardons et plaisante comme eux : jadis un homme l'avait même quittée parce que ses seins, quand elle eut maigri de douleur, étaient devenus gros comme des noisettes. Elle ne communiait plus, sans qu'il y eût forcément lieu de voir en cela les influences de Monsieur de Bures ou de Monsieur Lancelot. Mais elle demeurait pieuse. Durant des années, elle était allée à la chapelle prier. Elle montait à la tribune, regardait le chœur et les dalles qui entouraient l'autel, se mettait à l'orgue. Elle disait qu'elle offrait cette musique à Dieu.

Monsieur Marais demanda comment se portait Monsieur de Sainte Colombe. Toinette rétorqua qu'il allait bien mais qu'il ne voulait pas jouer la pièce intitulée la Rêveuse. A six mois de là, Madeleine sarclait encore au jardin et plantait des semences de fleurs. Désormais elle était trop faible pour joindre la chapelle. Quand elle pouvait marcher sans tomber, le soir, elle entendait servir seule son père à table, peut-être par esprit d'humilité, ou par déplaisir à l'idée de manger, se tenant debout derrière sa chaise. Monsieur Pardoux prétendait qu'elle avait dit à sa femme que, la nuit, elle se brûlait les bras nus avec la cire des chandelles. Madeleine avait montré à Toinette ses plaies sur le haut de ses bras. Elle ne dormait pas, mais en cela elle était comme son père. Son père la regardait aller et venir sous la lune, près du poulailler, ou bien tombée à genoux dans les herbes.

CHAPITRE XXIV

Toinette persuada Marin Marais. Elle l'amena après avoir prévenu son père, et sans que Monsieur de Sainte Colombe dût le voir. La chambre dans laquelle il entra sentait une odeur de soie moisie.

« Vous êtes plein de rubans magnifiques, Monsieur, et gras », dit Madeleine de Sainte Colombe.

Il ne dit rien sur-le-champ, il poussa un tabouret près du lit sur lequel il s'assit mais qu'il trouva trop bas. Il préféra rester debout dans une espèce de gêne qui était grande, le bras appuyé contre la colonnade du lit. Elle trouvait que ses hauts de chausse en satin bleu étaient trop serrés : quand il bougeait, ils moulaient ses fesses, marquaient les plis du ventre et le renflement du sexe. Elle disait :

« Je vous remercie d'être venu de Versailles. J'aimerais que vous jouiez cet air que vous aviez composé pour moi autrefois et qui a été imprimé. »

Il dit qu'il s'agissait sans doute de la Rêveuse. Elle le regarda droit dans les yeux et dit :

« Oui. Et vous savez pourquoi. »

Il se tut. Il inclina la tête en silence, puis se tourna brusquement vers Toinette en lui demandant d'aller chercher la viole de Madeleine.

« Vos joues sont creuses. Vos yeux sont creux. Vos mains sont tellement maigries ! dit-il avec un air plein d'épouvante quand Toinette fut partie.

— C'est une constatation qui est très délicate de votre part.

— Votre voix est plus basse que jadis.

— La vôtre est remontée.

— Est-il possible que vous n'ayez pas de chagrin ? Vous avez tellement maigri.

— Je ne vois pas que j'aie eu de peine récente. »

Marin Marais ôta ses mains de la couverture. Il recula jusqu'à s'adosser contre le mur de la chambre, dans l'ombre que faisait l'encoignure de la fenêtre. Il parlait tout bas :

« Vous m'en voulez ?

— Oui, Marin.

— Ce que j'ai fait jadis vous inspire encore de la haine contre moi ?

— Il n'y en a pas que pour vous, Monsieur ! J'ai nourri aussi des ressentiments contre moi. Je m'en veux de m'être laissée sécher tout d'abord par votre souvenir, ensuite par pure tristesse. Je ne suis plus que les os de Tithon ! »

Marin Marais rit. Il lui dit qu'il ne l'avait jamais trouvée très grosse et qu'il se souvenait, autrefois, que lorsqu'il portait les mains sur sa cuisse, ses doigts en faisaient le tour et se touchaient.

« Vous êtes plein d'esprit, dit-elle. Et dire que j'aurais aimé être votre épouse ! »

Mademoiselle de Sainte Colombe ôta brusquement le drap de son lit. Monsieur Marais recula avec tant de précipitation qu'il détacha le rideau de lit qui se déplia. Elle avait relevé sa chemise pour descendre, il lui voyait les cuisses et le sexe tout nus. Elle posa les pieds nus sur le carrelage en poussant un petit cri, tendit l'étoffe de sa chemise de dessous, la lui montra, la lui mit entre les doigts, lui disant :

« L'amour que tu me portais n'était pas plus gros que cet ourlet de ma chemise.

— Tu mens. »

Ils se turent. Elle posa sa main décharnée sur le poignet plein de rubans de Marin Marais et lui dit :

« Joue, s'il te plaît. »

Elle cherchait à grimper de nouveau dans son lit mais il était trop haut. Il l'aida, poussant ses fesses maigres. Elle était aussi légère qu'un coussin. Il prit la viole des mains de Toinette qui était de retour. Toinette chercha l'embrasse, remit le rideau de lit et les laissa. Il commença d'interpréter la Rêveuse et elle l'interrompit en lui enjoignant d'être plus lent. Il reprit. Elle le regardait jouer avec des yeux qui brûlaient de fièvre. Elle ne les fermait pas. Elle détaillait son corps en train de jouer.

prenant appui sur la cloison et s'aidant de l'étoffe de ses robes, elle se remit debout et revint vers le lit avec la chandelle et le soulier Elle les posa sur la table qui était à son chevet. Elle soufflait comme si les trois quarts du souffle dont elle disposait étaient taris. Elle marmonnait aussi :

« Il ne désirait pas être cordonnier. »

Elle répétait cette phrase. Elle reposa ses reins contre le matelas et le bois de son lit. Elle ôta un grand lacet des œillets du soulier jaune qu'elle reposa près de la chandelle. Minutieusement, elle fit un nœud qui coulissait. Elle se redressa et rapprocha le tabouret que Marin Marais avait pris et sur lequel il s'était assis. Elle le tira sous la poutre la plus proche de la fenêtre, grimpa à l'aide du rideau de son lit sur le tabouret, parvint à fixer par cinq ou six tours le lacet à une grosse pointe qui se trouvait là et introduisit sa tête dans le nœud et le serra. Elle eut du mal à faire tomber le tabouret. Elle piétina et dansa longtemps avant qu'il tombe. Quand ses pieds rencontrèrent le vide, elle poussa un cri ; une brusque secousse prit ses genoux.

CHAPITRE XXVI

Tous les matins du monde sont sans retour. Les années étaient passées. Monsieur de Sainte Colombe, à son lever, caressait de la main la toile de Monsieur Baugin et passait sa chemise. Il allait épousseter sa cabane. C'était un vieil homme. Il entretenait aussi des fleurs et des arbustes qu'avait plantés sa fille aînée, avant qu'elle se pendît. Puis il allait allumer le feu et faire chauffer le lait. Il sortait une assiette creuse en grosse faïence où il écrasait sa bouillie.

Monsieur Marais n'avait pas revu Monsieur de Sainte Colombe depuis le jour où il avait été surpris par ce dernier en train d'éternuer sous sa cabane, trempé jusqu'aux os. Monsieur Marais avait conservé le souvenir que Monsieur de Sainte Colombe connaissait des airs qu'il ignorait alors qu'ils passaient pour les plus beaux du monde. Parfois il se réveillait la nuit, se remémorant les noms que Madeleine lui avait chuchotés sous le sceau du secret : les Pleurs, les Enfers, l'Ombre d'Enée, la Barque de Charon, et il regrettait de vivre sans les avoir entendus ne serait-ce qu'une fois. Jamais Monsieur de Sainte Colombe ne publierait ce qu'il avait composé ni ce que ses propres maîtres lui avaient appris. Monsieur Marais souffrait en songeant que ces œuvres allaient se perdre à jamais quand Monsieur de Sainte Colombe mourrait. Il ne savait pas quelle serait sa vie ni quelle

serait l'époque future. Il voulait les connaî-
tre avant qu'il fût trop tard.

Il quittait Versailles. Qu'il plût, qu'il
neigeât, il se rendait nuitamment à la Bièvre. Comme il faisait jadis, il attachait son
cheval au lavoir, sur la route de Jouy, pour
qu'on ne l'entendît pas hennir, puis suivait
le chemin humide, contournait le mur sur la
rive, se glissait sous la cabane humide.

Monsieur de Sainte Colombe ne jouait
pas ces airs ou du moins il n'interprétait
jamais d'airs que Monsieur Marais ne les
connût. A vrai dire Monsieur de Sainte
Colombe jouait plus rarement. C'étaient
souvent de longs silences au cours desquels
il lui arrivait parfois de se parler à lui-même.
Durant trois ans, presque chaque nuit,
Monsieur Marais se rendait à la cabane en
se disant : « Ces airs, va-t-il les jouer ce
soir ? Est-ce la nuit qui convient ? »

CHAPITRE XXVII

Enfin, l'an 1689, la nuit du 23ᵉ jour, alors que le froid était vif, la terre prise de grésil, le vent piquant les yeux et les oreilles, Monsieur Marais galopa jusqu'au lavoir. La lune brillait. Il n'y avait aucun nuage. « Oh ! se dit Monsieur Marais, cette nuit est pure, l'air cru, le ciel plus froid et plus éternel, la lune ronde. J'entends claquer les sabots de mon cheval sur la terre. C'est peut-être ce soir. »

Il s'installa dans le froid serrant sur lui sa

cape noire. Le froid était si vif qu'il avait glissé dessous une peau de mouton retournée. Cependant il avait froid aux fesses. Son sexe était tout petit et gelé.

Il écouta à la dérobée. L'oreille lui faisait mal, posée sur la planche glacée. Sainte Colombe s'amusait à faire sonner à vide les cordes de sa viole. Il fit quelques traits mélancoliques à l'archet. Par moments, comme il lui arrivait si souvent de faire, il parla. Il ne faisait rien de suite. Son jeu paraissait négligent, sénile, désolé. Monsieur Marais approcha son oreille d'un interstice entre les lattes de bois pour comprendre le sens des mots que ruminait par instants Monsieur de Sainte Colombe. Il ne comprit pas. Il perçut seulement des mots dépourvus de sens comme « pêches écrasées » ou « embarcation ». Monsieur de Sainte Colombe joua la Chaconne Dubois, qu'il donnait en concert naguère avec ses filles. Monsieur Marais reconnut le thème principal. La pièce s'acheva, majestueuse. Il entendit alors un soupir puis Monsieur de Sainte Colombe qui prononçait tout bas ces plaintes

« Ah ! Je ne m'adresse qu'à des ombres qui sont devenues trop âgées ! Qui ne se déplacent plus ! Ah ! si en dehors de moi il y avait au monde quelqu'un de vivant qui appréciât la musique ! Nous parlerions ! Je la lui confierais et je pourrais mourir. »

Alors Monsieur Marais, frissonnant dans le froid, dehors, poussa lui-même un soupir. En soupirant de nouveau, il gratta la porte de la cabane.

« Qui est là qui soupire dans le silence de la nuit ?

— Un homme qui fuit les palais et qui recherche la musique. »

Monsieur de Sainte Colombe comprit de qui il s'agissait et il se réjouit. Il se pencha en avant et entrouvrit la porte en la poussant avec son archet. Un peu de lumière passa mais plus faible que celle qui tombait de la lune pleine. Marin Marais se tenait accroupi dans l'ouverture. Monsieur de Sainte Colombe se pencha en avant et dit à ce visage :

« Que recherchez-vous, Monsieur, dans la musique ?

— Je cherche les regrets et les pleurs. »

Alors il poussa tout à fait la porte de la cabane, se leva en tremblant. Il salua cérémonieusement Monsieur Marais qui entra. Ils commencèrent par se taire. Monsieur de Sainte Colombe s'assit sur son tabouret et dit à Monsieur Marais :

« Asseyez-vous ! »

Monsieur Marais, toujours enveloppé de sa peau de mouton, s'assit. Ils restaient les bras ballants dans la gêne.

« Monsieur, puis-je vous demander une dernière leçon ? demanda Monsieur Marais en s'animant tout à coup.

— Monsieur, puis-je tenter une première

leçon ? » rétorqua Monsieur de Sainte Colombe avec une voix sourde.

Monsieur Marais inclina la tête. Monsieur de Sainte Colombe toussa et dit qu'il désirait parler. Il parlait à la saccade.

« Cela est difficile, Monsieur. La musique est simplement là pour parler de ce dont la parole ne peut parler. En ce sens elle n'est pas tout à fait humaine. Alors vous avez découvert qu'elle n'est pas pour le roi ?

— J'ai découvert qu'elle était pour Dieu.

— Et vous vous êtes trompé, car Dieu parle.

— Pour l'oreille ?

— Ce dont je ne peux parler n'est pas pour l'oreille, Monsieur.

— Pour l'or ?

— Non, l'or n'est rien d'audible.

— La gloire ?

— Non. Ce ne sont que des noms qui se renomment.

— Le silence ?

— Il n'est que le contraire du langage.

— Les musiciens rivaux ?

— Non !

— L'amour ?

— Non.

— Le regret de l'amour ?

— Non.

— L'abandon ?

— Non et non.

— Est-ce pour une gaufrette donnée à l'invisible ?

— Non plus. Qu'est-ce qu'une gaufrette ? Cela se voit. Cela a du goût. Cela se mange. Cela n'est rien.

— Je ne sais plus, Monsieur. Je crois qu'il faut laisser un verre aux morts...

— Aussi brûlez-vous.

— Un petit abreuvoir pour ceux que le langage a désertés. Pour l'ombre des enfants. Pour les coups de marteaux des cordonniers. Pour les états qui précèdent

Marin Marais le prit par le bras. Ils descendirent les marches de la cabane et ils se dirigèrent vers la maison. Monsieur de Sainte Colombe confia à Monsieur Marais la viole de Madeleine. Elle était couverte de poussière. Ils l'essuyèrent avec leurs manches. Puis Monsieur de Sainte Colombe remplit une assiette en étain avec quelques gaufrettes enroulées. Ils revinrent tous deux à la cabane avec la fiasque, la viole, les verres et l'assiette. Tandis que Monsieur Marais ôtait sa cape noire et sa peau retournée et les jetait par terre, Monsieur de Sainte Colombe fit de la place et mit au centre de la cabane, près de la lucarne par où on voyait la lune blanche, la table à écrire. Il essuya avec son doigt humide de salive, après qu'il l'eut passé sur ses lèvres, deux gouttes de vin rouge qui étaient tombées de la carafe enveloppée de paille, à côté de l'assiette. Monsieur de Sainte Colombe entrouvrit le cahier de musique en maroquin tandis que Monsieur Marais versait un peu de vin cuit et rouge dans son verre. Monsieur Marais approcha la chandelle du livre de musique. Ils regardèrent, refermèrent le livre, s'assirent, s'accordèrent. Monsieur de Sainte Colombe compta la mesure vide et ils posèrent leurs doigts. C'est ainsi qu'ils jouèrent les Pleurs. A l'instant où le chant des deux violes monte, ils se regardèrent. Ils pleuraient. La lumière qui pénétrait dans la cabane par la lucarne qui y était percée était devenue jaune. Tandis que leurs larmes lentement coulaient sur leur nez, sur leurs joues, sur leurs lèvres, ils s'adressèrent en même temps un sourire. Ce n'est qu'à l'aube que Monsieur Marais s'en retourna à Versailles.

Œuvres de Pascal Quignard (suite).

LE VŒU DE SILENCE, Fata Morgana, 1985.

UNE GÊNE TECHNIQUE À L'ÉGARD DES FRAGMENTS, Fata Morgana, 1986.

ETHELRUDE ET WOLFRAMM, Claude Blaizot, 1986.

LA LEÇON DE MUSIQUE, Hachette, 1987.

ALBUCIUS, POL, 1990.

KONG-SOUEN LONG, SUR LE DOIGT QUI MONTRE CELA, Michel Chandeigne, 1990.

LA RAISON, Le Promeneur, 1990.

PETITS TRAITÉS, tomes I à VIII, Maeght Éditeur, 1990.

GEORGES DE LA TOUR, Éditions Flohic, 1991.

*Composition Bussière
et impression S.E.P.C.
à Saint-Amand (Cher), le 29 janvier 1992.
Dépôt légal : janvier 1992.
1ᵉʳ dépôt légal : novembre 1991.
Numéro d'imprimeur : 246.*
ISBN 2-07-072474-3./Imprimé en France.

55430

LIVRE 'À' LOUER